LIBERTINE LONDON

For Jad, with love and thanks for
the many years
of making and sharing
our very own Libertine London life.

Also by Julie Peakman

Licentious Worlds: Sex and Exploitation in Global Empires (London, 2019)

Hitler's Island War: The Men Who Fought for Leros (London, 2017)

The Pleasure's All Mine: A History of Perverse Sex (London, 2016)

Amatory Pleasures: Explorations in Eighteenth-Century Sexual Culture (London, 2016)

Peg Plunkett: Memoirs of a Whore (London, 2015)

Mighty Lewd Books: The Development of Pornography in Eighteenth-Century England (London, 2003; reissued in paperback 2012)

Emma Hamilton: A Biography (London, 2005)

Lascivious Bodies: A Sexual History of the Eighteenth Century (New York, 2004)

ed., *A Cultural History of Sexuality* (Oxford, 2011), 6 volumes

ed., *Sexual Perversions, 1650–1890* (London, 2009)

ed., *Whore's Biographies in the Long C18th* (London, 2007–8), 8 volumes

LIBERTINE LONDON

Sex in the Eighteenth-Century Metropolis

Julie Peakman

REAKTION BOOKS

Published by
Reaktion Books Ltd
Unit 32, Waterside
44–48 Wharf Road
London N1 7UX, UK
www.reaktionbooks.co.uk

First published 2024

Printed and bound in India by Replika Press Pvt. Ltd

A catalogue record for this book is available from the British Library

ISBN 978 1 78914 847 3

CONTENTS

Covent Garden Ramble

One night in Covent Garden,
With Pleasure I did steer,
I met a pretty fair maid,
Taking of the air,
Her shoes were made of kerseymere,
Her stockings they were silk
Her shift was made of the best of
lawn;
And her skin was as white as milk,
She had a black and a rolling eye.

I took this charming creature,
I took her to an inn,
I swore I'd ne'er forsake her;
If that she would be mine,
I detain'd this charming creature
So long she would not stay,
She sigh'd and said I am a maid,

Pray let me go my way.
I hope you will excuse me,
I dare not stop out late.
For if my mother she should know
I would not for a groat,
My father he's a preacher,
A very holy man
My mother she's a Methodist,
And I'm a true Briton.

When I kiss'd this charming creature
I had my heart's desire,
This little dirty stinking slut
Set me all on fire,
She set me all on fire,
Which caused me to rue,
This little dirty stinking slut
She's one of the wicked crew.

Eighteenth-century song

TOTHILL FIELDS

John Rocque's map of London, 1746.

Prologue: Libertines in London

The term 'libertine' was often used in the seventeenth and eighteenth centuries to describe a certain type of upper-class man of sexually free behaviour. The *Oxford English Dictionary* defines a libertine as 'a person, especially a man, who freely indulges in sensual pleasures without regard to moral principles'. The word was originally used to describe the sexual freedom and philosophical free-thinking of French aristocratic men in the *ancien régime*, or writers of pornographic novels such as Crébillon, Diderot, Laclos and Sade, but it was also in common usage in England by the eighteenth century. For the British, the term meant much more than for the French. It could be applied not just to those of the upper class, but more broadly to men of indelicate tastes – and libertinism was not necessarily politely negotiated, but seized as a right. This libertine world was to include women, but libertine women differed greatly from their male counterparts in that they only had their bodies to negotiate with and held a lesser place in society. Their sexual freedom was also often connected less to sexual desire, and more to the sexual encounters they needed for their survival. Libertine women did not always receive pleasure from their experience; just as often, they were simply making a living. Others might wallow in sexual pleasure, follow their heart's desire and give themselves to men they loved. However, they were often still dependent on men and 'kept women' lost any freedom they might have had. Libertine women were free sexually from moral conventional codes, but their libertinism came at a price.

We can see a vast gap opening up when the term 'libertine' was applied to men and to women. Whereas libertine men were considered genial rakes, libertine women were seen as immoral; while sexual laxity in men was often a proof of manhood and virility, it was condemned in women. Indeed, women who were sexually incontinent were labelled in derogatory terms, as whores, harlots and strumpets. Women working in the sex industry were often seen as libertines, but would not necessarily have had the freedom of choice men had, and sex might well have made them miserable. 'Libertine' is therefore an imprecise and ambiguous word.

Men's sexual activities were given much more licence than ever before in the eighteenth century, and this might be associated with a fully blossoming sexual culture after the Restoration. Of course, there were different *types* of masculinity evident, such as the fop, the macaroni, the homosexual, the ruffian, the good Christian and so on, and some of these men (the good Christian, for example) may have thought it prudent to follow a certain type of upright sexual morality. However, the libertine male was largely unconstrained in his sexual enthusiasms and, to a large extent, let off the hook as regards his sexual conduct, unless it was with a 'reputable' woman or with another man. The idea of libertinism for men started in youth, with the acceptance of young men 'sowing their wild oats'. There was no such encouragement or allowance for young women. Yet plenty of women managed to find sexual liberty outside the confines of marriage, though this invariably meant a ruined reputation and ostracization from respectable society.

Certainly the English had a role for female libertines, who were frequently described in magazines, pamphlets, satires, songs, theatre plays, erotica and other forms of social media. See for example female libertines in comedic plays, such as John Dryden's *Marriage A-la-Mode* (1671), George Etherege's *The Man of Mode* (1676), Aphra Behn's comedy *The Lucky Chance; or, An Alderman's Bargain* (1686); poems such as James Ralph's *Clarinda; or, The Fair Libertine, A Poem* (1729); and fiction such as Behn's novella *The History of the Nun* (1689) and Defoe's *Moll Flanders* (1722).[1] These fictional libertine women's lives, however, were far from those of some of the real female libertines living in London. Even women whose reputations were still hanging by a thread (and who were not quite 'respectable') – coquettes, actresses and royal mistresses – while they were revered, were also castigated and often brought down for their moral laxity. This might not necessarily come about just because a woman was working selling sex, as a streetwalker, bawd or prostitute working from a brothel, but instead could be because she was making a public role for herself. Libertine women were *public* women. It is unlikely that a private or domesticated female would be seen as a libertine, except perhaps when her private life became public, as seen in seduction, abduction or adultery trials. But since their reputations were in tatters by then, 'libertine' was not necessarily an appropriate term for these women at all. Most libertine women had foregone a respectable life in order to use their sexuality to gain something from men. A female libertine's life was one not of gay sexual abandon, but hard work, in which she would use her sexual favours in order to gain some security (and even occasionally luxury), if not always accompanied by freedom or complete independence. Readers might think this a generalization, but there is enough evidence in this book to show how sexually available women were negatively regarded and how they struggled their way through life. No doubt there were women who revelled in sexual abandon or found sexual contentment with one or many men, but even they were dependent on a man's fancy or whim unless they managed to obtain an independent income.

The women who fitted the role of female libertine most closely were the high-ranking courtesans or actresses who could choose their sexual partners. They would not necessarily be in pursuit of sex with lots of different men, as libertine men might be with lots of different women, but would be looking for a wealthy man who could keep them. Even women who were sexually lax were keen to put up a veil of respectability to protect themselves from acquiring sordid reputations – for example, courtesan autobiographers such as Harriette Wilson and Julia Johnstone were very careful to project an image of respectability.

This book examines the role of women in the long eighteenth century (roughly 1680 to 1830) who came to be associated with sex outside of marriage and were verbally abused for indulging in sex for love, desire or a living, behaviour that men might display with no social diminution. It is this overriding double standard which made women's lives a misery. Men were to blame – male authors, doctors, legal representatives, judges and vicars, all those who made up the legal, medical, economic and social systems. Some so-called respectable women (the chaste single or faithfully married) bought into the idea of slut-shaming with a lack of empathy for those who more freely engaged in sexual activities. I want to dig beyond the usual tropes of 'bawdy London' to reveal the underlying (and deep-seated) misogyny of the attacks on these 'libertine' women and show how they were manipulated into certain roles. Limitations were placed on them, which forced them into using their sexuality to secure a place for themselves in life, whatever the station they had been born into. What, in the twenty-first century, we now call rape culture was insidious in society and more so in cities, London in particular, where networks of protection were more tenuous; although there was no conception of this all-encompassing phrase in the eighteenth century, there was at least a recognition of the prevalence of men's unabated lusts and the sexual vulnerability of women. Yet women had their own ruses. In spite of verbal and physical attacks, they fought back using their wit, guile, cleverness, brashness or whatever they had within themselves that taught them how to survive in a man's world.

George Cruikshank, *The Art of Walking the Streets of London, Plate* II, 1818, hand-coloured etching.

1
Rambles through London

In Holiday-Time, when the Ladies of London
Walk out with their Spouses, or think themselves Undone;
When Whores have a more than an ord'nary Itching
To visit the Fields, and so Ramble a Bitching . . .
Then I, like my Neighbours, to sweeten my Life,
Took a walk in the Fields; but for want of a Wife
Was forc'd to take up with a Lady of Pleasure,
Who I turn'd of at Will, and enjoy'd at my Leisure.

NED WARD, *A Walk to Islington* (1701)

For many libertines, the eighteenth century was a raucous time of dissipation and sexual immoderation. From the brothels of St James's to Newgate prison, sex was used as a bargaining tool and thrived on every street corner. Chance sexual encounters, secret assignations and adulterous liaisons were on offer, with many opportunities for erotic excitement for any Londoner with the inclination. While much of the city was fraught with danger, there was also an array of sensuous possibilities as passions spilled over into animated declarations of love, debauchery and overindulgence in food and drink. One writer remarked, looking back to the period of Charles II's reign from 1660,

> I am quite certain that men and women were far less self-governed than now; when for instance, they were in love, they were much more in love than now. The passion possessed them and transported them and inflamed them. Their pangs of jealousy tore them to pieces: they must get their mistress or they will go mad.[1]

Whether this was love or lust, Londoners craved and suffered for it.

The city attracted millions of people seeking new experiences. Some were in search of work. Some found sex unexpectedly, either through promises of marriage, seduction or rape. Streets were ill lit and full of alleys and ginnels, making it easier for crimes to be committed unnoticed. All sorts of vagabonds and riff-raff dominated the London underworld and everyone had to be on the lookout for vice and scams. Although link boys could be hired to light one's way home for a fee, they might lead a person into a trap. Rogues hung out on every street corner, their main activity being to coax money out of passers-by through trickery or extortion. Crimes were so plentiful in the city that a variety of names existed to describe the people who committed them. There were huffs (robbers who threw their arms over the victims' shoulders and took money from their pockets), rooks (housebreakers who used a jemmy), pads (robbers on highways), philo-puttonists (people using deceptions, such as an old woman pretending to be hard done by and left in a wretched state), riffins (who bent the corners of cards in gambling), shabbaroons (disreputable, mean-spirited ragamuffins), rufflers (beggarmen pretending to be maimed soldiers or sailors) and pimps (those who procured a sexual partner for another person in exchange for money or those who controlled or managed the activities of prostitutes). There were clapperdozen women, who begged on the street with stolen children, Abram men, who pretended to be madmen seeking alms, mumpuses, who pretended to be decrepit merchants or clergymen, and dommerers or dummerers, who faked being dumb. In his *Treatise on the Police of the Metropolis*, Scottish magistrate and statistician Patrick Colquhoun (1745–1820) asserted that 'Crimes of every description have their origins in the vicious and immoral habits of the people . . . Innumerable temptation occurs in a great capital where crimes are resorted to, in order to supply imaginary wants and improper gratifications.' However, he recognized that the cause was poverty, as evidenced by the 'extreme misery and wretchedness of London'.[2] As profligate parents swilled ale in the tap rooms of taverns, their urchin children were left to run about the streets. These mothers and fathers were responsible for rearing their children to be prostitutes and thieves, and the unregulated public houses they frequented were blamed for the decaying morals of the city where 'boys and girls of tender years are to be found engaged in scenes of lewdness and debauchery.'[3]

Thomas Rowlandson, *Drunken Lovers*, 1798, hand-coloured etching.

Villains and footpads (thieves and highway robbers who operated on foot rather than on horses) were particularly good at spotting rich pickings and awaited their prey in the dark corners of streets and on highways. Criminals hung around Hyde Park – Horace Walpole, 4th Earl of Orford and the youngest son of the prime minister, was attacked there as he walked home from Holland House in moonlight. Another time, a man on horseback robbed him when he was in his

John Collet, *Scene in a London Street*, 1770, oil on canvas.

chaise with Lady Browne; although the villain got away with his purse and the nine guineas in it, the noble lady had sense enough to fool him: 'I gave him a purse with only bad [false] money that I carry on purpose,' she told Walpole.[4] Sometimes gentlemen were brave enough to fight off their attackers. One late night as the Earl of Lincoln was passing near Drury Lane in his coach, he was set upon by a gang of villains ready to rob him. The *True Domestick Intelligence* for 5 January 1680 reported,

> they were prevented from their design, chiefly by the Earls personal valour, who immediately drew his Sword, and wounded the first man that presented to the Boot, which made the rest give back, upon which the Earl leaped out of the Coach, and with his own hand seized upon another of them.

The rest of the rogues rescued him and made a hasty escape.[5] Women were more prone to attacks, especially if walking out at night. Elizabeth Humphreys was raped on 28 March 1752 at eight o'clock at night while walking from Rotherhithe to her house in Highgate. John Stevens had seized his opportunity while on the king's highway and put her in fear for her life. Not content with the rape, he also stole her money.[6]

Evidently everyone, whether rich or poor, had to defend themselves from the onslaughts of unwanted robbery and sexual assault. No one would be more aware of the ups and downs of London life than journalist Ned Ward, who wrote accounts of his rambles around the metropolis for the amusement of his readers.

The London Spy

Edward Ward (1667–1731), most commonly known as Ned, was one of the great eyewitnesses of early London. Observing the Londoners that frequented the pubs, clubs and streets of the city, he described the various salacious characters of the town. First the men – the virtuous courtier, the debauched parson who will 'preach up Chastity, as a Cardinal Virtue, and yet shall be the first to debauch your Wife', the facetious hypocrite, the precise Quaker, the covetous miser, the prodigal son, the beau apprentice and the city lecher who is 'a Salamander, Living continually in the Flames of Lust'. Then came the women, who were scarcely any better – the insatiate wife whose 'Lips are full of Wanton Smiles, her Eyes of Lascivious Glances, Toyish Gestures, and her Discourse Veneral [*sic*] Lectures of Lechery' and the amorous maid who 'is a piece of Flesh compos'd of two contraries, Desire and Refusal, a Medium between Love and Lust; as Inconstant in their Thoughts as a Lunatick'. He saw the city mob as a 'rude Multitude ... an Untam'd Monster of many heads, lock'd up in the dark Dungeon of Ignorance and Inconstancy, more infected with errors than Augean Stable was filled with Ordure'.[7] The image Ward was creating was one of a London bustling with energy, a city full of people from all walks of life who were hustling for a living and enjoying sex where they could find it. Women, however, were seen as a constant temptation and men must be aware of their tricks.

Ward uses his wit and humour to reveal his sympathies with women and the underdog. He picked up on the overall misogyny in eighteenth-century society and poked fun at it through his satires, though some people may have taken him at face value. For this was a time in which women were seen as provocateurs, bewitching creatures who could entice men against their will and lead them into trouble.

A man tugged one way by a prostitute and the other by a religious lady: unknown artist, *The Contest Between the Spirit and the Flesh*, 1773, mezzotint.

His books, such as *Female Policy Detected; or, The Arts of a Designing Woman Laid Open* (1695), fulfilled the audience's desire for work on the subject of women, while feeding into their idea of women being to blame for men's sexual downfalls. In essence, he is mocking them as he declares, 'There is nothing more evident, than that several Young Men in this City, have been drawn aside, to their utter Ruin, by the attracting Sorcery of these bewitching Load-Stones.'[8] Young men must be constantly vigilant, he advised, if they are to avoid the lust and subtleties of those women, 'whose gay Apparel and false Pretence to Modesty, gives them cover in reputable Families'. The allure of women is difficult to avoid, and a man must be careful not to succumb, for, he warns, 'The Inducements of the Fair Sex are so prevailing a Propensity, in Nature so forcible, that it is hard to stand unmov'd, when tempted forward by the Charms of a subtle Woman, and drove by the frail Desires of an unbounded Lust.'[9] Women were seen as objects disguised by make-up and artifice in order to lure men into a trap; men must be careful of conceiving too good an opinion of a woman at first sight, 'for you see not the Woman truly, but her ornaments, Paint, Patches, and fine Dresses are to hide Defects; for Beauty, like Truth, is always best when plainest.'[10] Obviously, here he is deriding the idea that men might have no control over their sexual desire and that women are to blame for luring them into a sexual trap. He well understood that women of the streets were forced into a position to entice men into sex for money.

Ward played with his audience in his satires exposing the general perception of the fickleness of women and their potential for betrayal; when a woman praises her own good qualities, she is merely advertising herself as a product to be sought after, and any woman who complains about her husband will surely do the same to any other man;

> Be always zealous of a Maid who extols her own Virtue; a Wife who exclaims against her own Husband in his Absence; and a widow that courts your Company: for when a Woman praises her Virtue, 'tis as a Shop-keeper does a Commodity, desiring to be rid of it, and she that sticks not to lay open the Failings of her Husband to another, will to the same Man, lay open herself whenever he shall require it of her.[11]

In other words, a woman will have sex with the man she complains to, but then will complain about him in turn. Yet Ward was astute enough to expose the pimps and keepers of women, providing them with disingenuous warnings to be 'as careful how you live upon a Whore, as how you keep one; for by the former you will get nothing, and by the latter lose every thing you have got'.[12] Flattery will get you nowhere with women, Ward cautioned men; one must not fall for the insincere praises of women or their declarations of love, as they are cunning and their designs on men will lead them to ruin: 'Let no Woman charm you with the Musick of a smooth Tongue, for many can Talk well that Act ill.'[13] These homilies are followed by chapter upon chapter about the inconstancy of women, whose love is 'easy to be gain'd, but difficult to be preserv'd'. He alerts his readers to the innate malice of women and their explosive nature: 'Deal with a revengeful Woman as with a *Hand – Granado*, which you cast from you as soon as the Fuse is lighted, left it burst, to the Prejudice of him that fir'd it.'[14]

With so many obtuse rantings against women circulating in the city, in which women were seen as a species apart, built specifically for tempting and conning men, Ward was mocking society with his satires, reflecting society's own misogyny back at itself. He did, of course, depict men as either gullible fools or villainous tricksters, and shone a light on men's foibles. According to the books themselves, they were designed as pocket pieces for young men, who could use them to defend themselves against the wiles of the sly sex. They contained warnings of duplicitous womanhood in an attempt to deter men from running headlong into sex and marriage. In his book *A Pleasant and Profitable Discourse in Defence of Married Men, Against Peevish, Fretful, Scolding Wives*, Ward alerts readers to beware, as 'there scarce happens any notorious Murder, Cheat or Villainy, throughout the World, but a Woman is found to be at the Bottom of it.'[15]

According to actor and playwright Theophilus Cibber (son of Colley Cibber), Ward came from a questionable background and was 'of low extraction and irregular education'.[16] Nonetheless, he knew Latin and French and so was educated to some degree. As with many hacks of the time, he operated from a pub in London, his work emanating from the King's Head Tavern next to Gray's Inn, where he lived. In 1699 Ward began a twelve-page monthly journal called *The London Spy*, which was eagerly gobbled up by readers awaiting the latest scandals and tittle-tattle.[17] Published in eighteen monthly parts between November 1698 and May 1700, it covered a multitude of London experiences. Ward portrayed the atmosphere of the most downmarket places. With his ears to the ground, he quickly became known for witty and original stories as he soaked up the environs and local scandals. He described the vices and sights of London on a ramble round the city with his friend, staying the night at the 'Dark Houses' of Billingsgate, huge sailors' taverns. He watched as coarse fisherwomen sat about the fire with their baskets 'hanging on their head', taking nips of ale

A prostitute leading an old man into the bedroom: Thomas Rowlandson, *Touch for Touch; or, A Female Physician in Full Practice*, 1811, hand-coloured etching.

and brandy to keep warm while conversing in an unseemly fashion as watermen sat about eating broiled red herring or cheese and onion with bread. Breakfast in such a tavern might be a pennyworth of burnt bread softened in a mug of 'porter's guzzle' and improved with a sliver of Cheshire cheese.[18]

While many of his musings on whores may have been overplayed for effect, the essence of the descriptions ring true. Certain shops had a reputation as hang-outs for whores and better-dressed, higher-class whores could pull a larger sum than streetwalkers. In one of Ward's

After Marcellus Lauron, *The Cully Flaug'd*, *c.* 1680–1700, mezzotint.

satirical rambles, the narrator's friend pointed out some whores who were 'a kind of first-rate punks by their rigging, of about a guinea purchase', and that any milliner's shop was as 'seldom to be found without a whore as a bookseller's shop in Paul's Churchyard without a parson'.[19] Jilts around town – those women who capriciously abandoned their lovers – lured men to their fate with finery and the help of paint, powder and patches. Poorer whores were forced to accept a shilling for want of alternative employment. Other women sold accessories as a cover-up for the true services they provided, presumably to keep the constables at bay. A gathering of these 'fair ladies' could be found at the Royal Exchange. Though they called out 'Fine linen, Sir,' proffering gloves and ribbons, Ward was under no illusion as to what they were really selling: 'This place is the merchants' seraglio, a nursery of young wagtails for the private consolation of incontinent citizens.'

Even coffee-houses ran whores from their premises. One coffee-house was run by a 'Mother Beelzebub', a madam of a house of 'flogging cullies' who ran a flagellation service on the side. Flagellation was a fixation of the period, understood to help old men obtain erections.[20] The theory was that a good flogging would stimulate the circulation and increase the blood rush to the necessary parts. However, as seen in *Memoirs of a Woman of Pleasure* (more memorably known as *Fanny Hill*), the birch was also applied to young men. This piece of fiction by John Cleland shows Fanny whipping a young gentleman to whom she has been obliged to offer her services. According to Ward, the men who frequented these places loved nothing better than to submit to female flagellants: 'This unnatural beast gives his money to those strumpets which you saw, and they down with his breeches and scourge his privities till they have laid their lechery. He all the time, begs their mercy, like an offender at a whipping post, and beeches their forbearance.'[21]

At his most outlandish, Ward made up fantastical names for some of the clubs he supposedly came across, although some of them were undoubtedly real, as London was awash with strange clubs. In *The Secret History of Clubs*, he describes the Farting Club, the Misers' Club, the No-Nos'd Club and the Atheistical Club – all of which offered specific services for their members. The No-Nos'd Club was supposedly a gathering of those who had been unfortunate enough to lose their noses to syphilis. Ward wryly observed that 'an abundance of both Sexes had Sacrificed their Noses to the God *Priapus* and had unluckily fallen into the *Aethiopian* Fashion of Flat-Faces.'[22] Its members were made up of 'snuffling Stallions; young unfortunate Whoremasters; poor scarif'y Bawds; and salivated Whetstones', 'a Bridge-fallen Lady' and 'a Dub-Snouted Bully'.[23] The Beau's Club, alternatively nicknamed the Lady's Lap Dog club, operated in Covent Garden, where every afternoon men gathered together to gossip and talk about how much they idolized their mistresses; they compared outfits, invented new fashions, shared bawdy talk and drank the health of the women they adored.[24] A weekly dancing club or Buttock-ball was held in St Giles and was a 'Diabolical Academy' consisting chiefly of 'Bullies, Libertines, and Strumpets'.[25] Here, all sorts of vices could be catered for at a small price.[26]

One real meeting place was a club for homosexuals, which was kept under cover for fear of retribution. Ward described the Mollies' Club as consisting of 'a particular Gang of *Sodomitical* Wretches in this Town, who call themselves the *Mollies*, and are so far degenerated from all masculine Deportment, or manly Exercises, that they rather fancy themselves Women'. They imitated women's speech and mannerisms and performed mock birthing ceremonies with cushions feigning pregnancy while disguising themselves in women's night attire. They pulled faces and groaned, mimicking women in childbirth 'to be deliver'd of a joynted Babie they had provided for that Purpose, and to undergo all the Formalities of a Lying-in'.[27] Afterwards they christened the wooden 'baby', probably in mockery of both women and religion. One participant represented a midwife, another a nurse, the rest gossips; the father was congratulated, and a food spread was served. After wine, obscenities followed. 'No sooner had they ended their Feast . . . than they began to enter upon their Beastly Obscenities, and to take those infamous Liberties with one another.'[28]

Sodomitical practices were not confined to private places, but also occurred in central London parks. According to one newspaper article of 1747,

> Last Friday Morning a Soldier was haltered [*sic*] on the Parade in St. James's Park, after which he received 500 Lashes, and was drummed out of the Regiment, quite to the Admiralty Gate, for being found guilty of Theft, and Sodomitical Practices, a Paper with those Crimes written thereon, being fixed upon him.[29]

This not only shows the severity with which such sexual activities were viewed, but demonstrates the practice of public humiliation it was thought necessary to inflict upon men who committed these acts.

The Bawd's Initiating Club was equally distained. Situated near Clarendon House, Mayfair, it was run by 'a famous wither'd Lady' who, after dispensing her favours for as long as her beauty had lasted, had been forced into becoming a bawd in order to survive. The club established various rules and conventions: when any member converted another woman to prostitution, she was given ten shillings, provided that the woman introduced was under twenty, attractive and a virgin. An initiation ceremony was made to celebrate the new recruit. She was to be the first to drink from the shared punch bowl, tossing the cup over her head and declaring, 'Farewell modesty!' From then onwards, she was taught how to deal with all sorts of clients:

> how to File a Drunken Cully, Sweeten an Old Letcher; Whedle a constant Customer; Deceive a Keeping Coxcomb; Humour a Town-Rake; Jilt a Troublesome Bully; Bribe a Reforming Constable; Soften the Sterility of a Crabbed Justice; and how to pass at once a Sham-Saint and a Maidenhead upon a loose Quaker, or an Old Lecherous *Non-Con*.

The newcomer was also taught the ministries of harlotry and all the tricks of the trade – numerous sexual positions, how to dominate, when to play coy and when to be forward.[30]

A young woman new to prostitution would be fêted during her initial introduction to the town as she was fresh meat, but her days were numbered. Starting off as 'a celebrated Punk in *Drury-Lane-Pit*, for the first Year or two', she descended to a lower level thereafter, to 'a Tatter'd Furbulo Customer for the Eighteen-Penny Gallery', and thence to a '*Fleet-street* Stroler [*sic*], in a Sarsnet-Hood and White-Apron, only a fit Mistress for a *Water-Lane* Pick-Pocket'. She was likely to stay in this miserable position until either pox or poverty got the better of her. Her end was likely to be the Lock Hospital, 'where a thorough Salivation wither send her to the Devil', salivation being a 'treatment' used for the pox, but essentially not a cure; or her body patched up and 'her Rotten Carcase [sent] for some Foreign Plantation'.[31] The type of women who enrolled in this club were young girls who had been thrown out of domestic service, those without parents or those who lacked the means to get other types of employment. Always on the brink of some misfortune, the women were sometimes roughed up by bully boys. Their clothes were torn and they were given black eyes, and they were often found covered in scratches or riddled with the pox. Scraping the money together for some medicine to treat their venereal diseases (all of them useless) was difficult and doctors were unwilling to advance medicines without payment up front. One woman, tritely called 'Madam *Pockly*', was found 'Cursing and Damning her Surgeon for refusing to send her more Physick, till she had paid for the Cure of her last Clap'.[32] Once together, the women enjoyed themselves in their club, as they drank to excess, shared bawdy tales and boasted of their sexual adventures to one another.[33]

Market-women joined clubs for protection and to enjoy each other's company over a drink or two. There were several of these clubs, described as 'Flat-Cap Societies of Female Tatlers'. As soon as their business was over, they fell to drinking in the taverns around the markets where they worked. One of the main clubs was held at Clare-market (between Lincoln's Inn Fields and the Strand), where sun-worn old women peddlers of herbs and tripe sat down together and shared a meal and mutual conviviality; 'although they Drink like Wine-Coopers, they always eat like Ladies.'[34] While downing a quart of the best claret, they gossiped about their various affairs and told bawdy tales, asking who had been knocked up by whom and whose wife was in bed with whose husband.

The thriving sex life of London can be seen in adverts placed at the back of Ned Ward's publications ranging from jocular requests for the return of a maidenhead to a potion offering a cure for venereal disease. One advert in Ward's satirical pamphlet *The London Terraefilius; or, The Satyrical Reformer* of 1707, which attested to being 'Drolling reflections on the Vices and Vanities of both Sexes', boasted new inventions such as a 'Curry-Comb', which was a word generally used to describe a brush meant for grooming horses, but here appears to be a fine-toothed comb for combing out genital lice, or the 'Teasing Plague', as it was called.[35]

There is little doubt that Ward's racy writings landed him in trouble. In 1706 the *London Gazette* reported, 'Edward Ward, being convicted of Writing, Printing and Publishing several Scandalous and Seditious Libels . . . on Thursday last [was] fined for the same by the

London at night: James McArdell, *Teague's Ramble at Charing Cross*, 1747, mezzotint.

Court of Queen's-Bench 40 Marks' (a mark was thirteen shillings and fourpence). He was ordered to stand in the pillory for an hour a couple of times at different public venues: first, the following Wednesday at Charing Cross for an hour between twelve and two in the afternoon, with a notice stuck to his head denoting his offence; then again the following Thursday, at the Royal Exchange in Cornhill.[36] After Ward finished with writing, he turned to operating as a publican at the Bacchus tavern in Clerkenwell Green and later became a coffee-house proprietor near Gray's Inn, no doubt seeking some financial security and a less troublesome business in his later years. He died on 20 June 1731 and was buried in St Pancras's churchyard.[37]

Ward's journalistic efforts left a lasting imprint of London streets and lewd lives. These descriptions would be joined by others in further accounts, some of them fictionalized, such as the anonymous *The Midnight Ramble; or, The Adventures of Two Noble Night-Walkers* (1754). The story depicted a couple of jealous wives following their husbands around London trying to find what they were up to on their night-time excursions.[38] The eerie feeling of walking round London at night is reflected in the focus on darkness and difficulty in seeing. Only the moon lights their way, indicating the very real danger of prowling the streets at night; 'as the Moon was by this Time rose pretty high, they had Light sufficient to conduct them to their Habitations.'[39] One newspaper clipping from 1731 pasted within the book reported that on 'Monday Night (for the first Time) London Bridge appeared most gloriously illuminated by the Addition of nineteen globular Lights . . . which all must own will greatly contribute to prevent the Robberies so frequent in this City.'[40] At the time, and until Westminster Bridge was opened in 1750, London Bridge was the only crossing of the Thames and connected the City to the suburb of Southwark. It would not be until the following century that it became the first bridge to be illuminated by gas, on 31 December 1813.

The Streets of London

The population of London during the reign of King George II in 1750 was anything between approximately 650,000 and 750,000 people. It was spreading, but not rapidly. St Katharine Docks were crowded, filled with people who made a living on the river. Whitechapel was already crammed with poor working men and women and relatively free of clergy or rich folk. Smithfield was full of thieves and pickpockets. In comparison, the City was ordered, but unfortunately the areas outside its walls were not – and its walls were gradually disappearing. As houses were built close to them and upon them, the walls were covered up bit by bit. Moorfields and Marylebone were still open

Woman falling headfirst through an open cellar door: Isaac Cruikshank, *Whither my Love! Ah! Whither art thou gone*, 1798, hand-coloured etching.

fields. Bloomsbury was up-and-coming, a crowded suburb north of the Strand. Westminster was a great city; Southwark housed half a million people.[41] Until 1760 the London city gates were closed at sunset, but they were eventually pulled down.

Filth covered the roads, which were rarely cleaned, except for thoroughfares. Rubbish was simply thrown in the streets. Dung from horses and bullocks passing through filled the air and the roads. Cattle were driven through the streets to the abattoir on Tower Hill, with huge numbers of cows, sheep and pigs coming up from Kent across the bridge and up to market at Smithfield. The mess and smells they made, along with those of horses, were part and parcel of London streets. With no proper sewers in place, added to this was the fetid mess from the cesspits, which invariably overflowed. Pavements were a veritable hazard as chamber pots were unceremoniously emptied onto pavements, and tavern cellar flaps, through which people could fall, were often left open. Beggars and vagrants darted through alleys as pickpockets slunk about waiting to steal watches and purses. Ballad singers stood on street corners selling their penny sheets of music and whores sat in the openings of hairdressing and milliners' shops. The streets were busy with the noise of workmen and tradesmen calling out their offers of services – tool sharpeners grinding knives, chair

Unknown artist, 'Two women fighting in the street as a crowd cheers them on', 18th century, etching.

menders bashing at wood, pot-sellers and china fixers shouting for sales. Food sellers hawked shrimps, greens, mustard, milk, lavender, fish, tarts and even fresh water. Lobster stalls filled Fish Street Hill and Southmarket was awash with broom men, butchers and cutlers.

Amid the mayhem, vehicles ran through busy thoroughfares and many a poor person about their business was in danger of being run over. The papers were full of reports of young London apprentices being hit by carts. The *True Domestick Intelligence; or, News Both from City and Country* for Friday, 31 October 1679, provided graphic details of such a death:

> On Tuesday last a Coal Cart with two Horses was going over London Bridge loaden with Coals: A boy of about eight or nine year of Age being pin'd up against a Wall, could not escape, but the Cart wheel catcht hold on him, and run quite over his Head, and squeez'd out his Brains.

The driver was committed to prison.[42] The sordid details of such accidents were commonplace in newspapers, reflecting the amount of violence on London streets, which was so familiar that people were no longer shocked at these horrific descriptions of brutal deaths. Natural morbid curiosity simply enticed readers to read on.

Fights in the street were common, and women were often the main protagonists. The *Daily Post* for Saturday, 9 May 1724, reported that 'two Women were fighting in Phonix-Street, and a Crowd gather'd about 'em, a Child of 6 Years old was push'd under a Dray and the Wheel squeez'd out its Brain'.[43] (It seems that squished brains were a frequent occurrence.) Family quarrels often spilled out into the streets. The *Daily Journal* for Tuesday, 3 November 1730, reported an incident that had taken place on the previous Sunday at one or two o'clock in the morning. A cry of murder was heard in the house of Moll Harvey near Hedge-Lane. The constable of the night watch seized the two women who were fighting and quarrelling and confined them in the Round-House. One of the women was a servant in the house and was discharged; the other, Mary Wildman, was the wife of a known thief who had been hanged at Tyburn (now Marble Arch) some six months previously. She had prior convictions for assaulting constables and was held by the watch, but made her escape with the assistance of men from Moll Harvey's gang after one of the men holding her fell asleep.[44]

Jealousy was often the reason for women fighting. Sarah Kelly and another woman were caught fighting in Church Lane, near St Giles. Kelly had stabbed her rival 'in so dangerous a manner, that her recovery is doubtful'.[45] Another reason was poverty, as seen when women fought over food. In one report, two beggar women were found quarrelling over victuals that had been given to them by a servant maid. A lamp-lighter tried to part them, but one of them fell upon him and 'thrashed him in an unmerciful manner', despite having a child tied to her apron. Fighting with anyone who came in reach, she was eventually caught and bundled into a carriage to take her to Bridewell prison.[46] Women fought without any rules or boundaries. A fight between two women in Noble Street near Goswell Street ended when one of them died after the other bit her finger so violently it caused 'Mortification' (probably gangrene).[47] Riots caused by oyster women around Sweeting's Alley at the Royal Exchange were common, one reporter remarking, 'They really are such a nuisance to the Alley . . . There is never a night hardly passes but they breed such riots, that it is really shameful to have it any longer permitted.'[48] These women, who opened oysters at coffee-houses, often got into arguments with each other.

Sex was frequently fuelled by drink and drinking alcohol to excess was common. Diarist Samuel Pepys admitted to being constantly 'foxed' with drink and he was a known groper. Women were just as prone to over-imbibing; Pepys recalled that on one occasion a lady dining at Sir William Bullen's house drank a pint and a half of white wine at one sitting. Nearly every courtesan's memoir speaks of bottles of champagne being drunk; the elite and the middling sort drank fortified wine, punch, port and whisky more freely, and most lower-class men and women would be familiar with cider, beer, porter and gin. Walter Besant, a famous Victorian campaigner, reckoned that serious drinking had begun in 1730 and had been kept up for the next hundred years.[49] Even contemporaries recognized that over-drinking was common, as seen in a newspaper report from 1739:

> Last Friday a Porter in Newport-street near St Martin's Lane, was so indiscreet as to lay a Wager of Half a Crown that he would drink a Quart of Geneva and two Quarts of Beers; the Geneva he drank and one of the Pots of Beers, which rener'd him incapable of seeing, hearing, or stirring, whereupon

Gin court scuffle during a St Crispin's Day celebration: George Cruikshank, *Battle of A-gin-court (Petty France)*, 19th century, etching.

> he was immediately put to bed, where he lay in a miserable Condition for almost Five Days, and then expir'd.[50]

Increasingly, poor people spent their money on gin, as it was so cheap. The evidence of the popularity of gin lies in the fact that by 1736 there were 7,044 gin shops in London and 3,200 alehouses that secretly sold gin.[51] Gin was blamed for the escalation of people fighting: in an open letter to the mayor of London, the Grand Jury of the City of London wrote of 'our Duty to complain of the late suprizing Increase of Gin Shops, and other Retailers of distilled spirituous Liquors' and the 'most dreadful and lasting ill Consequences'. They believed there was a daily increase in both profanity and immorality due to the passions being inflamed by these spirits, leading to a surfeit of cursing, swearing, and fighting in the streets; worse still were 'Women throwing off all Shame and Modesty in the open Day; and in private no common Lust alone is satisfied, but Rapes and Sodomy are perpetrated, Vices which have prevailed more of late Years than they were formerly observed to do'.[52] Some of the inns in the city no longer exist and were pulled down in the middle of the Victorian period – the Bell of Warwick Lane, Belle Sauvage of Ludgate Hill,

John Collet, *Shop-Lifter Detected*, 1787, hand-coloured mezzotint.

the Blossom on Lawrence Lane, the Black Lion on Whitefriars Street, the Four Swans in Bishopsgate and the Saracen's Head on Friday Street, to name a few.[53] In 1796 the annual consumption of ale and porter in the metropolis was estimated at an astonishing £2,311,466 worth a year.[54]

No official police force existed, but there was a disorganized system consisting of parish constables, beadles and the watch. From the 1730s, local improvement acts often included provision for paid watchmen or constables to patrol towns at night, while rural areas had less formal arrangements. Constables were elected and unpaid, watchmen were paid sixpence a night and beadles were employed by livery companies to enforce disciplinary measures decided by the courts. However, it was becoming increasingly difficult to find a suitable number of honest men to protect certain areas in London. Apothecaries were deemed necessary to serve the parish and take up ward offices, as they were well educated and honest. It was therefore unsurprising that the churchwardens of Westminster and other inhabitants of the city were concerned about the passing of a bill to exempt apothecaries from serving parish and ward offices and appealed to the House of Commons, declaring, 'It is very difficult to find a sufficient Number of Substantial Persons, fit to serve Parish and Ward Offices.' Many of the people recruited were uneducated and not altogether honest, and in 'mean Trades'. In desperation to fill the roles, the parish of St Paul's had in the previous seven years employed 'Constables, Surveyours of the Highways, and Scavengers, each to serve Two Years together'.[55]

Women were frequently arrested for robberies and pickpocketing. A common ploy was to pick up an intoxicated fellow coming from a tavern and proposition him. The woman would then lead him to a dark alley where a gang of fellow rogues would pounce on him and rob him of all his possessions. Apprehended, they often ended up before the Old Bailey. One of them was Susan Grimes of St Giles-in-the-Fields, who was indicted for stealing a watch and some money off a drunken Irishman, James Fitzgerald. According to him, he had met her on the streets at eleven o'clock at night and walked her back to her lodgings, where he paid the landlady a shilling for his bed. Supposedly there was a tussle, during which she stole his watch and hid it somewhere 'inside her'. Grimes's report differed from Fitzgerald's, as she related that Fitzgerald had accosted her near Newgate when she was on her way to her lodging in Charles Street. He took hold of her and asked her where she was going. She told him to go about his business, but he followed her home. Her landlady opened the door, and then Grimes again asked him to leave her alone. He grabbed her hand and said he would come in for a drink, and seemed well acquainted with the place. It sounds as though her lodging house was some sort of tavern (or possibly a brothel), as he called for two or three quarts of brandy. According to her deposition, having no money to pay for it, he pawned his watch to her for five shillings. He then proceeded to molest them both. She continued, 'He was so impudent, that we were both found to fall upon our Knees to keep his Hands from under our Petticoats. Then he would have gone up to Bed with me; which I refusing, he threatened to swear my Life away.' She called for a watchman, but they were both taken into custody. The jury obviously did not believe the Irishman, for Susan Grimes was acquitted.[56]

The trial records are full of such stories, and many other women were not so fortunate. Seventeen-year-old Eliza Mills and eighteen-year-old Caroline Williams were caught stealing a purse worth sixpence and five sovereigns from woollen draper George Abel of 7 Powell's Place, off the City Road, on 10 October 1823. He had picked the girls up sometime between eight and nine that evening on Bridges Street, near Drury Lane. It was unlikely he thought them anything but prostitutes. He bought them some apples and invited them for a gin. Who would refuse such a generous offer? The trio then went to the back room of a house in Eagle Court, White Hart Yard, where the crime allegedly took place. Both girls were found guilty; Mills was to serve a year in prison and Williams to be transported. This was a horrific sentence for such a small crime, evident of an obvious stacking of the odds of men with money against women without any. Williams received the harsher sentence as she was older and seen to be more culpable. There is also every likelihood that this was not her first offence. The Transportation Act of 1718 allowed the courts to sentence felons guilty of offences to seven years' transportation to America. In 1720 a further statute authorized payments by the state to the merchants who contracted to take the convicts to America, but not all persons sentenced to transportation were actually transported; some either escaped, were pardoned or had their sentence transmuted to a lesser one. By the early nineteenth century, as part of the revisions of the criminal law, transportation for life was substituted as the maximum punishment for several offences that had previously been punishable by death.[57]

Despite all the crime, there was an assumption that people had a constitutional right to ramble through London's exuberant streets. Even disorderly women were given passage; Lord Chief Justice Holt, when trying Ann Dickens in 1709 for causing an affray, declared: 'What! Must not a Woman of the Town walk in the Town Streets? . . . Why a light Woman hath a right of liberty as well as another to walk about the streets!'[58] However, as we will see, women were constantly being apprehended for being out at night and the reasons given were far from clear. The streets of the metropolis were teeming with social and economic opportunities, as well as sexual possibilities, and all classes and types of people would mingle and try their chance. As Dr Samuel Johnson was to exclaim of Charing Cross in 1775, an observation which could be applied to much of London, the place contained the 'full tide of human existence'.[59]

Thomas Rowlandson, *Catching an Elephant*, 1812, hand-coloured etching.

2

Streetwalkers

A Walking down Fleetstreet
For to meet young Nelly,
There did I chance to meet
The merry merry Gally,
I ask'd her the Price,
She said a Guinea,
And I said it was too much,
And called her my Honey.

ANON., 'Whore Eight o' Penny', 1744

In *Drury Lane* you still may find
Girls which live by their Tails;
All Females wh're to Sport inclin'd,
When best of Trading fails.
Here 'tis the mistress of the Town,
Will turn up for your fair Half-Crown.

ANON., *The Town Mistress; or, The Street Walker* (1726)[1]

London's streets were full of women trying to eke out a living selling sex. All sorts of derogatory names were given to them – whores, strumpets, harlots, jilts, 'Ladies of Pleasure' and 'Women of the Night' – all of them associated with prostitution. Throughout their lives, their status might change; they might start off as 'Whores of Fashion' and end up as streetwalkers, or start off as streetwalkers and work their way up to become courtesans. Others who came from a poverty-stricken background started off as streetwalkers and never rose from their position. Streetwalkers were at the lowest station among other women in prostitution; their job was to pick men up on the streets or in public places. Some of them had sex in alleyways, dark corners of streets or parks; others might opportune in the streets or taverns, but had dismal lodgings where they could take men back for sex.

In London, as in other major cities, contemporary observers complained about the gangs of whores who hung out on every street corner. A writer for *The Tatler* in 1709 declared that London's Covent Garden 'from Cellar to Garrett is inhabited by Nymphs of different orders so that persons of every rank can be accommodated'. Yet establishing the numbers of prostitutes was nigh well impossible as their work was clandestine. Contemporary estimations varied wildly from 20,000 to 30,000 or 40,000 over the century. Saunders Welch in his *A Proposal to Render Effectual a Plan to Remove the Nuisance of Common Prostitutes from the Street of this Metropolis* (1758) estimated that there were approximately 3,000 prostitutes active in London at mid-century,[2] within the area covered by the London Bills of Mortality. He also thought that 2,500 of them were unable to bear children. Yet a visiting Prussian officer named Johann von Archenholz, writing in the late 1780s, reckoned there were 50,000 in London, of whom 13,000 resided in Marylebone alone.[3] This was perhaps a more realistic figure, as it matched that of Patrick Colquhoun, a magistrate and the founder of the Thames River Police. He believed there were around 50,000 prostitutes in the 1790s, but, for his estimation, he included all women who lived with men without having gone through a recognized service of marriage.

Seen as the dregs, streetwalkers were described by one writer as 'having been always accustomed to lowlife, or else through extravagance, the desertion of former charms or other incidents, reduced to poverty and therefore ply the common streets, and endeavour to haul men by force to their disgustful embrace'. As with many other contemporaries, the author appears to lack compassion for the most destitute of prostitutes, as 'necessity compels them to prostitute their carcases for the smallest consideration, and to every reptile of the earth'; they were often full of venereal disease and 'rather antidotes than incentives to venery'.[4] With their looks lost to age and a poor standard of living, they were unable to keep up appearances (if they could ever have afforded to in the first place) and invariably became destitute. Sixpence to a shilling was the normal price for a streetwalker or 'a little profligate wretch' as Boswell called one impoverished woman he picked up. These women were often vagrants without any other means of making a living. Many were displaced peasant women, shunted out of the country towards the towns to look for work.

Various tracts and pamphlets reinforced the idea that streetwalkers were a particularly abhorrent class. One clergyman littered his tirade with references to the Bible. He thought any whore was bad enough, 'a Term of Dishonour and Disgrace', but a *Street-whore* was classified as at the bottom of the pit: 'She is Shame to her Sex, a Grief and Blemish to Her Family.' The ranter vilified all women who sold sex for a living: 'A plying Prostitute is an abandon'd Wretch, a walking *common-Shore, a Light-house* to the Wife, and *Ignis fatuus* to Fools. To be seduced by such, is like going gradually and deliberately into a *Pest-house;* or bartering our Reason for a Distemper.'[5] This stream of abuse towards streetwalkers seen in *A Conference About Whoring* (1725) was a common trope of eighteenth-century writers and these women were singled out for particularly nasty misogynist attacks.

While professional prostitutes were often seen as those who worked solely selling sex and had no other income, the trade was rarely that clear-cut and was as diverse as the women who were embroiled in it. The reasons for taking up prostitution were manifold, but it was mainly due to lack of available support from elsewhere. Girls and young women had often been seduced or raped while working in another family's house, or orphaned, their parents either dead or absent. They had often entered into prostitution early, usually around twelve to fifteen years of age, but most of the women ranged from fifteen to their early twenties. Some decided on a life of prostitution because they had been rejected by their families after a failed love affair of which their relatives did not approve, others because they had been seduced by a man on promise of marriage, then deserted with no one to fall back on. In general, though, most of the women were from poor backgrounds, with poverty being the main catalyst for women turning to making a living from sex: hundreds of prostitutes who were hauled in front of London magistrate John Fielding between 1730 and 1830 were born into pauperism.

The majority of contemporary commentators preferred to see prostitutes as a distinct group separate from the labouring poor

After John Collet, *The Continence of a Methodist Parson; or, Divinity in Danger*, 1776, mezzotint with etching.

because they were thought to form part of the 'idle undeserving poor'. However, in reality, poorer prostitutes, both individually and collectively, formed part of, and were accepted as, plebeian Londoners. Their temporary move into prostitution reflected the fluid social identity of the labouring poor. They were not set apart from their community, but often lived within poor neighbourhoods, such as Spitalfields or the slums of Covent Garden, and shared common lodgings. Some women rented private rooms while others worked from 'petty brothels' along the Strand, Fleet Street and Ludgate Hill; these women tended to be better dressed than the ordinary streetwalker, kitted out with the help of their bawd, usually older women who ran the brothels. They could be found at places of leisure and entertainment such as gin shops, taverns and theatres, since this is where they picked up their trade. Endeavours to get clients drunk at brothels were frequently made, bawds providing drink at exorbitant prices, women then pilfering what they could from clients' pockets. Other lower-class women frequented parks, jelly houses (a type of restaurant where rakes picked up prostitutes), drinking dens and the like in order to pick up clients. Transactions also took place in their lodgings, in brothels or in the backstreets.

Prostitution was a transient profession and women weaved in and out of the trade depending on the work available. Seasonal employment meant women fell on hard times when harvest was over, when a theatre closed after a season or when work simply dried up; then they might take up prostitution on a spasmodic basis. At the best of times, work opportunities for single women were few and far between, mainly jobs in the dress trade or domestic service. Milliners and mantua-makers, who made items of women's clothing, were particularly known for their sideline in prostitution, and for fixing men up with other women. In London, young girls who made money selling nuts or fruit round the piazza in Covent Garden or in the theatres might turn to casual prostitution.

Domestic service was seen as responsible for forcing many young girls onto the streets, as they lost their homes when they lost their jobs. Indeed, any live-in job could easily be lost if it became known that the women had had sexual liaisons. According to one anonymous contemporary commentator, 'The Town being overstock'd with Harlots, is entirely owing to those Numbers of *Women-Servants*, incessantly pouring into it from all Corners of the Universe, and those Debaucheries practic'd upon 'em in almost all the Families that entertain them.'[6] Female servants were often turned out after the master of the house or his son seduced or molested them. Once female servants fell out of favour with their employers, without a reference, they were left in an extremely vulnerable position.

Streetwalking was taking place all over London and no woman was safe from harassment by the local watch. However, being a streetwalker was not illegal and instead a variety of other charges were made against them. Elizabeth Allen was charged in Aldgate for being an 'idle and disorderly person being taken up late in the night and for being a Common night-walker'.[7] Mary Spouse was picked up by a constable at the same time in West London for 'strolling the streets last night and this morning endeavouring to pick up men and known to be an old offender'. On 2 July 1736 Sarah Bennet was caught picking up men on Holborn bridge. It was often loud cussing that brought streetwalkers to the attention of the constables. On 6 May 1736 one constable of the City of London found Mary Hooke near Temple Bar swearing and talking bawdy in a very obscene manner. Mary Armstrong was charged by the constable for Whitefriars for being out late at night and 'endeavouring to pick a Strange Man, being a notorious, cursing, swearing, idle disorderly person and common night-walker'.[8] Group sex was an activity the constables sometimes came upon on their night watch. Mary Truby was arrested in Ivy Lane with John Fryer, Edward Harding and Ann Pentors in 1924, 'all taken together late in the night secreted under a stall in Newgate Market, the said Mary Truby exciting the other two to commit lewdness together . . . the Constable taking the Boy with his Breeches down'.[9] Couples were fornicating in parks, even in coaches; Margaret Palmer was found 'in a lewd action with a strange man in a Hackney Coach'.[10]

Trade was briskest around Covent Garden, Pall Mall, St James's and Piccadilly in the West End, and in Shadwell and Wapping in East London. Other areas included Hyde Park, Charing Cross, the Strand, Fleet Street, Holborn and Chick Lane, Cheap Street and Leadenhall Street, East Smithfield, Petticoat Lane, Whitechapel, Vauxhall Gardens and Southwark. Marylebone tended to be at the upper end of the market, but Hyde and St James's parks were used for open-air sex on the grass. There were also well-known drinking dens, such as Bob Derry's, known as the Cyder Cellar, at 20 Maiden Lane, between Covent Garden and the Strand. It was intended as a concert hall where women and men might have a glass or two of cider and sing along with the music. However, the place fell into disrepute under the management of Derry and it became a dissolute drinking hole, its attraction being that it was open at all hours when everywhere else was shut. Different classes of people mingled here and fights often broke out, with much lewd behaviour. Other song and supper rooms emerged in the early 1800s, such as Offley's (previously known as the

Burton tavern) in Henrietta Street, Evans's two blocks away in King Street, and the Coal Hole down on the Strand.

Women might also pick clients up in taverns and coffee-houses. One report on the Denmark Coffee-House in Bridges Street stated, 'This seminary, though no nunnery [brothel], may perhaps boast some of the most agreeable votaries of Venus anywhere to be met with, King's place not excepted. There are but four in number on the house list, but then they are choice pieces, and merit all the compliments they receive.'[11] Gentlemen's magazines gave information about where you could find women for sex and provided descriptions of the women available. An article in the *Covent Garden Magazine* for January 1773 described the nineteen-year-old Nancy Carter: 'rather short, but with a most agreeable countenance, a fine pair of amorous eyes, which express the strongest passion, a pretty mouth, and a very good set of teeth'. Presumably at a time when rotten teeth were common, retaining them was a feat worth applauding. What is more, she was said to bear a strong resemblance to the courtesan and actress Sophia Baddeley, which was in her favour. The author goes so far as to describe her bosom: 'The two hemispheres of delight, which incessantly pout to be pressed, are white, firm and plump.' Also on offer was Miss Charlotte Turner, who was tall with black hair and black eyes, and very good-natured and chatty, resembling Mrs Abington; Miss Parker was still in her prime despite having had a child; and Miss Sparks (alias Miss Bridgman) 'seems to have recovered her health, and to come into the *em-bon-point*'.[12] These women charged five and threepence for a temporary favour, and half a guinea for a night's lodging. Male readers wrote in to thank the editor for giving details of these women and their whereabouts, offering suggestions of their own; 'As it seems to be the nature of your plan to publish an account of all the nunneries and nuns in this great city, I thought it would not be disagreeable to give you some intelligence of a lady (she goes by the name of Miss Green, or Mrs Mac Daniel) of that call,' who resided in a private apartment at a hairdresser's in Fenchurch Street and was reckoned to be 'a very genteel girl, though not very handsome in her face, and really treats her customers with a great deal of civility'.[13]

Venereal disease was rife, particularly among streetwalkers. In the early part of the eighteenth century prostitutes with venereal disease were sent for treatment to the 'foul wards' at one of London's general

A streetwalker accosts her client: Thomas Rowlandson, *Lust and Avarice*, 1788, hand-coloured etching.

hospitals. Frances Jones was sent straight to St Bartholomew's hospital after being pulled in for being a 'diseased person'.[14] Sarah Morban was picked up for 'being a Stroller' and the court was informed that she was 'in a very bad condition with the foul disease'. She was ordered to be taken to St Thomas's hospital in Southwark for a cure (although there was no cure, only treatment).[15] Miss Hannah Mills was picked up by Constable Benjamin Glentworth of Whitefriars 'strolling with a strange man late last night, and being a notorious old offender and a loose, idle and disorderly person' was sent to the same hospital for the same treatment.[16]

The London Lock Hospital and the Lock Asylum for Women were opened in 1747 to help provide medical treatment for poor men, women and children afflicted with venereal disease: around 26,800 were treated there between 31 January 1747 and 3 March 1800.[17] Benefactors included Robert Walpole, the Duke of Bedford and the courtesan Fanny Murray. The actor David Garrick and John Lacy gave benefit performances in support of the hospital. Women donated money, among them Mrs Garrick, Hannah Moore, Lady Mary Fitzgerald and Isabella Cavendish. The hospital claimed to be a penitentiary with religious instruction given to the patients on the wards. Female patients had to obey a strict set of rules. They were not allowed to talk to each other, except in the presence of the matron, or to leave the premises unless accompanied by her, and they were expected to attend church. Regular hours were enforced: after rising early in the morning, inmates had prayers at 8 a.m., dined at 1 p.m., prayed again at 8 p.m. and went to bed at 9 p.m. They were not allowed to drink, play games or read books.

The accounts of the Lock Hospital and their activities expose the beliefs of the founders and committee of the charity. While seemingly understanding women's plight and their wretched condition, they also shamed them: 'no persons are more miserable or mischievous than those unhappy women who disgrace our streets, and subsist

Refurbishment (or building) of Lock Hospital: Thomas Williamson, *The Opening of Pandora's Box*, 1802, etching with watercolour.

upon the wages of iniquity,' reported one committee. At least they recognized that others had abandoned them in their hour of need: 'Young women, having been seduced, deserted, and banished from their friends, are frequently left without any other resource than that of entering the recesses of debauchery, the general consequence of which are increasing wickedness, a ruined constitution, a premature death, and, as far as we can see, everlasting destruction.' However, women were seen to be responsible not only for the spread of disease, but for the corruption of young men as 'they throng our streets, lie in wait for the incautious, and corrupt the rising generation'. Prostitutes were a scourge on society and were seen as responsible for personal and national destruction: 'We may without exaggeration assert that a common Prostitute is an evil in community not dissimilar to a person infected with the plague: who miserable himself, is daily communicating the contagion to those, that will propagate still wider the fatal malady.'[18] No person who had once been a patient there would be readmitted.

Policing the Streets

The policing of prostitution in London was uneven and spasmodic, reliant on a mixture of watchmen, beadles and constables. With no central system in existence, each parish was left to its own devices. In 1735 an Act of Parliament allowed for the appointment of paid watchmen in St James's, Piccadilly and around St George's, Hanover Square. St George's was typical in that it hired 38 watchmen, four beadles and a watchhouse keeper. A series of further watch acts saw virtually every parish of the metropolis establish its own watch patrol by the end of the century. The acts were a reaction to increasing crime in London, which up to then had been policed only by householders and citizens. The Act of Parliament relating to the St Martin-in-the-Fields watch gave the reason why these watches were established: 'to prevent as well the Mischiefs which may happen from Fire, as Murders, Burglaries, Robberies, and other Outrages and Disorders'.[19] Night-watchmen patrolled the streets between 9 p.m. and sunrise and their job was to caution and arrest any suspicious-looking characters. Beadles were employed to oversee the watchmen. Anyone apprehended was taken to the watch tower, which acted as a short-term holding prison. This was also the base for the watchmen and the beadle and the place where they kept their equipment, including their thick coats and hats, lanterns to light their way, a staff for their defence and rattles to raise the alarm. Meanwhile, constables were responsible for the watch and possessed the power to arrest any criminals, including vagrants and the 'idle and disorderly', which included prostitutes. Indeed, they had powers to arrest anybody who offended against a loosely defined set of behaviours. Constables were elected by local parishioners, but if they preferred not to serve, they hired substitutes. Every so often Justices of the Peace would order them to clean up the streets and arrest vagrants, prostitutes and any 'disorderly persons'.

Various women were picked up in parishes around London for small misdemeanours pertaining to sex: Frances Palmer, Mary Shelton, Mary Davis and Jane Blewitt all appear in the Bridewell prison records in 1693 charged for being 'common nightwalkers', 'known to be lewd persons and not able to give any good account of themselves'. They were sent to do hard labour.[20] The charges applied to prostitutes were broad and often quite vague, ranging from 'vagrancy' to 'lewd or disorderly behaviour' or simply being 'a lewd woman'. Mary Dickinson was 'charged on oath for being a lewd woman and for being picked up by a gentleman in the street late last night and [being] one that can give no good account of herself or her lawful way of living and hath no legal settlement but is a common vagrant'.[21] Elizabeth Piercey was accused of being a 'common night-walker' and Margaret Buttler for being 'a very lewd person'.[22] Hannah Aysh was described as 'being an idle Vagrant person' after being hauled in from the streets at an 'unreasonable tyme of night', then abusing the constable. It seems she was a habitual trangressor, as it was noted that she had been arrested previously 'for night-walking', would not be reformed and so was thought in need of punishment. Mary Squires, Mary Turner, Elizabeth Emexton, Jane Knight and Elizabeth Gill were also brought in for night-walking, among countless others. About twenty other prostitutes were on charges at the same time.

Women were also picked up for other misdemeanours, including pilfering or stealing coins, pewter dishes, yards of cloth and anything else they might easily lay their hands on; Mary Hodges was caught at the Maypye alehouse in Newgate for pilfering a pewter pot and a pie and for being loose, idle and disorderly. Often sex and pilfering went hand in hand. Alice Fry was brought in for pilfering and Anne

Thomas Rowlandson, *Quaker in Love*, *c.* 1815, hand-coloured etching.

Godfrey for 'picking up strange men at three o'clock this morning in Farringdon'.[23] If a prostitute was caught, her punishment was to be paraded round the town in a horse-drawn cart, then placed in the pillory to be pelted with garbage. If it was her first misdemeanour, she might be given a small fine, but recidivists were treated harshly and were more likely to be sent to Bridewell prison for a stint of hard labour; this meant hacking hemp, as depicted by Hogarth in his *A Harlot's Progress* (1732). While poor whores with fewer means to pay fines could not escape a sentence, richer whores paid fines and bribes to get themselves off the hook. Those most likely to evade punishment altogether were the ones who knew lawyers: working around the Temple area therefore helped, as the women who sold sex in that area would be more likely to be acquainted with men in the legal profession, who might assist them. Young lawyers were only too willing to accept the services of these women in lieu of payment. When women visited them, they carried papers in their hands to appear as if they were on delicate business of the law.

In some cases, it is difficult to see what they might have been doing in public to allow for arrest. Hannah Sheppard was taken in as she was 'not able to give Account of her selfe' and sentenced to hard labour. It seems that any woman who was out late at night would be deemed idle and disorderly and was at risk of being arrested. Elizabeth White was picked up by watchman John Wheeler for being a 'common idle Night Walker taken strolling last night at an unreasonable hour and talking obscenely in the streets'; Anne Hussey was accused of being a common nightwalker with 'no visible means of a livelihood'.[24] Neither could a woman easily sit and have a drink in a pub with a man without attracting the uncomfortable eye of the law; Anne Hughes was arrested for being a 'common night-walker taken late in the night with a man in a publick house'. With others,

Whore beating hemp in Bridewell prison: William Hogarth, *A Harlot's Progress, Plate IV*, 1732, engraving.

Six fashionable young men after a drinking session, all with girls in their arms: unknown artist, *Bucks Progress, 12 o'Clock – Bagnio Scene*, *c.* 1796, engraving.

it was easier to see why they might have come to the attention of a constable, as in the case of Frances Munford, who was charged for being found in Field Lane 'in a very indecent and lewd posture with a strange man and being a disorderly idle woman'.[25] Many women were arrested either in brothels or while taking men to them. Anne Corbett and Anne Fuller were accused of being lewd caught in a 'late house' in Fleet Street, probably a known brothel.[26] Similarly, Mary Brookes picked up Thomas Leister and carried him to a notorious bawdy house in a courtyard near the Old Bailey. Sometimes, the situation became dangerous, with weapons involved; Elizabeth Tuckington was accused of picking up William P. Cooper and 'taking him to a house of ill fame where he was assaulted and threatened with a naked knife where she tempted him to lewdness and being a loose, idle and disorderly person'.

The oath of a constable was set out in print with instructions 'that he is to use his Endeavours that Night-Walkers be apprehended'; constables should also be vigilant against swearing and cursing and 'execute their Office with the greatest Effect, for the Suppressing of

Prophaneness and debauchery'.[27] While policing relied on the public to apprehend culprits within their own parish, a London constable was authorized to execute his office in any ward or parish within the city. He would hold the perpetrator at the watch-house in a cell overnight, then take them to Justices of the Peace the next morning. Constables were therefore always on the lookout for streetwalkers and often resorted to entrapment, as described in a London newspaper from 1680.

> On Monday night last, a constable in the City going about his occasions, was jostled by a couple of Ladies of Pleasure, who seemed at first to take no notice of them; but going further, one of them made up briskly to him, and ask'd him for a Bottle of Wine. The Constable demanded upon what terms they expected it? And after a small parly [discussion] they agreed for this Treat and a Pair of Gloves he should have whatever he desired of them. Whereupon they went immediately to a Tavern, where they took a Room, and call'd for a Bottle of Wine, and the Constable bid the Drawer [barman] get a good Fowl and lay it down to the Fire presently; and withal call'd upon the Drawer, and sent him for two pair of Gloves, and whispering the Drawer in the Ear, bid him go to his house and bring the short Staff with him.[28]

The women were suspicious, but the constable allayed their concerns with toasts and general chit-chat. On the return of the barman, the constable, commanding the gloves and the fowl to be carried home to his wife, handed the ladies over to a Justice of the Peace, who sent them for that night to the holding cell, and the next day to be whipped in Bridewell. While this would indicate some vindictiveness on the part of the arresting constable, he was given licence to act upon his initiative.

Despite this, there is evidence that some watchmen and constables simply turned a blind eye to prostitutes. When Westminster watchmen Hunter and Witherall apprehended one woman they knew to be a prostitute and took her back to the watch-house, the constable refused to charge her. There is also an indication that women refused to let themselves be arrested or fought back. Margaret Green, who was charged with being disorderly, refused to go away when ordered, and when John Joyce arrested Elizabeth Shage and Mary Loyde for being disorderly, Shage hit him and Loyde ran off with his rattle.[29] It would seem there was sometimes a connection between the arresting men and disorderly women – that the women were sometimes known to the men policing the area and that these men were unwilling to bother arresting the women. It is also evident that some women were unafraid of the men trying to apprehend them and felt in control enough of the situation to abuse them.

Prostitutes in Prison

Petty criminals such as pilferers, pickpockets, vagrants and whores served their sentences in Bridewell prison. The jail had been established in 1553 in a former royal palace. The original intention of its founders was to turn it into a place for imprisoning and punishing the disorderly poor. In addition, Bridewell hospital was established to provide a home and training for homeless children who would be given apprenticeships in the City of London. Boys who came from the families of poor citizens were referred by their local parishes or nominated by governors. It was jointly overseen, along with Bethlem hospital (also known by Londoners as Bedlam), by a court of governors who met every few weeks. The minutes from these meetings record the arrests of women selling sex in 1690 (and many more like them over the following century), and are now kept at the Bethlem Royal Hospital Archives. From these, we can glean information about the conditions of the prison, the treatment of the prisoners, what petty sex crimes were addressed there and the names of some of the women who were incarcerated for sexual misdemeanours. Over time the list of crimes that the prison dealt with was extended, and sentencing times became longer, with harsher punishments, although the idea of rehabilitation did not really exist at that time in the prison system.

Public floggings, with the women stripped to the waist, were common punishments for prostitution. This type of punishment was inappropriate enough for Ned Ward, journalist for the *London Spy*, to comment,

> I think it is Shameful Indecency for a Woman to expose her Naked body to the sight of Men and Boys as if it was design'd rather to feast the Eyes of the Spectators, or stir up the Beastly

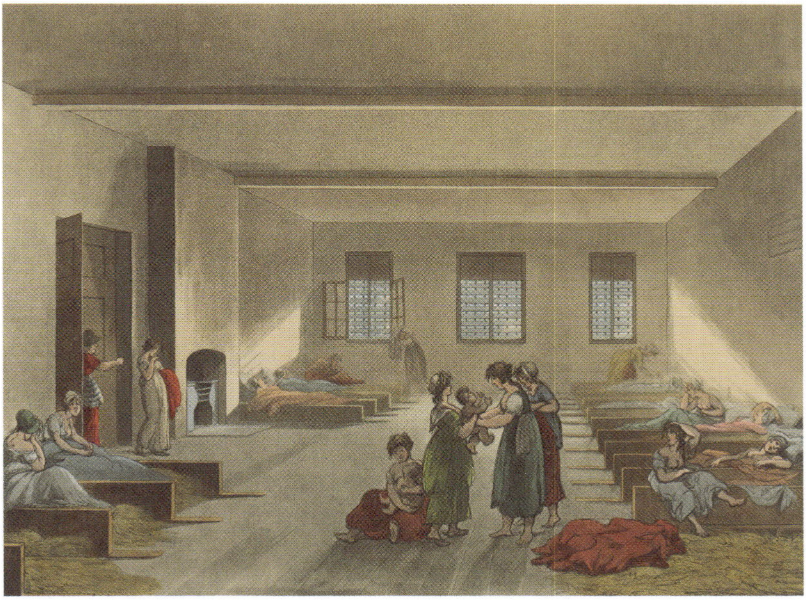

Thomas Rowlandson and Augustus Pugin, *Pass-Room Bridewell*, 1808, etching and aquatint.

> Appetites of Lascivious Persons, than to Correct the Vice, or Reform Manners.[30]

Prisoners were supervised by an overseer who would lash out at them if they were not working effectively. Inmates' hygiene left much to be desired; Ward commented, 'They smelt as frowzily as so many goats in a Welsh gentleman's stable.' All ages of women were inside. 'Some seemed so very young, that I thought it very strange they should know sin enough, at those years, to bring them so early into a state of misery.' Others were so old that it was surprising they were still operating. Some in between were 'in the meridian of their years, were very pretty, but seemed so very lewd that, Messalina-like, they might be tired but never satisfied'.[31]

Conditions inside the prison were unhygienic, with no place to wash, and only filthy straw to sleep on. No one emerged without a body covered in lice. The stench of the prison cells was overpowering, full of human excrement and unwashed bodies. Within the darkness, cockroaches and rats ran freely all over the place. Typhus was rampant and a common killer in gaol. If a prisoner were to survive their incarceration, a bribe must be made to the keeper of the gaol and everything from food to water had to be paid for. A new prisoner was liable to be stripped of all his or her possessions unless a bribe was paid. Those with money paid for separate cells, although these were hardly better than the communal cells where people were huddled together. For a hefty sum, lodging might be found in a superior room of the keeper's house, where the richest prisoners could buy themselves out of a hellhole and into reasonable accommodation with furniture and a bed with clean sheets. Friends and family could visit and books and newspapers be brought in; even a visit by the local whores could be accommodated for a fee.

Conditions in Bridewell began to improve at the end of the eighteenth century. Two of the most pressing considerations of the prison committee were decisions on the maintenance of the building and the general conditions of the inmates. A review was made of the state of both the men's and women's prisons to see if they could be extended. Various repairs and refurbishments needed to be made to the joists and flooring of the hall, as members of the committee found them to be 'in a very ruinous and dangerous situation'.[32] A surveyor was called in to assess the costs of repair, and estimated that converting the room on the second storey of the centre building between both courtyards into an infirmary for men would cost £186 12*s* 10*d*; converting the upper room over the women's prison into an infirmary for women would cost £126 4*s* 10*d*.[33] They also ordered the conversion of the old watch-house into an apothecary shop at the cost of £19 7*s* 6*d*, because a space where the apothecary could make up medicines and treat his patients was needed. A couple of months later the committee ordered the steward to buy two new bathing tubs for the men's and women's prisons. To address the problem of lice, it was ordered that the prisons and the inmates should be fumigated twice a week. This consisted of dousing them with vinegar and again with tar cooked in an iron pot for that purpose. The porter and the matron were in charge of ensuring the men and women were properly fumigated. The committee also ordered extra beds, blankets and sheets to be sent from Bedlam for the apprentices.[34]

New stocks were ordered for the women's prison on 6 November 1783 in case any of the women behaved in 'a Riotous or Disorderly manner or [were] Guilty of any Indecent or Filthy Behaviour'. The toilets were to be kept clean by the prisoners under the direction of the matron; they were to 'throw a Quantity of Water down the

Necessarys sufficient to keep them Clean'.[35] Beds were not allowed for prisoners, who instead slept on straw, but by 9 December 1790 it was decided that it was cleaner for men to sleep in hammocks and they were to be shaved once a week, on Fridays. Both men and women were provided with a new set of clothes on entry to the prison; their own clothes were fumigated and returned to them when they left. By the end of the eighteenth century a new set of rules had been introduced, with the abolition of whipping of women in Bridewell prison in 1792 and the segregation of men's and women's spaces. However, solitary confinement had been introduced, which would make life in the prisons a lot less bearable.

Newgate prison was reserved for those committing the most serious of crimes – highway men, thieves, rapists and murderers. The prison stood on the corner of Newgate Street and was situated next door to the Old Bailey.[36] Often women working in the sex trade were accused of stealing from their clients and would end up facing more serious charges, which would be heard at the Old Bailey. In certain cases, prostitutes such as Sally Salisbury and Deborah Churchill would languish in Newgate accused of murder. Those who could afford to pay for their accommodation would fare well, but for the poorest of the prisoners confined to the common side, prison life was a living hell. Overcrowding and poor sanitary conditions allowed 'jail fever' to spread, killing many inmates; in the ten years from 1755, 132 inmates died in Newgate.

The idea that London was a vice-ridden capital was expounded upon by Anglo-Dutch philosopher and satirist Bernard Mandeville when he wrote, 'It is believed that London is more pester'd with low Villany than any other Place whatever.' However, even what we would consider minor offences now, such as stealing ribbons, cloth or a handkerchief, might lead to a sentence of hanging. Counterfeiters too were considered serious criminals, women among them. Executions had taken place at Tyburn in the earlier part of the eighteenth century but were moved to outside of Newgate prison in 1783, where crowds could still come and watch the hangings. Invariably sex would be used as a comforter. In his enquiry into the state of the prison, Mandeville pointed to 'the Licentiousness and other Disorders of Newgate', complaining, 'It is an encouragement to Vice, that the most dissolute of both Sexes, and generally young People too, should live promiscuously in the same Place, and have Access to one another.'[37]

He also attacked the public route to hangings at Tyburn as an attraction at which the worst sorts of people congregated:

> All the Way, from Newgate to Tyburn, is one continued Fair, for Whores and Rogues of the meaner Sort. Here the most abandon'd Rakehells may light on Woman as shameless: Here Trollops, all in Rags, may pick up Sweethearts of the same Politeness: And there are none so lewd, so vile, or so indigent, of either Sex, but at the Time and Place aforesaid they may find a Paramour.[38]

The prisoners would get drunk along the way to still their fear. In order to escape their fate altogether, some women would 'plead their belly' to avoid hanging, although once they gave birth, they would be hanged anyway. Babies delivered in Newgate were given to the workhouse or to the parish to look after. Prisoners with children who had nowhere to place them had to take them into prison with them. A few brothel-keepers were prosecuted at the Old Bailey, but most cases of prostitution came to be prosecuted in Sessions of the Peace and at the Court of the King's Bench.

The Case of Deborah Churchill

Many of the women working around Drury Lane and other parts of London ended up in serious trouble because of vicious men they had become involved with. Deborah Churchill, a known prostitute and pickpocket (*c.* 1677/1682–1708), was one such case.[39] Churchill had an inauspicious start to life; both her parents had died before she reached her fifth birthday and by the time she was fifteen, she was pregnant. By her own admission, she 'began very early to be loose and ungovernable, and so by degrees arrived to that pitch of Wickedness, which brought her to Ruin', although her involvement with exploitative men seems to have been the real cause. Given the sexual climate of the times, once she had lost her virginity, there was not much opportunity to salvage herself. At some time she moved from her home town of Norwich to London and began working in the brothels around Drury Lane, sometimes using the name of Miller. After being arrested for murder, she ended up in Newgate prison and recounted her life story to the chaplain, Paul Lorrain.

Lorrain attended to prisoners' religious needs twice a day in the Newgate chapel, praying with them and encouraging their repentance. As one of the inmates, Churchill made regular confessions and related her life story to him, an account which he later had the temerity to publish. During her incarceration, Churchill was obviously in a state of high anxiety and trepidation and 'cried bitterly for her past Follies', which is understandable given that she was facing death. Lorrain stated that she cried about her 'Abuse of the good Education which her Parents and Friends (Persons of great Worth) had given her, who in her younger years was by them carefully brought up in Religion and good Manners'; however, she admitted she had 'wickedly thrown off all those good things' and 'abandon'd herself to all manner of Filthiness and Uncleanness with greediness'. More than likely, after her parents died, she was left without proper guidance.

According to this account, she married John Churchill, an ensign in Major-General Farringdon's regiment, and they had two children. Her first husband had been 'a very unkind and bad Husband to her, had thereby given occasion to her going astray'. Her second husband she married in the Fleet prison on the agreement that they would not live together, but it is unclear why (unless her first husband had died, it is unlikely that she could have been legally married to her second husband as divorce was impossible for the poor). In any case, it is obvious that she made poor choices in men, as she took up with guardsman Richard Hunt for the next seven years, who also acted as her pimp. On 12 January 1708 a brawl broke out between Hunt and a Martin Were in a Drury Lane tavern after the latter insulted Churchill. Two of Hunt's friends, William Lewis and John Boy, were also there. Churchill was accused of encouraging them to kill Were, supposedly calling out, 'Crucify him!' The three men escaped, but she was taken in as an accessory and condemned to death on 26 February 1708. She denied being with the men during the murder but accepted her sentence as punishment for her previously misspent life. By this time she had become the archetype of the penitential sinner and was a well-behaved prisoner, but it shows how easy it was to pin murders on women while men escaped without due punishment.

Churchill was temporarily reprieved on 1 March, having been inspected by a midwife and declared pregnant, but her sentence was reinstated when the pregnancy was found to be false. According to Lorrain, at the same sessions five men and four other women had been found guilty of similar crimes, but only Churchill was not reprieved:

> Deborah Churchill, formerly condemn'd for Murther, and then respited, was now call'd to her former Judgment, and order'd with the rest to prepare for Death. Of these ten Persons, Churchill only is appointed to die, and the rest have (by Her Majesties gracious Reprieve) a further opportunity to shew to the World their Repentance and Amendment of Life. I hope they will take great Care (and God give them Grace) so to do.[40]

However, Churchill continued to deny being involved in the murder or having incited anyone to commit such a crime. She admitted Hunt was an acquaintance of hers whom she had been with for seven years, living 'in a lascivious and adulterous way'; she was besotted with him despite his violent personality. It was obvious that Hunt was an aggressive character and would easily have been provoked to murder. Even she realized he was 'a very passionate and dangerous Man', to the extent that she had sometimes been afraid for her life. When they went out together, she said, 'he was always very quarrelsome, and ready to draw upon anybody that he fancied did affront him.' Whenever this happened, she attempted to restrain him, as she knew he would either 'do mischief' to her or another person at some point, but 'she was so bewitch'd, that she could not leave off his company.'

While in prison, she admitted that she was not pregnant, but had persuaded the midwives to say she was so she would not be put to death. The chaplain had the audacity to suggest that she 'had done very ill to induce those Women, who declared her to be with Child, to do (perhaps out of their misplaced pity) such a wicked thing, as to take a false Oath for her'. When faced with death, who would blame a woman in her position? She answered that the midwives swore only 'to the best of their Knowledge', as no one knew at the time whether she was pregnant or not, not even her. Most importantly, while she admitted she 'could not plead Innocence, but was a great Criminal before God' (because of her sexual immorality), she always denied inciting the murder and 'did not look upon herself to be guilty of Blood-shedding'. While she 'wept most bitterly' during her confessions, her repentance was for 'the foul Sin of Uncleanness', not because she had murdered or injured anyone. It was her past sex life that she lamented, nothing to do with the accusations against her. Her sexual indiscretions were the matter that perturbed her most, a burden placed there by a judgemental society that had little compassion for sexually active women. The first man she had sex with left her pregnant, and her subsequent sexual encounters were all with unsuitable men. Essentially, it was her so-called fornication that led to her downfall, not any murder she had committed.

Churchill was in evident distress at the position she found herself in, condemned for a deed her male cohorts had committed, but forced into feeling guilty because of her sexual activities. Somewhat bravely, she cautioned other young women against falling in with the wrong company. Facing the onlookers waiting for her execution, she warned, 'I desire all Persons, especially Young Women, to take Warning by me, and take care how they live; for my wicked Life has brought me to this shameful Death.' Even at the end, with nothing to lose, she denied having committed the murder: 'I kept company with a Young-man, who committed the Murther for which I am here to suffer. I did not prompt him to it, nor was near him when he did it. But it was my misfortune to be concern'd with him.'[41] What is saddest of all is her knowledge that her children 'were likely to suffer for her Faults'. Her last thoughts were for them as she turned to the nurse (presumably overseeing the execution) and 'earnestly begged of her to take care of her poor Children'. In a paper 'written with my own hand' on the day of her execution, Deborah wrote of her grief at leaving them. Her hanging was done via a cart in which she was placed when she arrived; once a noose was put around her neck, the cart withdrew, thereby slowly strangling her.

While Lorrain's account of Churchill's life made her out to be a penitent, another account of her life, *The Whole Life and Conversation, Birth, Parentage and Education of Deborah Churchill*, was more salacious altogether, and reminiscent of whore biographies.[42] The frontispiece dramatically declared that Churchill had been 'Condemn'd some time since for the Barborous Murder of Mr William Ware in Drury-Lane, and now brought down to her former Judgement'. According to this version, she was born in Essex, the daughter of a parson, and brought up in a genteel manner, going to wait on a 'Lady in Town'. Here, she met her first seducer, 'where in the Family she was Debauch'd', then kept for two or three years. According to this version, she was a very beautiful woman, but once her looks left her she was probably abandoned and so forced to take up work as a prostitute.[43] Supposedly one of her many lovers was a gentleman going to Ireland who promised to take her with him and pay her well, but for some reason, she left him and returned to London. Her usual haunt, as with the other whores, was the playhouse where she met her first husband, Mr Churchill, who is said to have settled £40 a year on her for life. This is unlikely, as it would have been enough to keep her away from prostitution if she had wished. The murderous incident that ruined her life came about when Were approached her, taking her for a whore. When she responded in a haughty manner, he called her a bitch. Out for revenge, she sent her maid to fetch Hunt from a nearby tavern. William Lewis and Hunt ended up killing Were, a crime for which she was blamed.[44]

While Churchill thought herself a wicked woman, it is difficult to see anything other than an orphaned child being taken advantage of sexually at an early age, then abandoned to her fate. How wicked she had actually been is highly questionable. She only ever admitted to being led astray and having sex with a variety of men, yet she still condemned herself for being a sinner. Unless she was an astute liar, which is unlikely from her confessions to Lorrain and her desire to atone for her self-professed sins, it seems obvious that Churchill was not the murderer. She was simply another poor woman who had been thrown like garbage into London's cesspool by an uncaring society. That society inflicted such guilt on a woman merely because of her sex life exposes deep-seated misogyny, even in a morally lax capital like London.[45] She was executed for murder at Tyburn on 17 December 1708, aged 31 according to Johnson, and 26 according to Lorrain.

The life of a woman in middling and lower-class prostitution was generally short. She often entered it at an early age, her time 'on the town' lasting only as long as her looks. Thousands of women were reliant on men buying their bodies, for which harsh punishments were directed at the women if they were caught. Some constables at least knew the women local to their area and were reluctant to apprehend them. However, the most hardened to the life of a poor prostitute, those who made their voices heard and swore and fought back, were more likely to end up in Bridewell, or Newgate if associated with further crimes of stealing. There was little in the way of compassion for women with few alternative employment opportunities; rather they were seen as an eyesore on the London streets.

3

Brazen Bawds

Thus do the Bawds drive on their Trade of sin
By whom unthinking Fools are soon drawn in:
Her Feet are snares, infectious is her Breath
The Pox her Punishment, her end is Death.

ANON., *The Constables Hue and Cry after Whores & Bawds* (LONDON, *c.* 1700)

London's brothels were flourishing in the eighteenth century, offering services of all kinds, so much so that they had become a major problem for local authorities. Churchwardens and overseers of St Martin-in-the-Fields were so concerned about the sexual anarchy on their doorstep that they called a meeting in 1689 to discuss how to suppress the brothels currently operating in several alleys off Covent Garden and Drury Lane. Little was done in the long run, as by the following century the same area would be found clogged back-to-back with taverns, inns and bawdy houses all running illicit sex for sale. Some of the most salubrious sex establishments existed around Mayfair and were aimed at the high end of the market. Here, titled men and wealthy businessmen paid over the odds for the most desirable women. In turn, women in these places had the possibility of finding a better class of clientele. At the lower end of the market, bawds clapped out from their own days on the town offered the more unkempt whores who were struggling to keep themselves alive. These women were paid a pittance, but at least they had some kind of protection and a roof over their heads. However, they were obliged to have sex with whoever turned up on their doorstep, and did not have the luxury of declining men, as did those higher up the ladder.

Typically bawds ran their business from a lodging house, a tavern or a coffee-house, engaging a group of prostitutes whose sexual services they would sell. Scottish statistician Patrick Colquhoun thought there were approximately 5,620 licensed brothels operating in London alone, but many operated illegally. One German gentleman visiting in 1725 believed there were 107 brothels in and around Drury Lane alone. The disparity in figures was mainly due to the fact that these places were difficult to identify, and operations frequently moved. Brothels also went under the guise of bathhouses or bagnios, where 'assistants' would provide extra services. Bagnios offered bathing and sweating along the lines of a Turkish bath and came to be known as 'Hummums'. The first in London was opened in a basement to the rear of the Piazza Tavern in the Little Piazza in Covent Garden in 1681 and was run by John Small. When Casanova visited London in 1763, he frequented the baths and thought them well worth the money and more economical than most brothels he had encountered. In his memoirs he recalled, 'I visited the bagnios where a rich man can sup, bathe and sleep with a fashionable courtesan of which there are many in London. It makes a magnificent debauch and only costs 6 guineas.'[1] There he saw the well-known procuress Mrs Wells and

Brothel scene: Thomas Rowlandson, *A Sketch of Nature*, 1784, stipple engraving with etching.

the celebrated courtesan Kitty Fisher dressed up ready for a ball while awaiting her aristocratic lover.

Bawds had a bad reputation in general, but they were tolerated – so long as men wanted sex. They were responsible not merely for facilitating the provision of sex services for men, but for procuring young women into the business. Because of this purposeful corruption of girls and young women, bawds were often reviled by the public. Their *modus operandi* was to take on the appearance of kindly old souls, seek out vulnerable young women, offer them bed and board, then secure them into debt. Clothes would be provided for the young woman, which they would be accused of stealing if they refused to work or tried to abscond. The bawd might introduce a young woman to moneyed 'gentlemen' with whom she was expected to have sex in order to pay off her debt, which effectively bound her to the trade. Maria Ann Cooke was accused of stealing clothes from widow Hannah Swinchurch, whom she in turn accused of running a brothel:

> She gave me a shilling a week, and if I did not bring home a man with me every night, I might as well be buried alive: she keeps a bad house, and turned out three girls as naked as they were born; she gave me things to pick up men in, and I thought I had a right to them.[2]

Young orphans milling around on the streets of London were most vulnerable to the advances of avaricious old crones on the make. *The New Cheats of London Expos'd* (*c.* 1780) advised visitors to London to be on their guard against 'the iniquitous practices of the metropolis', especially warning the most innocent country people of 'all the various cheats, frauds, villainies, artifices, tricks, seductions, stratagems, impositions and deceptions, which are daily practised in London'. Among a long list of cheats, readers are instructed to beware all bawds, bullies, pimps, procurers, jilts and whores. Some bawds also acted as a fence for stolen goods that their charges managed to steal from clients; as the police committee noted, the owners of Westminster brothels were 'Bawds, Thieves, [and] Receivers of Stolen Goods'.[3] Procurers were depicted as being of slatternly appearance with no teeth, infected with the pox which eventually killed them off. London bawds were the worst, described as 'the most infamous and destructive, beyond description . . . a wretch, who being lost to all sense of modesty and humanity, is

Isaac Cruikshank, *Dividing the Spoil!! St James's and St Giles's*, 1796, hand-coloured etching.

capable of any action, base and injurious as it may be to society, to serve her own infamous purposes'. New girls were introduced to sex by more experienced whores already in the establishment, and 'five or six of her choice whores . . . are let loose to play upon you at their discretion.'

An ingrained belief existed that women were often responsible for introducing sex to other women, a theme that circulated in various pornographic accounts. This type of scenario had already been well established in seventeenth-century French pornography and its early eighteenth-century English translations, as seen in *Venus in the Cloister*, in which an elder nun introduces mutual masturbation to a novice; *The School of Venus*, where schoolmistresses teach their pupils about sex; and *A Dialogue between a Married Lady and a Maid*, where an older experienced female friend explains the loss of virginity.[4] While there was an acceptance that women introduced other women to the intricacies of sex, there was no hint of true Sapphism. No serious lesbianism was suggested or any permanent sexual inclination of women towards other women – it was just the first step on the way to heterosexual sex, which was seen as 'normal'.[5]

A list of some of the chief culprits, giving their names and their usual haunts, was provided in *The Constables Hue and Cry after Whores & Bawds*, published around 1701. Among the women who could be found accused of running brothels 'of all sorts and sizes' were Moll Carr and Peg Pierce of Moorfields, Doll King of Salisbury Court, Mrs Elizabeth Wenford of Covent Garden, Mary Green of Saffron Hill, Bess Lanturn of Rosemary Lane, Jane Shelley of Kings Street, Westminster, Amy Softbelly and Kate Wood in Wapping and Prudence Appleby of Redriff. Attached at the back of the book was a satire on bawds, accompanied by warnings to 'all Young Persons, to avoid such obnoxious and bewitching Companions'. The document was jocularly (supposedly) signed by men with surnames that imply inadequate penises such as John Falshort, William Wantool and Adam Lost-Yard.

One of bawds' most common ruses was to sell young women as virgins when they had already had various clients. If the sale was of a country girl, it did not matter if she was a virgin or not, so long as she looked the part and appeared fresh-faced, unlike those who had been 'on the town' for a while. Virgins fetched more money, up to ten shillings each, but their virginity was often faked. Methods of 'repairing' or faking hymens were common knowledge and obviously a running joke.[6] Any bawd clever enough to follow this scheme was seen to be 'a wonderful preserver of Maidenheads, for tho' she Lends them out, to every new Comer, she never let's them be lost'.[7] Lydia Bennet in Knightsbridge supposedly had a clinic for stitching up hymens,[8] but faking virginity was less painful, cheaper and probably more common. This practice can be seen in John Cleland's *Memoirs of a Woman of Pleasure* (1748/9), a pornographic novel in which Fanny Hill, a prostitute in a brothel, hides a blood-soaked sponge in the bedpost. She uses this during intercourse to make it look as if the customer has taken her virginity:

> In each of the head bed-posts, just above where the bed-steads are inserted into them, there was a small drawer so artfully adapted to the moulding of the timber-work, that it might have escap'd even the most curious search, which drawers were easily open'd or shut, by the touch of a spring, and were fitted each with a shallow glass tumbler, full of a prepar'd fluid blood; in which lay soak'd, for ready use, a spunge; that requires no more than gently reaching a hand, taking it out, and properly squeezing between the thighs, when it yielded a great deal more of the red liquid than would save a girl's honour.[9]

Other real-life prostitutes used animal offal or some similar bloodied flesh to misguide their clients into assuming they had just had sex with a virgin.

The make-up of brothel-owners changed over the years and by the eighteenth century, brothels were more often run by women than men (as they had been in the medieval period, with its Southwark 'Stews'). Male 'bullies' were employed to act as protectors or front-door men to keep out trouble-makers or assist prostitutes in fleecing customers. While they worked for bawds and whores in order to defend them from unruly clients, they were also part of the sexual threat to women, generally intimidating them by relating dismal tales of murders and rapes they had committed. Two kinds of bullies operated: those who hovered about and belonged to petty brothels, and those who lived upon fashionable whores. The former were made use of in order to introduce men from the country or strangers from outside London into compliance with the extortionate demands of the bawds' whores, but also acted as accomplices to female pickpockets; the latter acted as bodyguards, 'affect[ing] the dress and airs of men of rank and fortune, and by strutting occasionally by the side of a gay lady, add[ing] a consequence to her and themselves'.[10] This induced more gullible 'cullies' or clients to pay out more than they might otherwise have done.

Bullies were used to keep marauding youths or disagreeable clients in check, and were good at extracting money from those who refused to pay up. Gangs of young men called Mohawks were particularly threatening to bawds and prostitutes, as they would beat up women on the streets and smash up brothels; bullies were kept on hand to deal with them. Operating under the cover of night, Mohawks would also break into residential houses and shops and mug gentlemen on their way home from their clubs. A newspaper reported their offences in an article on 'The Town-Rakes; or, The Frolicks of the Mohocks or Hawkubites'. Their behaviour could scarce be called frolics, as they were particularly violent and difficult to control. The newspaper reported, 'These Barbarities have been carry'd on by a gang of 'em for considerable time, and many innocent Persons have receiv'd great Injury from them.'[11] They carried clubs and bats with which they split people's noses, made cuts down their backs, and overturned coaches. They rolled one woman down a hill in a tub. The *Daily Journal* for 13 April 1721 reported that complaints had been made of several similar scandalous societies 'who distinguish themselves with the impious Characters of the Hell-fire, the Demi-dragoons, the Thunder-Club, the Sulpher Society, the Merry Mohawks, etc.' William Hickey related tales about them in his memoirs:

> In the winter of 1771, a set of wild young men made their appearance . . . from the profligacy of their manners and their outrageous conduct in the theatres, taverns and coffee house in the vicinity of Covent Garden, created general indignation and alarm, actually driving away many sedate persons from their customary amusement in an evening. They were disguised under the title of Mohawks and as such severely attacked by the public newspapers, which, instead of checking them seemed to stimulate their excesses.[12]

According to Hickey, the group were elite young men whose chief, Rhoan Hamilton, led Mr Hayter, the son of a wealthy merchant banker, Mr Osbourne, an American law student, and Mr Frederick, said to be the son of the king of Corsica. They usually met at Lovejoys in order to plan their evening of mayhem, which often ended in violence.

Bawds and prostitutes could be arrested for 'keeping a disorderly house', although additional crimes of pickpocketing, assault or fraud might also be added to the charges. Women were occasionally brought before London's Old Bailey for proffering young girls for sex, like Alice Randall, accused of 'entertaining Evil-disposed Persons therein'. At her trial on 31 May 1693 a witness for the prosecution told how he went to the house one evening, and while upstairs, Randall offered him a young girl, who pulled up her coat and put his hands on her belly, saying, 'If you'll pay for it you shall have enough of it.' His reaction was to beat her with his cane two or three times. Such beatings were often a side-effect of having to sell sex for a living. There was no comment about what the witness was doing in the house in the first place. At the same session, Elizabeth Ely was indicted for keeping a 'House of evil Repute' in Flower-de-luce Court off Fetter Lane. In this case, the commotion they were making in the house, 'Swearing, Roaring and Damning all the Night long, drinking to such a pitch, that they would fall out, and cry out Murder', would have made the brothel an easy target. Several lewd women who were enticing the youth of the city were reported as living there, but the problem reached further, as the apprentices were stealing their masters' goods to give to the women. Both Randall and Elizabeth Ely were fined twenty shillings each and made to give sureties (a pledge or guarantee) for their good behaviour for a year, and to remain in prison until they paid the money.[13]

The authorities seemed particularly keen on shutting down homosexual brothels. Mother Clap had been found guilty on 11 July 1726 of keeping a homosexual brothel in Field Lane, Holborn. She was ordered to stand in the pillory in Smithfield and pay a fine of twenty marks, and sentenced to two years' imprisonment. Giving witness to the events, Samuel Stevens said he had found nearly fifty men making love to one another (as the men themselves called it); he declared,

> Sometimes they'd sit in one another's Laps, use their Hands indecently Dance and make Curtsies and mimick the Language of Women – O Sir! – Pray Sir! – Dear Sir! Lord how can ye serve me so! – Ah ye little dear Toad! Then they'd go by Couples, into a Room on the same Floor to be marry'd as they call'd it.

Clap herself supplied their liquor and seemed to enjoy their company, as the witness stated, 'They talk'd all manner of the most vile Obscenity in her Presence, and she appear'd wonderfully pleas'd with it.'[14]

While it was mainly women who were known for keeping London brothels, at least one man was running a homosexual brothel. Julius Cesar Taylor was indicted for a second time in October 1728 for keeping a disorderly house, and 'entertaining wicked abandon'd Men, who commit sodomitical Practices'. Taylor's opportunity for running a homosexual brothel had been made possible by the void created by the arrest of Mother Clap a couple of years earlier. He had allegedly assaulted John Burgess with an intent to commit sodomy. He had been caught the previous August sitting in John Burgess's lap, committing 'such indecent and effeminate Actions, as are not to be mentioned'. He was fined ten marks and five nobles and ordered to give surety for his good behaviour for one year. His fine was higher than the ones given to women, as the crime of sodomy was considered much worse than simply running a brothel. During the trial, the type of entertainment at the brothel came out, including details about the initiation ceremonies: 'When any Member enter'd into their Society, he was christened by a female Name, and had a Quartern of Geneva thrown in his Face; one was call'd Orange Deb, another Nel Guin, and a third Flying Horse Moll.'[15]

Some taverns hired out back rooms where men could take women for sex, as depicted in the third plate of William Hogarth's *A Rake's Progress* of 1735. Once the regular taverns had closed, a shack in front of the church near the piazza of Covent Garden known as Moll and Tom King's coffee shop remained open for much of the night and was renowned as a picking-up place popular in the 1720s and '30s. According to the pamphlet *The Life and Character of Moll King* (1696–1747), 'Every Swain, even from the Star and Garter to the Coffee-House Boy, might be sure of finding a Nymph in waiting at *Moll's Fair Reception House*.'[16] However, couples had to go elsewhere for sex and Moll pointed them to bagnios. She refused to allow beds in her own shacks so as to avoid accusations of running a bawdy-house.

Since often 'memoirs' were not written by the people themselves, the 'memoirs' of Moll King were most likely written by a hack to make money from her notoriety. This makes it difficult to know exactly how much of it is true. According to them, she was born in Vine Street

William Hogarth, *A Rake's Progress, Plate III*, 1735, engraving.

in 1696. She was taken to work as a servant in the house of a Mrs Atwood in Charles Court in the Strand, but was unsuited to her job. At some point after leaving there, she married Thomas King, but left him for a while after finding he had been with another woman. Instead, she went on the town herself and became 'amongst the gayest Ladies of the Town', meeting up with other well-known whores such as Nanny Cotton and Sally Salisbury. Various aliases emerged over time: she passed as Elizabeth Adkins (her given name), Moll Bird, Mary Mary and Maria Godson. Her husband, Thomas King, had been educated at Eton College and King's College, Cambridge, so was not without connections, which would have helped with their business. Her memoirs suggest he had also worked in the sex trade, having been a waiter in a bawdy house in Covent Garden. Evidently, she returned to Tom at some point, and they set up their business together selling coffee at a penny a dish to the market-stall owners from their coffee-house on the south side of Covent Garden Square, opposite Southampton Street. At night, their coffee-house turned into a tavern catering to 'a great many Gentlemen of Fashion and some of the gayest Ladies of the Town' until two o'clock in the morning. Her business became famous for its nightly revels.

The customers operated in their own language, which could only be understood by those in the know, like a sort of early Polari: this was obviously intended to conceal what was being said by those who spoke it.[17] Presumably, this type of conversation also gave a feeling of inclusion in certain select company at Moll King's shack. A dictionary of meanings was printed in *The Humours of the Flashy Boys at Moll King's* in 1732. Even the bills were summed up in what customers called 'Cant' language: 'There's a Grinter's Gig, is a Si-Buxom; two

Unknown artist, *Moll King*, *c.* 1738, engraving.

Cat's Head, a Win: a Double Gage of Rum Slobber, is Thrums' may be roughly translated as 'There's a hog's cheek, that's sixpence, two half-pennies, a penny: a pot of porter, is threepence.' Whole conversations appear to have been held in this way. One customer said to Moll, 'You must tip me your Clout before I derrick, for my Bloss has nailed me of mine; but I shall catch her at *Maddox's* gin-Ken, sluicing her Gob by the Tinney; and if she has morrie'd it, Knocks and Socks, Thumps and Plumps, shall attend the Froe-File Buttocking Bitch,' which translates roughly as 'You must give me your handkerchief before I leave, as my woman has stolen mine, but I shall find her at Maddox's ginhouse swilling gin in front of the fire; and if she has stolen it, I will thump the pickpocketing bitch.'[18]

After her husband died, Moll King found herself entangled in many quarrels, ending in an indictment for violently assaulting a young man in her establishment. In the expectation that the youth would not continue with such an increase in legal costs, she moved the case from Hick's Hall to the court of the King's Bench, where the expenses were much higher. The trial was brought before a jury, but despite all her witnesses, she was found guilty, sentenced to a fine of £200 and made to provide sureties for good behaviour for a year. Moll stood her ground and refused to pay, saying, 'if she was to pay Two Hundred Pounds to all the insolent Boys she had thrash'd for their Impudence, the Bank of England would be unable to furnish her with the Cash.'[19] She remained defiant in prison, but since the fine became the property of the High Bailiff, cutting a deal was the only way he would get some money out of her; he let her off for payment of half the sum, so at least that way he received something. Another twenty or more indictments were served on her before the Grand Jury at Westminster Hall for keeping a disorderly house, but since she kept no beds there, there was not enough evidence to convict her. It is thought that she bribed the justices as well as the defence witnesses, as they failed to appear in court, so it is unsurprising that she escaped conviction.

London's Infamous Bawds

Two of the most infamous bawds were Mother Cresswell (*c.* 1625–*c.* 1698) and Mother Wisebourne or Whyburn (1653–*c.* 1720).[20] Both procured young girls and set them up in business. Cresswell's father was a reputable liveryman, yet despite the fact that she came from an

After Marcellus Lauron, *Elizabeth Cresswell*, 17th century, engraving.

upstanding Protestant family, she attained a prominent position in the sex trade. She was well known to the London public and her position as the top procuress in the city was legendary. Writers and social commentators, such as John Dunton, mentioned her in pamphlets and tracts.[21] Her family had moved from her birthplace in Knockholt, near Tonbridge in Kent, to Camberwell soon after she was born. As with many women in her position, she had started off as a prostitute, working in the East End in Aldersgate, at Clerkenwell and in Shoreditch, then running brothels in Moorfields and Camberwell. By assuming the appearance of a decent and modest woman and regularly attending church, she managed to evade the law for some time. She came to the attention of the authorities in July 1658 when she was in her thirties, by which time she was running a disorderly house in Bartholomew Close.

By the following year, her pretence was gradually unravelling and she was once again hauled up before the magistrates for running a business in Shoreditch. She appears to have wheedled her way out of a guilty verdict, possibly through bribery, as plenty of witnesses testified on her behalf, but she also had well-positioned clients who no doubt saved her in order to protect themselves. A decade later, the Bawdy Riots of 1668 broke out, sparked by Dissenters annoyed by the king's proclamation against private lay worship while ignoring any action against the hundreds of brothels in London, among other more complicated political and economic reasons. The riots involved overlapping groups including apprentices, servants and artisans, and it has been suggested that the apprentices were frustrated about their employment conditions and attacked brothels; under the terms of their contracts, they were not allowed to marry, but nor could they afford the service of the whores in the brothels.[22] Samuel Pepys described 'great talk of the tumult at the other end of the town about Moorfields among the prentices taking liberty of these holidays to pull down bawdy houses' with armed soldiers out in force.[23] Thousands of young men armed with iron bars, staves and various weapons had taken to the streets to wreck brothels in Moorfields, Shoreditch, East Smithfield and Holborn. Cresswell's was one of those attacked: apprentices broke in and smashed up her furniture and crockery. One of her clients, possibly also her lover, was Sir Thomas Player MP, who held the office of City Chamberlain and would provide protection for her after the riots in 1668.

Further public interest was stirred up by the satirical sheet *The Poor Whores' Petition* of 1668, which was allegedly made by Cresswell and her partner in vice, Damaris Page. Supposedly written by them in response to the riots, it contained a plea to King Charles II's mistress Lady Castlemaine, asking her to come to the aid of her 'sisters' and to help pay for the rebuilding of their bawdy houses. Apparently, Cresswell re-established her business after the riots and continued unharmed, as thirteen years later she received another conviction, which was reported in the *Impartial Protestant Mercury* in November 1681: 'The famous Madam Cresswell was, on Tryall of *Nisi prius* at Westminster, convicted after above Thirty years practice of Bawdry . . . some of her Does [women] most unkindly testify against her.'[24] Although the crime of procuring was usually dealt with in the magistrate's court, in this case someone had brought a civil action against her at the Assizes.

Unknown artist, *The Mob Attempting to Pull Down Peter Wood's Bawdy House in the Strand*, c. 1749, engraving.

Cresswell's dubious activities made her the focus of various jibes: her character appeared in Thomas Otway's play *Venice Preserv'd* (1682), she was satirized in *A Letter from the Lady Cresswell to Madam C. [Cellier] the Midwife* (London, 1680) and she even appeared in salacious erotica, as well as *The Whore's Rhetorick* (London, 1683). She died in 1698, and some had reported her as having a 'hacking cough', so it is possible she died of tuberculosis. In her will, she left a considerable amount of money and an estate attesting to her successful business.

Once a bawd's position in the sex trade had become well known, contemporary pamphlets came out outlining their life stories. Hacks were well attuned to the fact that a few shillings could be made out of a bawd's notoriety and any salacious details they might write about them. These pamphlets and small booklets were more often than not a mixture of fact and fiction and portrayed bawds as grasping and avaricious, with various tricks on hand to fleece their customers. Cresswell's death left the trade open for other bawds to take up the spot of London's top brothel-keeper. The story of Mother Wisebourne was told in a sixty-page booklet, *The Life of the Late Celebrated Mrs Elizabeth Wisebourn* (1721) by 'Anodyne Tanner MD', which was sold for a shilling.[25] The 'Anodyne Necklace' was an alleged cure for venereal disease; the pseudonym is given by way of a joke.[26] As with many other procuresses, Wisebourne managed to go about her business for so long without arrest because of her well-connected clientele. In Wisebourne's case, it was the depraved Duke of Wharton who used his influence to keep the arm of the law at bay on her behalf.

As the daughter of an Anglican clergyman, Wisebourne came from a genteel background, and was born in the City of London in 1653. At the age of 24, she married Edward Brook and within a couple of years was operating a discreet business near Drury Lane, running young women such as Sally Salisbury, Elizabeth Minshull, Diana Cardogan and Elizabeth Stanley.[27] After her marriage floundered, in 1707 she became involved with Johann Jacob Heidegger, a Swiss man destined to help her with her business. His father had been a well-known clergyman in Zurich, but it is doubtful that it was their common religious background that drew them together. He put on Italian operas in the Haymarket and threw lavish masked balls, his hand in the entertainment business no doubt of assistance to Wisebourne's own establishment. Though her biography asserts that Wisebourne studied medicine in Rome, this is more likely a reference to her expertise at treating her whores for venereal disease and procuring abortions, since she was 'always furnished with a Closet of Medicines'.[28] Any bawd involved in the profession had to have a well-equipped medicine cabinet and a good doctor on call for early intervention. Bawds carried various herbs and potions to use when any sign of pregnancy occurred in the prostitutes under their employ. Wisebourn died circa 1720.

Another notorious bawd operating in London was Mother Needham (1680–1731), who ran a high-class brothel in Park Place, near St James's Street. As with other bawds, she recruited daughters from poor families, but became known for her malicious treatment of the young girls who worked for her. The Society for the Reformation of Manners reported their findings on 10 April 1725: 'The famous Mother Needham, *alias* Bird *alias* Howard *alias* Blewitt was again apprehended on Sunday last April 4th for keeping a Disorderly House. 'Tis likewise said she has made ample discoveries relating to several of her own profession.' She was arrested for being an accessory to a known felon, a fact reported in the *London Journal* on 2 November 1721. On 23 July 1724 she was again in the news after a search at her house the night before had revealed 'two Women in Bed with two gentlemen of Distinction'. The women were sent to Bridewell prison to serve hard labour. The London public evidently abhorred Needham: when she was convicted for keeping a disorderly house on 24 March 1731 and sentenced to stand in the pillory on 30 April 1731,[29] the mob pelted her so hard that she died a few days later. A flurry of publications came out cashing in on her notoriety and death, such as *Mother Needham's Lamentation* and *Mother Needham's Elegy and Epitaph.*[30] In

Moll's arrival in London, greeted by Mother Needham: William Hogarth, *A Harlot's Progress, Plate 1*, 1732, engraving.

the *Dunciad*, Alexander Pope wrote of her: 'To Needham's quick the voice triumphal rode,/ But pious Needham dropped the name of God.'

Needham had been involved with the unsavoury character Lieutenant-Colonel Francis Charteris (*c.* 1675–1732), who was known as the Rapemaster-General because of his violent assaults on young women. Both Needham and Charteris were portrayed in Hogarth's *A Harlot's Progress* (1732) and their relationship was depicted in a satirical poem published upon Charteris's death in February 1732, *Don Francisco's Descent to the Infernal Regions*, which shows them meeting in hell. By the time he met Needham, Charteris was already infamous for his sullied military career, having been accused of falsifying muster records in February 1711, allowing men who were in debt to enrol in his company for a bribe. Known as a card cheat, a thief and an embezzler, he had grown wealthier by gambling and loaning money at extortionate rates of interest. He had raped a young girl, Sarah Selleto, in the Scotch Arms in Pall Mall, an encounter which left her with an illegitimate child. He employed Needham to procure young country girls to send his way and kept a 'seraglio' at his country estate at Hornby Castle, near Lancaster. He had undeservedly received a king's pardon for his first conviction of rape, and was then charged with another rape on 28 December 1728.[31] The later rape case he was involved with was one of the most notorious of his time and involved Mother Needham; she had sent him Anne Bond, a young servant, whom he had violently attacked and raped. At the Old Bailey trial on 17 February 1730 he was found guilty of rape and sentenced to death, but his sentence was commuted after intervention by his relative the Earl of Wharton (who had assisted Needham in evading the law), to much public outrage.

The Crimes of Jenny Diver

One prostitute-come-pickpocket working in London was to become embroiled with Mother Needham and would eventually set up her own brothel. *Drury Lane in Tears; or, The Ladies of Pleasure Mourning* (1740) claimed to be the 'genuine account of the life intrigues of Jane Webb otherwise known as Jenny Diver', 'diver' being a slang term for a pickpocket. Webb must have been well known as a whore and pickpocket for the hacks to have written about her. She had fallen under the influence of Mother Needham, who was described as 'that insinuating old Bawd'. Needham was evidently quick to sniff out new flesh for her sex trade, as Webb allegedly commented, 'having got Scent of several giddy headed young Girls in our Neighbourhood, [she] made use of many Allurements, by her Female Correspondent in that Part of Town, to entrap one or more of us.'[32] Webb quickly became the centre of attention of the many male callers to Needham's house.

Disagreements and fights between women and their bawds were commonplace and often ongoing. Webb complained that Needham did not buy her enough things, and admitted violence against her: 'I once cut the Old Women's Hand in five Places, with a Quatern Pot, for which I was severely punished' by 'an old Stalion' whom Needham kept in the house. He beat Webb so badly with a 'Crab Tree Cudgel' (hardwood stick) that she was left unable to walk or to do business. Needham eventually called for a surgeon and apothecary to attend to her so she could stand again. Webb showed her scars to the other women in the house as evidence of what Needham did, but all the women were kept locked up and it was near impossible to escape. In an attempt to assuage Webb, Needham plied her with new clothes, but instead Webb patiently awaited her revenge on the old fellow who had beaten her. Once he and Needham fell to fighting over a couple of guineas Webb had stolen from Needham's pocket, Webb picked up a penknife and, under the pretext of protecting Needham, slashed his nose so badly that he carried the scars to his grave.

Webb had managed to save thirty guineas with the intention of setting up on her own business, which caused another row between her and Needham. According to the pamphlet, Webb 'fell upon her Tooth and Nail' and she was taken into custody at the gatehouse in Westminster. Imprisoned for the next seventeen weeks, she was taught all the 'tricks of the town' by the other female prisoners, women trying to survive as she did. When she was finally allowed out, she bumped into Needham in King Street in Westminster and a scuffle broke out. Needham threatened her and called her a 'barren bitch', but Webb took advantage of the crowd that had developed around them, telling them who Needham was and what she had done to her. Procurers were generally hated by the public and the crowd sided with Webb, heckling Needham and beginning to tear at her clothes. Needham narrowly escaped real harm by hailing a cab and retreating.

Webb set up in business for herself, hiring a house and some other women. Initially, the trade went well and they pulled in lots of custom,

After John Collet, *The Female Bruisers*, 1770, engraving.

but soon the house was making a bad reputation for itself – the girls were so busy pickpocketing that they were ending up before the civil magistrate's court on a regular basis. Most of the women were jailed, hanged or transported and the business broke down, leaving Webb to fall back on pickpocketing. How true this tale was can be compared to her last confession while waiting for her execution. It is in the Old Bailey trials that we find an appendix of her confession while in prison, where we find her real name is in fact Mary Young (with the added alias of Murphew).[33] Pickpocketing was an easy and common crime for women and children, needing only a bit of nerve and sleight of hand. Large public gatherings were the best places to operate as they made it easier to 'dip' unnoticed into people's pockets in crowds and more difficult to spot the perpetrator. Executions, fairs, markets and church services were good venues for the thefts as the victims' attention was elsewhere. Slipping a hand into a victim's pockets or cutting fabric to take the whole pocket, a pickpocket might retrieve handkerchiefs, jewels, purses or money. With the bloom of youth fading, Webb had become increasingly reliant on pickpocketing for her income. She had worked in pickpocketing for around fifteen years when she had first arrived in London from Northern Ireland. She knew nothing of her family, having been brought up by an old woman she called 'Nurse'. From her own account, later recounted to the prison chaplain, she had been taught reading and writing and was exceptional at needlework. A young man had travelled with her on the ship to Liverpool, but he was promptly arrested on landing for stealing his master's watch. Though her intention was to make a living by honest work in London, such business was not forthcoming. Instead, temptation was put in her way when her landlady introduced her to a small gang of thieves.

Criminal gangs became a new source of concern for eighteenth-century authorities. They usually consisted of a small group of loosely connected people, either friends, family or neighbours, who came together in order to commit crimes more effectively. Typically, one would brush up against the victim or bump into them as a distraction; another would pick their pocket, and then pass the stolen items on to a third and possibly fourth person to avoid being caught red-handed. Picking the pockets of women was easy, as pockets were not sewn into the fabric but tied on, and therefore easily snipped off. Though men were also involved in the business, more women than men ended up as defendants in trials. Webb did not hesitate in joining the gang, and money started to pour in fast. She became so good at pickpocketing and thinking up new scams that she was soon given an equal share of everything the gang stole, either by dipping into gentlemen's jackets, loosening jewellery undetected or cutting off women's pockets.[34] In one ingenious scam, she acquired two false arms to cover her supposedly pregnant belly and sat in a meeting house between two elderly ladies, quietly pilfering their watches. Other tricks saw Webb disguised as a pregnant woman pretending to fall in St James's Park, while the gang filched what they could from the people trying to help her.

Aliases were a common ploy of criminals and were used to avoid harsher sentencing when they were prosecuted for a second or third crime. Since there was no fingerprinting, DNA or method of verifying a person except by observation, it was easy to take on a different identity using an assumed name. Webb's criminal activity eventually caught up with her and on 13 January 1738, she was sentenced under her real name, Mary Young, to a whipping for stealing 'a Coral with eight Silver Bells, a Child's Cap, a Diaper Napkin, and a Frock' from Andrew Turner.[35] Next time she was caught, she knew she would receive a heftier sentence if she went under the same name as it would count as her second offence. On 11 April 1738, now 38 years old, she used the name of Jane Webb when she was caught stealing a purse from one Mrs Rowley in Canon Alley, Paternoster Row. The incident was overseen by a bookseller in St Paul's churchyard, Mr Addy. When the trial came up at the Old Bailey, he gave evidence that he had seen Webb assisted by her criminal gang:

> I was looking out of my Window to see the Crowd at the Rehearsal, and had observ'd the Prisoner, with the Assistance of her 2 Fellows, to have pick'd a great many Pockets that Morning: But this Lady was robb'd under my very Window. I observ'd the 2 Men to shove the Gentlewoman against the Prisoner, and saw her put her Hand into her Pocket, and afterwards clap something into her own. I was positive she took Money out of this Gentlewoman's Pocket, and put it into her own; so I told her, if she would Prosecute her, I would take her, for I knew her. She had been an Hour and Half, or 2 Hours, about the Alley that Morning, and had pick'd a great many Pockets.[36]

Addy knew Webb and went after her. Although she was apprehended and taken to the Lord Mayor, it was pointless searching her, as the men with her had acted as receivers. Despite the fact that Webb's friends Mary Cherry, Ann Garter, Frances Fletcher, Mary Robes, John Taylor and Thomas Webb came forward as character witnesses to say what an honest woman she was, they were not believed. Webb was sentenced to be transported at the sessions of the Old Bailey on 15 April 1738.[37] Since she was prosecuted under the name of Jane Webb, with no way of identifying her as the same woman with previous convictions in her name, she escaped hanging and was sentenced to transportation, though the *London Evening Post* identified her as Jenny Diver. On 7 June 1738 she was put on a ship bound for America, the *Forward*, but managed to wangle her way back to repatriate with her gang.

On 16 January 1741 she was indicted for assaulting Judith Gardener in Sherborne Lane and stealing twelve shillings.[38] This time Webb was prosecuted under the name of Mary Young. Again she worked in a small trio: her accomplices were Elizabeth Davies (alias Catherine Huggins) and a man who escaped. Both the women were charged with

Pickpockets: Henry Heath, *The Rule of Three*, *c.* 1827, hand-coloured etching.

highway robbery. While Davies's sentence was reduced to transportation, there would be no such reprieve for Webb, though both women pleaded their belly. While imprisoned, Webb gave an account of her life:

> As I am in a few Days to suffer for what I most justly deserved, and am to give an Account to the righteous Judge of all Things for my past wicked Transactions, I thought it a Duty incumbent on me, as I could no other Way make Restitution, to publish an Account of my past misspent miserable Life.[39]

She was hanged from London's Tyburn Tree on Wednesday, 18 March 1741, along with nineteen other criminals. At her own request, she was buried in St Pancras's churchyard.

Despite the concern of the authorities over the number of brothels in London, their attempts to quash them had little permanent effect. As long as clients kept looking for sex, bawds would find girls and young women to satisfy them. Some of the most infamous bawds escaped sentencing for some time, as they came under the protection of wealthy well-connected men. When they were eventually convicted, the mob sought vengeance against them, because they were so despised as procurers. More often than not, bawds operated with other men and women in closely knit gangs to add petty pilfering or stealing to their crimes.

4
The Celebrated Courtesan

> Lucy Locket lost her pocket,
> Kitty Fisher found it:
> The deuce a farthing was there in't –
> Only the binding round it.
>
> NURSERY RHYME, 1775

The most celebrated whores were elevated to the title of courtesan and included actresses, singers and dancers. The most successful tended to be the most attractive in terms of beauty, charm and wit but also were able to hold an interesting conversation, dance, sing or provide some other sort of entertainment. All of them were lauded in print and paintings; they were the pin-ups of their day and set the fashionable trends around London. While they came from different backgrounds, all of them had fallen into disrepute at some stage in their lives, often because of a single initial sexual misdemeanour; some had clawed their way out of a life of poverty to become the centre of attention among the *bon ton*. Once they had made it to their exclusive position, they were frequently seen at the most stylish places in London and their outings made the news.

'Whores of Fashion' were among the select women in the sex trade who aimed themselves at man of rank and fortune, usually with a train of followers. At the top of their game, they resided in the gayest part of town and reserved themselves for those most able to pay. Good taste and good breeding made them 'a mighty toast among the red coat gentry', the officers in the army, as well as titled men. Courtesans were costly and demanding, warned author Richard King, and if they agreed to become your lover 'they must have a handsome settlement, elegant lodgings, plate, china, and all things suitable to a woman of rank'. A courtesan's fidelity, however, was short-lived and 'will last no longer than you can maintain her in extravagance'.[1] King also cautioned that 'the smallest of her favours are not dispensed without a considerable acknowledgement [payment], to keep up her acquaintance, in a short course of which, so many incidental expenses will occur, as require an ample fortune.'[2] In other words, a man had to be considerably wealthy to be able to afford to keep a courtesan in the manner she demanded.

Growing calls for information on courtesan's love affairs resulted in revelations about their scandalous behaviour. Even reports on their daily activities were deemed worthy of interest. Readers clamoured for domestic details of their public and private lives, any nuggets hidden from view and, more particularly, sexually intimate details if they could get them. Their daily activities became fodder for countless gossip columns published in newspapers, pamphlets, gentlemen's journals, ladies' magazines and even full-length books. Stories about these alluring women became increasingly popular during the eighteenth century and were often based on real-life events, usually with added titillating fictional anecdotes.

Courtesans were at the centre of a cult of celebrity and certain factors were present that allowed for this development. Changes in technology allowed for mass printing and the circulation of news. Leather-bound biographies were available for the elite; smaller pamphlets made stories about courtesans more easily accessible for the less well-off. This, combined with a rise in romantic literature, meant that the market exploded with lurid material, amorous stories and public exposés of courtesans' domestic arrangements. At the same time, privately sponsored public spectacles in small theatres, pleasure gardens and concerts were all part of an increase in consumerism among the British public, which would spur the rise of celebrity figures.

This increased visibility meant that courtesans, actresses, mistresses of well-known men and titled divorcing couples became public property. A person's private life was no longer safe. Questionable morality no longer necessarily dragged a person down, but might well elevate them to a higher status. Libertine women who had made a name for themselves, either from their beauty or their reputation, particularly those seen to be free with their sexuality, became the centre of public attention as the masses developed a fascination with them. The distinction between 'good' and 'bad' celebrities became increasingly blurred as even the most disreputable people became glorified figures in certain public areas. One of these women was a Miss Smith of Duke's Court, Bow Street, 'a well-made lass, something under the middle size', who was 'of true Messalinalian breed'.[3] She had transformed herself from a mere fallen young women to a woman of the town. This meant adhering to certain etiquette such as speaking only to potential suitors who had been formally introduced to her by a known acquaintance. A courtesan must go out for daily jaunts to be seen at regular intervals by her admirers, expected to have an apartment and a coach provided for her and regularly frequented the top entertainment establishments.

Men shared knowledge between themselves on where to find the most attractive and willing women and about the best top-class brothels. Not only was this information disseminated in coffee-houses, taverns, gentlemen's societies and men's clubs, but whole books, magazines and pamphlets on the subject were available. The well-known *Harris's List* was only one such book of information doing the rounds, but other material, such as the *Covent Garden Magazine* and the *Gentleman's Magazine*, carried pointers as to where these women might be found with references to their daily habits: where they went riding, where they went to concerts or when they might be seen in their fashionable carriages. The *Covent Garden Journal* gave a list of male keepers and their more upmarket current mistresses: some of the codenames of those listed can be deciphered, as they were named merely with missing syllables or vowels: 'Among the ladies you may pick and chuse; for none of them can lay claim to be immaculate, it is plain they are all come-at-able, and there is no doubt that everyone had her price.'[4] *Kitty's Attalantis* was a list that was more derogatory to women and referred not only to high-class courtesans, but included some of the women from lower classes; it pointed men to 'the gaudy Miss Stew___d . . . she formerly belonged to the Opera-House, but whether quitted or not for a better trade, is a mystery to me. The *Naked Lad* in *Bedford Street* will conduct you to her apartments.'[5]

These women found wealth in all types of beaux, from kings and nobility to captains of ships, military leaders and Members of Parliament – no one escaped their attractions. John Wilkes favoured Fanny Murray, passed on by Sir John Montagu, the 4th Earl of Sandwich. The Prince of Wales was notorious for his flirtations with a number of well-known actresses. Even the respectable Horatio Nelson was to fall for the charms of a married woman, Emma Hamilton, wife

William Hogarth, *John Wilkes*, 1763, etching and engraving.

to the ambassador of Naples; Emma's fake memoirs, which came out just after her death in 1815, added new life to an old scandal.

While being a courtesan was the summit of the sex trade, she could never rely on the maintenance of this success and was ever-dependent on the whims of men. She could never be sure when this status might be whipped away from her and she was also at the mercy of possible

Charles Spooner, *Nancy Dawson*, *c.* 1762, mezzotint.

pregnancy, the ravages of age and the pox. For many women, life as a mistress, courtesan, actress or prostitute oscillated between riches and destitution – and debtors' prison. Nancy Dawson (1728–1767) was one such woman who edged her way up as an actress and courtesan only to fall back into picking men up in drinking dens when she fell on hard times. Born Ann Newton, probably in Devon, she walked a fine line between the acting profession and prostitution. She was orphaned when she was young and began working for the Griffin puppeteers, with a side-line in acrobatics and dancing. Though she made her stage debut at Sadler's Wells in Thomas Betterton's opera *The Prophetess* on 1 February 1758, the work was seasonal and she fell back into whoring each time the season was over. She ended up in Weatherby's drinking den, run by Mother Weatherby, where the infamous Lucy Cooper also worked. Yet at her peak, her lovers included captains, peers of the realm and royalty, among them Prince Henry Frederick, Duke of Cumberland.

The attractions of women for men were varied and sometimes unusual. The *Covent Garden Magazine* expounded on 'Keeping, Keepers and Kept-mistresses', revealing,

> One woman is kept at an extravagant rate, because she weights thirty stone, and has the largest pair of tetons in Europe; another, because she is very thin that you may span her waist; a third, because she is so completely marked with the small-pox, it is impossible she can ever have that disorder again; a fourth because she would make an excellent school-mistress, and is more expert at the application and flourish of the rod, than Ticklepitcher, of Barnet.

While the act of flagellation had become a favourite in the elite brothels such as that of Theresa Berkeley in Charlotte Street, it is unlikely a man would keep a mistress unless she had qualities other than simply a deft hand with a birch. However, it would seem that another penchant, previously overlooked, had led one titled gentleman to keep one particular woman to service him in an uncommon way:

> a nobleman who has made himself pretty conspicuous, as well as ridiculous for his amours, keep[s] at this time a lady entirely upon the *bon ton*, who administers no other gratification to him than *licking his eyes,* which he declared with rapture is the greatest bliss a woman can communicate.

Another fetish was highlighted by the same magazine: 'Combing of a woman's hair, is well known to be a common passion among the debilitated debauchees.'[6] In the same article, one man was reported to be paying a kept lady £1,500 a year 'for the felicity of paring her corns, with which she is much afflicted, and cutting her toenails'. One woman kept by the elderly Sir Orlando Bridgeman, 'never desired a keeper to do more for her than pay her debts, and make her a good settlement – She chose to cater for herself in all other respects.' This may have been an allusion to Lucy Cooper, who, despite being the kept mistress of Bridgeman until his death, continued to do business elsewhere. Although he set her up in her own establishment in Parliament

John June, *Flagellation*, 1752, engraving.

Street, she continued to frequent Weatherby's, as she appears to have liked the low-life company.

Mrs Elizabeth Weatherby was the infamous bawd who was responsible for bringing Lucy Cooper to the attention of the rakes of London. Weatherby's establishment at the Ben Johnson's Head on Russell Street was a 'hell-hole', according to diarist William Hickey, a place secured by bolts, keys and iron bars and watched over by a 'cut-throat looking rascal'. Inside was in uproar, 'men and women promiscuously mounted upon chairs, with two bare-bosomed women engaged in a fighting match covered in bloodied scratches'. From such a den of thieves, highwaymen, pickpockets and vagabonds was Lucy launched onto the town, probably in the early 1750s.

Though Bridgeman had left her an annuity, Cooper reportedly drank her way through it. By the time Hickey knew her, she was already in debt. At a meeting with a group of his friends in the Shakespeare tavern, his friend Tomkins told the company that he had received a letter from Lucy Cooper saying that 'she was almost naked and starving, without a penny in her pocket to purchase food, raiment, or a coal to warm herself.' The men had a whip-round (Hickey put in ten guineas despite being short of money himself) and they raised £50 for Cooper in order to pay off her debts so she could be released from the King's Bench. Hickey thought this 'perhaps saved the life of a deserving woman, who in her prosperity, had done a thousand generous actions'.[7] Without a wealthy protector, Cooper was no doubt already feeling the ravaging effects of her lifestyle and she died in 1772. Cooper was only one of many women who was fêted when at her zenith, only to fall into difficulties and debt when she was no longer wanted.

A Blazing Comet

One early example of a courtesan who pushed her way upwards was Sally Salisbury (*c.* 1690–1724), one of Mother Wisebourne's 'girls'. Salisbury fulfilled many of the requirements demanded of a courtesan, 'It must be confessed, that she can be very entertaining Company when she pleases; has a surprising Vivacity, and Redundancy of Thought, a Ready Turn of Wit, and is very sprightly at Reparteé.'[8] She was to become so famous that a flurry of pamphlets burst on the scene that celebrated her life story: they include *The Genuine History of Mrs. Sarah Prydden, usually called Sally Salisbury and Her Gallants*, 'regularly containing, the real story of her life' sold at pamphlet shops during 1723 for a shilling a copy, and *Authentick Memoirs of the Life and Adventures of the Celebrated Sally Salisbury* which sold for 2*s* 6*d*.[9] Broadsheets were also printed about her in *The Effigies, Parentage, Education, Life, Merry-Pranks and Conversation of the Celebrated Mrs Sally Salisbury* and *Sally Salisbury's Letter to Frank Rigg*, and songs were named after her, such as 'Sally in our Alley' and 'four new songs' printed in *Sally Slisbury's* [*sic*] *Garland*. Although the tales about her life frequently diverge, and parts were undoubtedly fabricated to fill in gaps or provide entertainment value, there is sufficient agreed facts to create a composite version from the many eighteenth-century biographies and reports about her.[10]

Born Sarah Pridden (there are different spellings, also Priddon or Pryddel) in Shrewsbury in around 1690, she was the daughter of a bricklayer, Richard, and his wife, Mary. The family, including her three sisters, Peggy, Molly and Jenny, moved to London when Sally was three years old and lived in an alley off St Giles High Street. Richard Prydden was a man known to be forever in debt, with 'his

John Smith, after Sir Godfrey Kneller, *Sally Salisbury*, *c.* 1720–25, mezzotint.

well-known Enemies', the bailiffs, constantly knocking at the door of the family house.[11]

At this time St Giles was one of the worst areas in East London, full of slums with families squashed together in 'rookeries'. Destitute people struggled to make a living by pickpocketing, thieving, prostitution and gambling. Murder and rape were common in the area amid cockfighting, gambling dens and brothels. According to one biography, the young Sally devoured storybooks and newspapers, so she was keen to educate herself. She danced to earn some money to help the family, and showed an early aptitude for theatricals. While still only around six or seven, she could do a turn, 'having by Nature a

Sprightliness and Agility of Body'.[12] By her teens, she took up a series of employments undertaken by the poor in order to scrape a living: at various times, she shelled beans and peas, sold nosegays and made matches. She became apprenticed to a milliner in Dukes Place, then an orange seller at the Playhouse at Drury Lane, and sold newspapers at the corner of Pope's Head in Cornhill. News about her charms were already spreading around town. Reports came out about 'the beautifulest Wench, who sold papers about *Cornhill*, that ever appear'd on a sunny Day; and that several Boys had given her half a crown, for an Hour of her Love; that being her usual Price'.[13]

After entering a dancing competition at fifteen years of age, she fell into the clutches of a Dutch sea captain with whom she went off to Holland, but the relationship did not last. On her return to London, she opened a coffee shop and took up with a Colonel Salisbury, whose name she adopted. He felt forced into fighting a duel in defence of Sally's honour, losing an arm in the process, and later ended up in a debtors' prison, leaving Sally with no protector. Her business must have failed, as she moved into lodgings at a distillers in New Street by St Martin's Lane, and she fell into the lower end of prostitution. At one stage, she was carted off to the House of Justice after an argument with her landlady, but escaped sentencing by paying off her creditors.

Sally supposedly regaled her friends with the story of when she first met Mother Wisebourne. As she stood naked, the bawd inspected her like a piece of merchandise and 'felt every Limb one by one, touch'd her to see if she was sound; as a *Jockey* handles a Horse or Mare in *Smithfield*'.[14] Wisebourne's ultimate aim was to pass Salisbury off as a virgin, which was such a profitable business that Wisebourne revirginized her girls on numerous occasions. It was said 'That the venerable old Vice-aider [Mother Wisebourne] did something to Mrs. *Sally*'s Body, which was Secret to them, and then sold her Virginity to a Person of Quality.' By this means, it was alleged that Salisbury

> was dispos'd of to 26 different Lords and Gentleman as a Maiden; being sometimes an Esquire's Daughter privately flown from her solitary friends in the Country; at other Times she was a wealthy Tradesman's Child in Cornhill . . . ; At other Times she was a Nobleman's Niece, or the usual Cant of a young Miliner or Parson's Daughter.[15]

By this time her status had risen, and her finances were good enough that she had managed to establish herself in a select house. She employed a full entourage of servants, including a cook, a chambermaid, a housemaid and a footman, and began to entertain rich noblemen. The *Original Weekly Journal* reported in 1719, 'We hear that Salisbury Sally, a noted Lady of Pleasure, is setting up a Chariot and has hired a Coachman and two Footmen.'[16] Salisbury had reached her peak.

The poet Matthew Prior allegedly fell under Salisbury's spell but his attempts to seduce her were side-stepped in a trick she played on him. Supposedly, after she had flirted with him, Prior had become so aroused that he was ready to agree to anything. He rushed into a nearby room, intending to have sex with her, but she told him to lie down in her lap where, unbeknown to him, 'she clipped off the ends of his Periwigg'.[17] This anecdote was probably a joke made by the author at Prior's expense in an attempt to discredit him. It was also said that Salisbury had a malicious side to her nature that was brought out by her association with the Mohawks, a bunch of elitist thugs who prowled the night looking for trouble: '*Sally,* they say, learn'd her bullying Way, by going o-Nights among the *Mohocks*, drest like a beautiful Youth: And this is most certain, because she was once taken by two Constables, and would have been punished, had they not rifled her Breeches and discover'd her Sex.' Known for their vicious and bullying manners, the Mohawks had been arrested in 1712 for killing the landlady of a tavern in the Strand but, because of their aristocratic class, had been acquitted after subterfuge and bribery. As a consequence, they enjoyed a sort of immunity from criminal justice since no one dared to cross them.

Further scandal erupted when Sally was sent to Bridewell in 1713 after a drunken riot in Mother Wisebourne's house involving Robert Henley, later Lord Northington and Lord Chancellor. Salisbury was renowned for her sarcasm, drollery and sharp retorts, as well as her entertaining anecdotes. Considered 'a celebrated Wit, among a great variety of Noblemen that esteem'd her Smiles',[18] with this skill she began to attract the attention of some of the most eligible wealthy men, among them the elderly Lord William Bentick, Charles Fitzroy, Duke of Richmond, his half-brother, the Duke of Albans, Lord Bolingbroke and the Earl of Cardigan. She also claimed to have had an intimate encounter with the Prince of Wales, later George II, but then every whore in town claimed to have had an encounter with a king at one stage or another.

A scandal erupted after she stabbed one of her lovers with a bread knife in the Three Tuns tavern on Chandos Street, Covent Garden. The incident was described by Lady Wortley Montagu in a letter to her friend dated 25 December 1722:

> The freshest News in Town is the fatal accident happened three Nights ago to a very pretty young Fellow, brother to Lord Finch who was drinking with a dearly beloved Drab whom you may have heard of by name of Sally Salisbury. In a jealous Pique she stabbed him to the Heart with a Knife. He fell down dead immediately but a Surgeon being called and the Knife being drawn out of his Body, he opened his Eyes and his first words were to beg her to be Friends with him, and he kissed her.[19]

The 'pretty young fellow' was the Honorable John Finch, third son of the 2nd Earl of Nottingham. He did not die, but the case was brought to trial soon after the incident. Sally was mortified at her own actions and pleaded his forgiveness, but she was sent to Newgate prison. To his credit, Finch desperately tried to have the charges dropped. Despite his actions, Sally was indicted in February 1723 for assaulting and wounding Finch with intent to murder. Initially nothing came of it as 'she was sick and could not be brought to her Trial, without danger of her Life', so her trial was deferred unto April 1723.

Quick to cash in on her new-found notoriety, books, pamphlets and broadsheets were rushed to book stalls and coffee-houses. Her picture was advertised in various newspapers as a 'curious Print, finely done in large Mezzotinto of the celebrated Mrs Sally Salisbury'.[20] Newspapers and journals also were busy reporting on the stabbing. The *British Journal* for 9 February 1723 expounded that

> Mr. Green, Surgeon of St Bartholomew's Hospital, is added to the Number of those who attended the gentleman, some time since (as formerly mention'd) stabb'd by Sally Salisbury; and tho' he is not yet reputed past Danger, he is much better than at any time since this unhappy Accident happen'd.[21]

Sally Salisbury stabbing Sir John Finch, illustration from William Jackson, *The New and Complete Newgate Calendar; or, Villany Displayed in All Its Branches* (1795).

The *Evening Post* for 23 February reported,

> Yesterday Sally Salisbury was carried from Newgate before Judge Eyre in order to be admitted to Bail; but the same being opposed on the Part of the Gentleman wounded by her, the Matter was strenuously argued by Council *Pro* and *Con*, and the Surgeon Oath not being Satisfactory that he was thoroughly out of Danger, (he having been ill since the said Surgeon has seen him) she was remanded back to Newgate.'[22]

The *Daily Journal* for 28 February 1723 commented that she was indicted for a 'high misdemeanour' at Hicks Hall.[23]

When she was finally brought to trial, she was accused of having

> violently, and with Malice fore-thought upon the Honorable John Finch Esq; made an Assault, and with a Knife, then in her left Hand, stab'd him in the left Part of his Body, near the Breast, and between the fourth and fifth Rib, and thereby gave him a Wound of the Length of one Inch, and Depth of three Inches, of which Wound he long languished.[24]

According to the trial report, Finch had been having a quiet 'Pint of Mountain Wine' to warm himself against the elements of a cold winter's night before he made his way home on the evening of 22 December 1722. He had gone to the tavern around midnight (the barman, John Thorpe, said it was 2 a.m., not midnight, but this was found to be incorrect). Thorpe then went to bed and left Finch asleep in front of the fire with his scarlet cloak wrapped around him, leaving the barmaid in charge. Salisbury came in around fifteen minutes later and demanded 'a pint of frontiac' (frontenac wine). The maid had called the barman to come down and he had taken in drinks, a French roll and a bread knife to cut it with. Salisbury had seized the knife and thrust it into her lover. Upon being stabbed, Finch declared 'Madam! You have wounded me!' upon which the barman called for the surgeon to attend him. The surgeon told Sally that it was a dangerous wound and she said, 'I was the person that gave it; and if he dies I don't desire to live a minute longer.'[25] Even so, they did not leave the tavern immediately and more drinks were ordered, although Finch did not drink anything. The two of them later left together. The incident had apparently erupted because Sally discovered that Finch had given her sister an opera ticket and she thought he had 'designs on her'. The defence suggested that the crime 'appears to have been committed in a sudden start of Passion when she knew not what she did'.

There is some confusion over exactly what happened after the trial. The *London Journal* for 20 April 1723 reported that Salisbury was to be released at the next session of the Old Bailey on the request of the injured gentleman.[26] Public demonstrations of jubilation at her release took place in Drury Lane and various other places in town.[27] However, the jury found her guilty of assaulting and wounding, but acquitted her of intent to kill and murder, as was reported in the *Daily Post* for 25 April 1723.[28] She was sentenced to pay a £100 fine and given one year in prison, plus sureties for good behaviour for two more years.[29]

By May, Salisbury had settled into prison, furnishing her room to make herself more comfortable.[30] She was now back in her stride, entertaining men from her cell. Among them was a sea captain with whom she spent the night drowning her sorrows in drink. The *British Journal* reported, 'As their Apartments are contiguous, their Intercourse is frequent, and their Conversation very free and familiar; and they often drown their Sorrows in *Champagne* and *Burgundy*. Notwithstanding his present Opulency, should the government detain him long, *Newgate* and *Sally* may reduce him to his primitive Occupation of a Crab-Catcher.'[31] This was an obvious pun on the captain's seafaring reputation, but also an allusion to infestation with 'crabs' or venereal lice.

Conditions in London prisons were dire and the death rate was high. After spending many months in prison both before and after the trial, Sally was obviously suffering, as the *Daily Journal* reported she was 'very ill and lame in Newgate'.[32] By the following week, the *London Journal* was reporting her worse. A physician and apothecary had attended to her but she remained 'much out of Order with a dropsy'. It appears that this did not stop her drinking, as despite her illness 'she is said to make very free with the bottle.'[33] She received visits from callers while in prison, not all of them pleasant. One 'Person of Distinction' who was admitted to her chamber was 'very rude to her', upon which the officer sent him away.[34] By November, Sally was dangerously ill with consumption, still in Newgate.[35] On the 10th she was visited by two physicians who believed she would not live another 24 hours.[36] She died of fever on the morning of Tuesday, 11 February 1724, a couple of months short of finishing her sentence. The *London Journal* for 1724 reported that 'the famous Sally Salisbury died on Tuesday . . . of a Consumption . . . preceded by a fever so that she was almost reduced to a skeleton.'[37] The 'jail fever' that killed Sally was more than likely typhus, a notorious disease transferred through head and body lice. The disease was associated with destitution and close confinement 'where great numbers of the human race are collected together and especially where poverty much prevails'.[38]

By 13 February her corpse was lying in an undertakers in Holborn ready to be taken to St Andrew's church, Holborn, for burial.[39] Six gentlemen carried her coffin and four mourning coaches attended her funeral. She was interred in the vault.[40] The *London Journal* for 15 February 1724 summed up her life: 'like a *Comet*, her Blaze was bright but of no consequence; Scarce had she appear'd like the Sun, before she disappears like a Meteor.'[41] An ode to her came out:

> Here flat on her Back, but unactive at last,
> Poor Sally lies under grim Death;
> Thro' the course of her Vices she gallop'd for fast,
> No Wonder she's now out of Breath.
>
> The Goal of her Pleasure she drove very hard
> But was tripp'd up e'er half way she ran;
> And tho' every one fancied her. Life was a Yard,
> Yet it prov'd to be less than a Span.[42]

In her honour, a Mr James Bradely named his racehorse after her.[43]

Shining Stars

An illuminating summary of some of the top courtesans, some of them recognizable actresses of their day, was available in *Characters of the Present and Most Celebrated Courtezans*, which provided mini-biographies of Mmes Armistead, Baddeley, Hatton, Farrar, Gay (Farrar's sister) and Mahon, as well as women who are less remembered now, such as Kit Frederick, Bette Coxe, Mrs Bone and Miss Ambrose. Bette Coxe, like so many of her compatriots, gave inconsistent and contradictory accounts of her birth and parents, sometimes when 'in her cups' asserted she was the illegitimate daughter of a lord, and, according to the summary, 'looks so much like a gentlewoman, she certainly must have good blood in her veins'.[44] Her story bears witness to how easy it was for a man to completely derail a young woman's life. Coxe's notoriety began in 1764 when she was 'discovered' as a sixteen-year-old in a hovel in Windmill Street by a Captain Fox, having just given birth and been abandoned by the child's father. Fox took her to his house, where he kept her for a fortnight, 'the object of his cruelty and sport all day, and of his lascivious impotency by night'.[45] Having bored of her, he dropped her off with Charlotte Hayes, a well-known London madam, where she flourished as a courtesan: 'After three years indulgence in every pleasure and amusement that London could afford, while she was in the zenith of her glory, and in the broadest blaze of beauty, she quitted the public situation of general attainability, and yielded to the solicitation of the enamoured Colonel Coxe.'[46] This appears to have been her get-out-of-jail-free card, as he lifted her out of prostitution to share his fortune and home and was genuinely fond of her. According to the author of her story, she took advantage of her position and supposedly, whenever he was away, gave open house to all her friends and 'converted his house into a temple of debauchery', throwing orgies of sex and drink. How true this was is impossible to tell, but it is hard to believe that she would willingly wreck her life so thoughtlessly. She was eventually dismissed by Coxe and returned to Hayes, taking up lodgings in Curzon Street, Mayfair. It was here that she managed to connect to rich men, including the Earl of Ashford and the Honourable Henry Nevill, 2nd Earl of Abergavenny, who kept her for five years while he was still a student at Christ Church, Oxford, sometime in the early 1770s.[47] How she ended her days is not known. Bette Coxe is just another woman whose star shone brightly for a short while and was snuffed out by the ravages of prostitution.

Portraits and mezzotints played a key role in the notoriety of women such as Kitty Fisher (*c.* 1741–1767) and Emma Hamilton (1765?–1815), who were both painted by famous artists such as George Romney and Joshua Reynolds. These women were also connected to erotica circulating at the time, with in-jokes for those in the know. Thomas Rowlandson drew a cartoon of Emma naked in reference to her modelling days as the Goddess of Health at James Graham's Temple of Health, which he had opened at the Adelphi in 1780; this was in mockery of her poses or 'Attitudes' of famous classical figures, which she presented to visitors in Naples after her marriage to Sir William Hamilton, ambassador to the king of Naples. Similarly, Kitty Fisher was so famous a courtesan in her day that she had her portrait painted by Joshua Reynolds no fewer than five times: her name appears in his sitters' books for 1761, 1762, 1764 and 1766.[48] Artist Nathaniel Hone's portrait of her from 1765 is perhaps the most famous, as he cleverly made a pun on her name: he painted her sitting next to a cat trying to catch a goldfish in its bowl, indicating that she was a fisher of men. Edward Fisher's mezzotint after the Reynolds painting was available in shops all over London; 'her face appeared in print-shop windows' at

Thomas Rowlandson, *Lady Hamilton's Attitudes*, *c.* 1800, etching.

the same time as pamphlets concentrating, often in graphic detail, on her amorous pursuits, which were widely available for sale.[49]

Many courtesans were lauded only for a short time while at the height of their youth and beauty. Kitty Fisher's turn in the limelight started around 1758 and ran for about seven years.[50] Just like Sally Salisbury, Fisher had started out working in a milliner's shop, a trade frequently connected to prostitution. Some debate surrounds who was responsible for her initial downfall, but suggestions have been that Ensign Anthony George Martin was the man responsible for first seducing her.[51] *The Sun* newspaper concurred that it was Martin, the 'natural' (illegitimate) son of a sea merchant and a Portuguese woman, a handsome man and known Lothario who went by the name Military Cupid.[52] It is said she broke off their affair due to his lowly position as an ensign, although she retained a fondness for him for the rest of her life. Captain Augustus Keppel may also have been her first seducer.[53] She worked her way up and during her best years lived at Carrington Street in Mayfair.

As usual, publishers were quick to cash in on any gossip. Fisher's fall from her horse while riding in St James's Park on 12 March in 1759 was thought significant enough to reach the newspaper gossip columns. The accident caused a flurry of poems and pamphlets to be published, among them *Horse and Away to St. James's Park; or, A Trip for the Noontide Air Who Rides Fastest, Miss Kitty Fisher or her Gay Gallant.* Fisher and a friend, both attended by officers and servant, had been returning on horseback from Hyde Park:

> one of the Ladies was in black riding-habit, and mounted on a horse singularly marked they flung down the Green Park in an easy canter; but they no sooner entered within the palls of St. James's, but the Lady in black lost her seat, shrieked out, and tumbled to the ground: – Numbers flew to her relief; her distress and genteel Appearance awakened our curiosity and pity. Upon our coming up, we found that it to be the celebrated Miss K----y F-----r: her military attendant had raised her from the Ground. ---The Nymph was in tears, but rather from Apprehension of her Danger than the sense of Pain; for whether it was owning to any thing her Heroe [*sic*] said, or from finding the danger over, she, with a childishness, stopped the torrent of tears, and burst into a fit of Laughing.[54]

The *Universal Magazine* even published a poem about the incident:

> Dear Kitty had thy only fall
> Been that thou met'st with in the Mall,
> Thou had'st deserved our pity,
> But long before that luckless day,

Edward Fisher, after Joshua Reynolds, *Kitty Fisher as 'Cleopatra Dissolving the Pearl'*, 1752–63, mezzotint.

> With equal justice we might say,
> 'Alas poor fallen Kitty!'[55]

A couple of days later a small handbook came out called *The Juvenile Adventures of Miss Kitty F____r*, advertised in the *Public Advertiser*. Fisher reacted with anger, writing to the *Public Advertiser* in March 1759 to complain of the intrusion into her life, that she 'had been abused in the public papers, exposed in Print shops, and to wind up the whole, some Wretches, mean, ignorant and venal would impose upon the public, by daring to publish her Memoirs'. This same newspaper advertised a second volume a few days later.[56] By 1762 ditties were being published in the same paper dedicated to Kitty Fisher, alongside an advert for the Anodyne Necklace, at five shillings, a proposed cure for venereal disease.[57]

At the height of her fame, Fisher's conquests included many prominent and titled men, the absolute proof of a high-class courtesan; among them were Sir Thomas Medlycott, heir of a landowner in Somerset; Admiral George Anson, 1st Baron Anson of Soberton; Thomas Bromley, 2nd Baron Montfort; merchant Joseph Salvador; John Montagu, Earl of Sandwich; Field Marshal Earl John Ligonier; and William Stanhope, 2nd Earl of Harrington. Certain paramours

Francesco Narici (attrib.), *Giacomo Casanova*, 1768, oil on canvas.

offered to marry her, including John, 2nd Earl Poulett, and Henry Herbert, Lord Pembroke, who provided Fisher with £1,000 per year, and £1,000 for 'present decorations'.[58]

Casanova insisted on meeting Fisher when he visited London in 1763 and was apparently impressed by her magnificent dress and charm. Years later, in his memoirs, he recalled,

> Mrs. Walls [Wells, a famous bawd] told us that one day this Fisher swallowed a thousand pound bank-note on a slice of bread-and-butter [though a similar tale was told of Fanny Murray]. The note had just been given her by Atkins, brother of the beautiful Mrs. Pitt.[59]

She allegedly told Prince Edward that he was no longer welcome when he left her what she saw as the paltry sum of £50 after being allowed to join her for tea at her house in New Norfolk Street. Her fame even gave rise to plays – Kitty Willis in Hannah Cowley's comedy *The Belle's Stratagem* (1781) was supposedly based on her.[60]

Under the pseudonym of Mrs Brown, Fisher lived with a Mr Chetwynd, supposedly acting as his housekeeper until he died of consumption. She found a husband in the son of a Kentish squire, MP for Rye John Norris, marrying him first at Trinity church in Haddington, Scotland, in 1766 and then on 4 December 1766 in London at St George's, Hanover Square, by special licence of the Archbishop of Canterbury.[61] Still only in her late twenties, she became ill with consumption and went to Bath to take the waters.[62] She died at the Three Tuns in Stall Street and was buried in the Norris family vault at St George's Church, Benenden, Kent, on 23 March 1767.[63] She was still being talked about four years after her death in the scandalous memoir of Admiral Keppel and another courtesan named Mrs Wells, printed in the *Town and Country Magazine*.

For most courtesans, life at the top was short-lived. They rose to fame, shone brightly for a few years, then disappeared with their health worn out. If they were lucky enough, they found themselves a man with money whom they could marry. If they did not, they might take to running a brothel themselves when they were no longer the flavour of the month. When they were at their height, publications frequently portrayed them in an admirable light and they were considered celebrities. Admired for their forceful personalities, they made a lifestyle for themselves in a society that generally ostracized those who operated outside a certain moral code. Of course, this does not necessarily mean that these women would have been seen themselves as forging a role as free-thinking feminists of their day, but they might at least have retained some level of control and self-determination. While these libertine women operated on their own terms, they lived in a society that was set against unmarried women having sex. Sadly, all too often, with few alternative opportunities, they ended their lives ravaged by illness and poverty.

5

Public Opinion: The Way with Whores

> A girl quits a place, and turns whore: if there is not a bastard to be murder'd, or left to the parish, there is one or more wary youths drawn in to support her in lewdness and idleness.
>
> DANIEL DEFOE, *Augusta Triumphans*

Public reactions to prostitution came from contemporary commentators, novelists and magistrates and from the popular press. The authorities, observers and social critics had complicated and often conflicting attitudes to the topic, and their perceptions about why women became prostitutes varied widely. Should prostitution stay or should it go? Was it best to provide registered brothels and allow prostitutes to operate from them? This would at least mean that fornication was better contained and could be monitored. Or should prostitution be banned altogether, with all the whores taken off the streets, put in prison and given a good whipping as punishment? None of the options seemed suitable – and those authorities who had tried to eradicate it in the past had never succeeded. The municipal authorities recognized that prostitution was endemic and occasionally made half-hearted attempts at clean-up sweeps, but for the most part, they thought that it had a social value in that it kept male predators away from the 'respectable' women of London. It had been impossible to enforce any ban and any previous attempts to do so had simply seen the profession go underground to be run by unsupervised bawds and pimps. Certainly, in that way no taxes were to be raised. On the one hand, the idea existed that the prostitute was an agent of destruction: she was regarded as to blame for her own degraded state. On the other, she was to be pitied, as usually there was a reason for the situation she found herself in.

Thomas Rowlandson, *Vauxhall Gardens*, 1785, etching and aquatint.

Concerns about the visibility of prostitutes on the street were frequently raised at council meetings. At a meeting of aldermen and the common council of Farringdon at St Andrew's churchyard on 11 December 1799, a complaint about the increased number of 'Common Prostitutes' that had been made by several 'respectable' inhabitants of the area around Fleet Street was heard. The committee resolved 'That the common council of each precinct [was] to give such directions to the watch and constables to attend to their duty in order to clear the streets of the prostitutes, as they shall think expedient.'[1] They may well have been under the impression that London spaces were full of fornicating couples as some men and women were content to sexually indulge themselves in public places. Parks, pleasure gardens, commons and river banks were well-known places of sexual assignation. Pleasure gardens offered courting couples a place to meet, while prostitutes picked up clients there. After a trip to Vauxhall Gardens, William Byrd wrote in his diary how he and a friend had picked up two women there and 'carried them into the arbour . . . and about 10 o'clock we carried them to the bagnio, where we bathed and lay with them all night and I rogered [*sic*] mine twice and slept pretty well, but neglected my prayers.'[2] St James's

Park also acted as a pick-up place. Diarist James Boswell wrote, 'As I was coming home this night I felt carnal inclinations raging thro' my frame. I determined to gratify them. I went to St. James's Park and like Sir John Brute, picked up a Whore.' Boswell was known for having prostitutes in the open, most notably on Westminster Bridge, declaring, 'The whim of doing it there with the Thames rolling below us amused me much.'[3] Homosexual men looked for trysts in known outdoor locations in St James's Park, Lincoln's Inn Fields, Moorfields and Covent Garden. Church porches seem to have been a particularly suitable place for sex: two men were caught with their breeches down against the railings in front of St Paul's Church, Covent Garden (although they were later found not guilty of sodomy). Another pair, John Painter and John Green of Stepney, were less fortunate; they were imprisoned after they were found together on the porch of St Dunstan's on the night of 24 August 1727 'in such an indecent Posture as plainly betrayed they were guilty of Sodomitical Practices'.[4]

While the most common place to have sex with a woman was in her own lodgings, it would seem that there was enough public fornication taking place outside in the open air of London to make the authorities believe that the city was a hive of limitless, illicit sexual activity. Various public discussions on the topic of whores and whoring made it even more noticeable.

A young man and woman having intercourse outside: Thomas Rowlandson, *Jolly Gipsies*, *c.* 1790–1810, etching.

On Whoring

Various tracts and pamphlets added to the debate on the subject of prostitution. In *Some Considerations Upon Street-Walkers* (1726), Daniel Defoe (*c.* 1660–1731) describes whores accosting him as he walks the streets of London:

> I have every now and then been put to the Halt, sometimes by the full Encounter of an audacious Harlot, whose impudent Leer shewd she only stoppe'd my Passage in order to draw my Observation on her; at other times, by Twitches on the Sleeve, lewd and ogling Salutations; and not infrequently by the more profligate Impudence of some Jades, who boldly dare to seize a Man by the Elbow, and make insolent Demands of Wine and Treats before they let him go.[5]

However, Defoe is decidedly on the side of the whores themselves, and attacks the members of the 'Reforming Society', otherwise known as the Society for the Reformation of Manners, for 'the paltry mean Behaviour of some of their ministerial Officers'.[6] He condemns their lack of sympathy for women who are reduced to prostitution because of desperation and were at 'the Extremity of Unhappiness', urged by necessity 'to become the Instruments of satisfying those Desires in Men which were given for a better Use'.[7]

Defoe's compassion for the poor and for prostitutes was fuelled by his religious beliefs and he had trained for the non-conformist ministry. He knew London well, having been born in Fore Street in St Giles, Cripplegate. After his religious training, he followed his father into business as a general merchant, dealing in a variety of products including hosiery, general woollen goods and wine. He was a risk-taker and knew about losing money, sharing the experience of some of the more desperate Londoners after spending a brief time in the Fleet prison in 1692 for a £700 debt (although in fact he faced debts upwards of £17,000 because of bad investment in shipping and declared himself bankrupt). He was later pilloried for sedition and spent time in Newgate. Though he is known as a novelist, his other works often deal with suggestions for economic and social improvement of society in general and London in particular. His sympathies lay with the needy; in his *Poor Man's Plea*, he attacks a society whose magistrates were 'punishing men for being poor, which is no Crime at all'. This identification with the poor can be seen in Defoe's heroes and heroines, who at various stages of their lives are punished for their poverty, if not by law, then by the rules of society itself. In his consideration of streetwalkers, he compares the laws of foreign countries regulating prostitution, where 'Common Whores are kept in a sort of decent Order; certain Places are allow'd them from which they must not depart, and certain Rules of Behaviour prescrib'd to them which they must keep to,' against the reformers whose laws make 'no Allowances for human Weakness, no Allowance, think of no Cure for Lewdness, but Amputation'. He suggests running a middle course between sinfulness and severity and attacks those dispensing justice in Britain.[8]

Another commentator on whoring who followed in Defoe's footsteps was John Dunton (1659–1732). Working from his shop, the Raven in the Poultry near the Royal Exchange, along with his wife, Elizabeth Annesley, he published political tracts, devotional sermons and practical manuals, as well as making attacks on the state of the law. His satire *The Shortest Way with Whores and Rogues* (1703) – written in the same vein as Defoe's satire *The Shortest Way with the Dissenters*, published a year earlier – was used as mock criticism of whores, whom he disingenuously placed in a category with the worst of criminals, such as thieves and murderers. Descriptions of the Keeping Lady, the Plyer to Bawdy Houses, the Common Night-Walker and the Bawd provided his readers with a detailed account of the types of women involved in the sex trade.

Dunton despised some judges and attacked both Sir George Jeffreys and Sir Charles Duncomb in his pamphlet *The Bloody Assizes* (1689). Jeffreys was a despicable bigot known for his corruption and cruelty, who had taken his enjoyment through watching prostitutes being stripped and flogged in public view. Duncomb was just as unprincipled; he was particularly influential because of his enormous wealth, yet even so was known for accepting bribes. Dunton's account of the victims who had suffered under Jeffreys sold over 6,000 copies. Daniel Defoe also attacked both Jeffreys and Duncomb in his satirical pamphlet *Reformation of Manners* (1702).[9]

Both Dunton and Defoe were playing to the moral climate of the times. They had become friendly after meeting in 1692, but a quarrel broke out after Defoe published one of Dunton's poems without his permission.[10] As a publisher though, Dunton was like the

Style of Sir Godfrey Kneller, *Daniel Defoe*, 17th–18th century, oil on canvas.

pornographer Edmund Curll – both men were content to publish smut as well as moralizing sermons, since publishing demanded no consistency of morals in the publishers themselves. Both were creative and imaginative, although they also easily picked quarrels, a fact that was later to ruin Dunton's career.[11] In *Proposals for a National Reformation of Manners* (1694), another of Dunton's publications, a list is given of successfully prosecuted bawds and prostitutes.

J. C. Armytage, after Eyre Crowe, *Defoe in the Pillory*, 1868, engraving.

Sanctimonious societies were supposedly aimed at rectifying the basest activities of lewdness, profanity, drunkenness, sabbath-breaking and other proclaimed immorality. Their main targets were prostitutes and homosexuals and the societies aimed their activities at ridding the city of them. Members actively went out to find prostitutes in order to have them prosecuted and imprisoned, then issued a list of their names as a warning to others. The first Society for the Reformation of Manners, which emerged in the 1690s, was established to deal with the mass of brothels in Tower Hamlets.

The fact that their prosecutions were brought privately meant that the societies were largely ineffectual as bringing a case against another person was both time-consuming and costly. Societies joined together to prosecute offenders who would then be quickly brought before a Justice of the Peace. Those who were prosecuted would be indicted, placed in a house of correction or asked to enter into a recognizance, a legal term for assurances that they would not disturb their surroundings or the people involved in the case, as well as not cause trouble for law enforcement in the future. Nearly 12,000 people were prosecuted by the society, most of them prostitutes who were sent to houses of correction. The records show that men occasionally stepped forward to offer sureties for women accused of lewd behaviour, to ensure they would turn up at court. Men were also seen among those picked up for soliciting; Thomas Cowper, listed as a 'gentleman' in his recognizance, was accused of 'picking up a woman in the street, and goeing along with her'.[12] One supporter of the society perhaps best summed up his feelings about prostitutes in his comment that they were 'lewd wretches, who openly lay Snares and Enticements' for young men.[13] These men were described as helpless victims in the face of the cunning wiles of prostitutes. Such beliefs circulated generally, a suggestion exemplified by Defoe in his *Some Consideration upon Streetwalkers* (*c.* 1735), when he urged the 'Man of Frailty' to escape from the 'dangerous beauty of the Wanton' if he was to escape utter ruin.[14] Such statements invariably allowed any young man who was arrested to accuse the prostitutes of having enticed him into lewd acts. While constables were legally allowed to arrest 'all suspicious persons that go abroad in the night', reformers were vigilant enough to enter brothels and catch their prey in the act.[15] Among the many people arrested were Robert Lewis, taken 'in bed' with a woman, and Richard Lary, taken 'with 2 Lewd women in an obscene posture'.[16] The societies drew up blacklists of people whom they had prosecuted, no doubt hoping to name and shame them. Defoe attacked the men of the societies – and the members were all men – for their lack of sympathy and a failure to recognize women's plight, an issue he would explore in his own fiction. He did in fact become a member of Edinburgh's Society for the Reformation of Manners in April 1707, but this was a cover for his real work of spying, as well as a way to give him access to other merchants.

In 1715 the societies asserted that by their endeavours over the last 25 years 'Our Streets have been very much cleared of those lewd Women, who used to solicit openly there to Debauchery; Night-Walkers have been supressed, and Gangs of detestable Sodomites dispersed,' as well as bawdy houses closed down.[17] Seven years later, they were still boasting about their good deeds as they gloated over the numbers of people they had prosecuted – 84,720 people for debauchery and profanity over the previous 32 years:

> Great Numbers of Baudy-houses, and other disorderly houses, have been suppressed and shut up, and the Streets were very much purged from the wretched Tribe of Night-walking Prostitutes, and most detestable Sodomites. Many young

> Men, taken with lewd Women, have, by their being brought to timely Shame and Punishment, been discouraged and turned from following such sinful Courses.[18]

How effective the societies were in clearing the streets of whores is debatable, a fact which even their own members recognized: 'It must be confessed, That Profaneness and Debauchery do still too much abound.'

In *The Night-Walker; or, Evening Rambles in Search after Lewd Women* (1696), Dunton again found a way of pandering to public interest in whores and whoring. He wandered the streets looking for prostitutes to talk to, then wrote up the results, cashing in on his conversations with them while supposedly encouraging them to read the Bible. Though he condemned the trade, in his autobiography in 1705, he admitted that unrequited lust was his reason for writing about lewd subjects. This stemmed from an earlier attraction, he confessed: 'I was wounded with a silent passion for a Virgin in my Father's house that unhinged me all at once.'[19] From his interrogation of the women about town, he came to the same conclusions as some other commentators when he learnt that women had become ensnared into prostitution because of poverty.

Dunton went further with *Bumography; or, A Touch at the Ladies Tails* (1707),[20] in which he assured his readers he wanted only to write such satire in order to expose lewd behaviour, particularly that of sodomites, declaring,

> I suppose none will think the worse of our Present Reformation, because they can tell us the Vile Practices of the He-strumpets and the Town-Cracks: And therefore I don't see why A Modest Touch at the Lady's Tails (with a Design to reform both those and their Morals) shou'd displease any but ignorant Block-heads, or Lewd Women, who think reformation a needless Thing.[21]

In his later years, Dunton became somewhat mentally unhinged and, in such works as *Whipping-Post; or, A Satyr upon Every Body* (1706), attacked everyone he believed had done him a disservice. In ill health and with his career in tatters, he was described by Pope as 'a broken Bookseller and abusive scribbler'.[22] Dunton died in 1733 and, at his own request, was buried in a non-conformist cemetery.

Another commentator of the day, Bernard Mandeville, was generally seen as a supporter of vice and an opponent of virtue in the eighteenth century, mainly for arguing that vice was beneficial to people if they were to attain any happiness. *A Modest Defence of Public Stews; or, An Essay upon Whoring* (1724, generally attributed to Mandeville) attacked members of reformation societies for inadvertently contributing to immorality, stating, 'it is no small addition to my grief to observe that your endeavours to suppress lewdness have only serviced to promote it, and that this branch of immorality has grown under your hands.'[23] Mandeville had settled in London from the Netherlands and started to practise medicine without a licence, an offence for which he was called to appear before the Royal College of Physicians in 1693. His *The Grumbling Hive* (1705), later reworked into the popular *Fable of the Bees; or, Private Vices, Publick Benefits* (1714), depicted the English as complaining bees, alluding to the hypocritical grousing of the London anti-vice moralists. He claimed that all professions had their vices, and wealth and power were not compatible with innocence and virtue. Indeed, 'If Courtezans and Strumpets were to be prosecuted with as much Rigour as some silly people would have it, what Locks or Bars would be sufficient to preserve the Honour of our Wives and Daughters?'[24] Venereal disease affected the innocent, who suffered along with the guilty, a fact Mandeville understood: 'Men give it to their wives, women to their husbands, to perhaps their children, they to their nurses and the nurses again to other children, so that no age, sex, or condition can be entirely safe from infection.' Mandeville proffered the argument for regulated prostitution in order to lessen the spread of the disease. However, the spread of disease was more often than not blamed on female prostitutes.

The Fictional Whore

As the public were reading commentaries about prostitution, they were also obtaining a different view on the subject from reading novels. Daniel Defoe's novel *Robinson Crusoe* had already met with great acclaim by the time *The Fortunes and Misfortunes of the Famous Moll Flanders* hit the market in 1722. The public were ready and eager to devour this new form of realistic literature, and *Moll Flanders* purported to be a real-life story. Readers felt they knew Moll personally as she reached the dizzy heights of wealth only to be plunged to the depths of poverty. They experienced the world of Moll through her actions and words. Such novels influenced people's attitudes towards whores and whoredom.

Moll Flanders explores the precarious existence of a woman who had a sorry start to life. She was born in Newgate prison, and her mother was transported to the colonies. She was brought up first by gypsies, then, after being found abandoned in Colchester when she was three, given to a parish nurse to look after. From then on we follow the ups and downs of her life as she is left to live off her body and her wits. To some extent, she follows the typical trajectory of many whores: orphaned as a child, she spends her youth in domestic service, where she is debauched by the son of her employers. The veracity of the tale was part of its appeal. The book was a phenomenal success and made Defoe a healthy sum. While Defoe had high standards regarding sex, marriage and servants, he knew that the natural law of survival made it difficult for many to hold to them. But the subject matter of the story – that of a woman of easy virtue – was something for which Defoe felt the need to apologize at the beginning of the book. He knew his material might shock some of his more polite readers. Towards the end of the book, he states in Moll's voice, 'As the publishing of this account of my life is for the sake of the just moral of every part of it, and for instruction, cautions, wrong and improvements to every reader.'[25]

A couple of topics were omitted, perhaps because they were thought too delicate for his audience's tastes: that of venereal disease, which almost anyone who had a sexual life outside of marriage would have contracted, and the sorry reality of infanticide. After the death of her first husband, Moll says that her children were 'taken happily off my hands'. She shows no concern over leaving her first two children with her in-laws and going off to look for another husband.

Defoe's Moll Flanders might have been seen as a wily whore doing her best to survive with the odds stacked against her. His later version of a whore's story, *Roxana: The Fortunate Mistress* (1724 edn), was a more serious and complex portrayal of a woman's conscience. Defoe provided an uncommon understanding of a woman in a difficult position struggling to survive in a man's world and demonstrated a sensitivity rare in portrayals of women of 'easy virtue'. While Roxana may well find and lose fortunes, she contemplates her life much more than Moll ever does. Again, her children are palmed off with her in-laws and she becomes the mistress to a series of men. Defoe examined

Lady Roxana, frontispiece illustration by John Ward Dunsmore to Daniel Defoe, *Roxana: The Fortunate Mistress* (1904).

the idea of female autonomy in Roxana, especially in her refusal to marry – 'the Marriage Contract is . . . nothing but giving up Liberty, Estate, Authority, and everything, to the Man.' Instead she retains her wealth and runs her own business. She becomes a popular hostess, entertaining the *beau-monde* of London, and eventually marries a Dutch merchant but is pursued by one of the first set of children she had abandoned. The problem of incessant childbearing as a reward for any possible sexual freedom is prevalent.

Central to both *Moll Flanders* and *Roxana* is the problem of money – the acquisition of it, the keeping of it, the safety of it and the losing of it. The concern of where to hide wealth was a problem for many. Banks had only recently been established and after the South Sea Bubble crash in 1720 people were unwilling to invest money in stocks and shares. Most people hid their money in trunks, but it was always in danger of being found and stolen by servants. Defoe showed how men were constantly trying to trick women into sex and out of their wealth. He forced his readers to confront the social questions of the day.

The first pornification of the fictional life-story of a whore came with John Cleland's *Memoirs of a Woman of Pleasure*. It embodies a male-dominated vision of sex and makes little attempt at showing female autonomy, as seen in Defoe's female characters. The protagonist Fanny is mostly passive rather than showing any true agency. This representation is at variance with some earlier British-made erotica that portrayed women as active, enjoying at least some level of sexual equanimity with men, often in shared jovial companionship. This delineation of mutual pleasure in pornography would later give way to depictions of less intimate relationships between men and women that contain more graphic bodily descriptions: sexual relations become more alienated and the characters' emotions are increasingly detached. Cleland's pornographic vision of sexual indulgence is also a sanitized version of the real world, with little drunkenness or problems with police and with the middling and upper ranks of society as the main protagonists. No mention is given of abortifacients or infanticides. Apart from a miscarriage, the only children born to Fanny are the wanted ones of her favourite lover, whom she marries. Perhaps unsurprisingly, pornography here gives a less truthful version of reality than non-pornographic novels.

Scene from John Cleland, *Memoirs of a Woman of Pleasure* (1766 edn), vol. I.

Whores' biographies provide another insight into the life of prostitution for the reading public. These books were mainly published in London and were written by hacks to pull in a few shillings per copy. For those with less money, smaller pamphlets and broadsheets were available and sold for a few pence each. The 'memoirs' of Nancy Dawson, Kitty Fisher and Fanny Murray held basic elements of truth, if somewhat exaggerated for readers' edification. Murray's biography was a hotch-potch of fact and fiction; she ended up as a courtesan after being seduced (some say raped) by Jack Spencer (1707–1746), grandson to Sarah, Duchess of Marlborough, who deserted her soon after. Beau Nash (1674–1761), friend of the Duke and Duchess of Marlborough, came to her rescue but she left him after a row and took up lodgings in Covent Garden under procuress Madam Maddox. From there on, her life went downhill as she succumbed to the pox after taking a series of lovers.[26] Her fortunes recovered when the pimp Jack Harris put her on his infamous *List of Covent Garden Ladies around 1747* and her rate rose to two guineas. Now she was attracting aristocratic clients like John Montagu, 4th Earl of Sandwich, and Sir Richard Atkins of

Richard Purcell, after Henry Morland, *Fanny Murray*, c. 1746–66, mezzotint.

Clapham, who provided her with money until his sudden death in 1756. Supposedly, to make amends for his father's behaviour, the junior Lord Spencer offered the actor David Ross £200 a year if he would marry her. The pair settled in London until her death in 1778.

Whores' 'memoirs' would become a popular feature of eighteenth-century literature, although the biographical facts could hardly be relied upon. Surprisingly, although they talked about prostitutes and debauchery, they avoided graphic descriptions of sex and tended to use euphemisms. Nonetheless, they gave readers an insight into the highs and lows of prostitution and offered the public a different picture of the sex trade.

William Hogarth's famous series of prints in *A Harlot's Progress* (1732) added to the imagery of the plight of the young country-woman coming to London and showed how speedily her life could be destroyed. The brutality and ruthlessness of London city life was displayed in full in five plates, beginning with a gritty portrayal of the seduction of a poor millineress, Moll, by a procuress, Mother Needham. The aristocratic man standing behind the bawd in the picture is Colonel Charteris, known rapist of young women, a symbol of the corruption of his class. Plate II shows that Moll has become mistress to a nobleman: transformed in a fancy dress, silk stockings and fashionable shoes, she apes the upper class. She has gained the accoutrements of a courtesan, including a monkey, a maid and a young Black servant in livery. A mask lies on her dressing table, reflecting her artifice, while a beauty spot indicates the first signs of covering up the pox. By Plate III, having lost some of her quality, she has descended into working from less salubrious establishments and now offers a flagellation service, as indicated by the birch hanging on the wall. Plate IV shows her in Bridewell, hacking hemp. The final scene shows Moll's inevitable death from syphilis, while two well-known doctors, Richard Rock and Jean Misaubin, haggle over whose is the best cure. Her teeth have fallen out on the floor, her child is about to be orphaned, and Moll's possessions are already being sifted through by an avaricious neighbour.[27] Hogarth's intention was to show his audience the contribution their own behaviour might have to the downfall of young women, specifically pointing to certain types and classes (the hopeless upper-class doctors and the thieving neighbour). The male counterpart to this was *The Rake's Progress*, which similarly follows the downfall of a libertine man.

Moll dying while doctors haggle over her: William Hogarth, *A Harlot's Progress, Plate V*, 1732, engraving.

Hogarth's prints of *Before* and *After* (1736) show the other side of the path to debauchment: seduction. The first image is normally interpreted as the scene of a young woman struggling to resist a lover's advances as he tugs at her clothes while his wig falls off. *After* shows her at the man's feet, clinging to his jacket in cloying gratitude for his having sexually satisfied her so well. But all is not what it initially seems. In *Before*, in anticipation of the man's advances, she has already taken off her corset, which now lies on the chair, and she has obviously invited him into her bedroom. The pomade on the floor, along with her beauty spots, commonly used to hide signs of the pox, indicate a previous knowledge of sexual chaos. She has certain reading material on the bedside cabinet that indicates her proclivities – the bawdy poems of Rochester, a novel (reading material thought to make a woman's imagination run wild) and a copy of 'The Practice of Piety', which acts as a satirical joke. The erotic picture on the wall of a cupid euphemistically shooting a rocket indicates she may not be as innocent as she makes out. These sorts of erotic pictures were commonly hung in brothels. The *After* image shows the woman perfecting a look of admiration while the gentleman looks as though he doesn't know what has just hit him – she is obviously well-practised at satisfying men. The hand on his jacket is suggestive of her requesting his money. The book that lies on the floor is inscribed *Omne animal post coitum triste* – every animal is sad after intercourse – and *Aristotle*, no doubt a reference to the erotic instruction manual *Aristotle's Masterpiece*.

From Brazen Whores to Seduced Maidens

The image of the prostitute changed over the eighteenth century and the prevalent idea of the brazen whore gradually gave way to that of the seduced maiden (though at times these images would run concurrently). Unmarried women who had sex were no longer seen as insatiable vixens but rather as prey who had been targeted and then seduced by men who took advantage of them; they were no longer considered lewd harlots who enticed men into sex and milked them of their money and possessions, but were seen as victims of circumstance. By the middle of the second half of the eighteenth century, the image of the woman as victim had become entrenched in novels such as Samuel Richardson's *Clarissa*; the idea also permeated magazines, as seen in letters published in *The Rambler* magazine for March and April 1751 that opined the need to rescue prostitutes. A typical narrative of a 'woman on the town' saw her as a daughter of the respectable lower middling sort (clergy or a half-pay army soldier), who had been debauched through the manipulations of a wealthy man of rank, either through persuasion, seduction, a promise of marriage or rape.

This idea can be seen in the founding of the Magdalen Hospital for Penitent Prostitutes in London in 1758 and the formulation of the belief that prostitutes could be rescued from vice.[28] Robert Dingley, director of the Bank of England, together with Jonas Hanway, commissioner of the Victualling Office, suggested establishing a safe retreat for prostitutes, a place where they might be 'rescued', rather than sending them to a house of correction. They believed that many of the women who had turned to prostitution had done so because of men's failures rather than by choice. Prostitutes were no longer considered painted strumpets who sinned because they were innately lascivious, but unfortunate women

J. Taylor, *Magdalen Hospital, St George's Fields, Southwark*, 1818, engraving.

who had fallen by the wayside.[29] Philanthropist Jonas Hanway in his *Thoughts on the Plan for a Magdalen House* (1758) held that recruits to the Magdalen House were not from the labouring poor but the daughters of poor tradesmen put into domestic service.

While the institution was not ideal, it was well intended. The failure of the hospital lay in its structure and its methods of control. A hierarchy of superiority was established within the institution, giving girls status based on their appearance, deportment and education. While 'Trusties' were allowed to wash and cook for themselves, newcomers were kept in a separate ward for one month before being moved to an inferior ward until good behaviour earned them a promotion to a better one. These places were more like prisons, with regulations strictly enforced and harsh punishments for those who did not adhere to them. Bed and meal times were set in regimental style; piety was encouraged, with hymns every morning and evening and grace said before and after every meal; insolent or foul language resulted in confinement to one's room for six hours, public admonishment by the chaplain for the second offence, twelve hours of solitary confinement for the third, and so on. A sliding scale of fines existed and failure to reform resulted in expulsion. Hanway saw idleness as the cause of evil and prostitution, so the aim of the reformers was to keep the girls busy.

Frontispiece illustration from Jonas Hanway, *Thoughts on the Plan for a Magdalen-House for Repentant Prostitutes* (1758).

By excluding hardened prostitutes and emphasizing seduction as the reason for women turning to prostitution, the charity supporters focused on the inmates' chastity and the instilling of modest behaviour. An inquiry by the Magdalen authorities for the period May 1786–May 1790 declared that 'about two-thirds of the whole number of women admitted were permanently reclaimed', but this is highly unlikely.[30] Without some ongoing economic support, once outside, many women would fall back into their old ways. Despite the philanthropic claims of the Magdalen authorities, they were essentially trying to control female sexual behaviour with a more carceral model of discipline rather than out of real concern for the women; the reformers were mainly male of the middling or gentry class, and there was a biased view of what these women needed. There is little evidence from female sex reformers at this time or from the prostitutes themselves as to what they thought of the subject.

The rise of the Proclamation Society against Vice and Immorality, which ran between 1789 and 1808 and was very similar to the earlier reformation societies, saw another clamp-down on 'immorality'. It was run by a group of men who had set up an organization to track down prostitutes and homosexuals and take them to court. The abolitionist politician William Wilberforce helped found the society, which remained small and select until his demise.[31] The society claimed to have been established to fight crimes against 'religion, morality and public decency'.[32] In doing so they had 'combined together as Guardians of the national religion and morals, and engaging to exert the force of law, and the authority of personal influence, in punishing and discouraging vice, and in distinguishing, countenancing, and rewarding virtue'.[33] Sixty members met once a year, the subcommittee once a week or as often as required. A subscription was raised of two guineas each. Addressing the problems at hand, they suggested that 'all suspicious persons, who have no lawful means of obtaining a livelihood, and who cannot give a good account of themselves might be deemed rogues and vagabonds,' and produced suggestions for how to deal with them, which included transportation for repeat offenders.[34] Similar to the reformation societies set up at the end of the previous century, their aim was to have raucous taverns and other establishments deemed immoral and shut down or pressure put on them to change; they insisted on the enforcement of the law, even against the publishing of Sunday newspapers, and set on persecuting the publishers of obscene books and prints, which were thought to produce 'mischievous effects' specifically on 'the morals of the rising generation'.[35]

Certain places of entertainment in London were targeted, one 'sheltering themselves under cover of an ancient privilege belonging to the Vinter's Company'. Its doors opened every night 'without restraint, to persons of every description, on the payments of a very small sum for admission, these places naturally become the resort of the licentious and abandoned of both sexes'. On Sundays, the most popular night, around five hundred people would assemble 'and exhibited a scene of the most horrid profanes and the most shocking indecency. Here . . . the young and unwary were led into the acquaintance of the most depraved and profligate. Here they were hardened against the sense of shame, and the dread of punishment.'[36] It would seem that despite their vigilance, sex continued to thrive and immorality to persist in resistance to the control of the anti-vice societies of London. In effect, the societies took a decidedly punitive attitude to anyone behaving outside their moral orbit and targeted the poorest and most persecuted people in London.

The two main opposing strands of public opinion came from harsh magistrates inflicting brutal punishments on prostitutes, buttressed by the reforming societies at the end of the seventeenth century and again at the end of the eighteenth century, and from writers and publishers who were keen to understand the plight of prostitutes and the effect of poverty in influencing their paths into the sex trade. Novels and whore biographies provided an alternative insight into the plight of prostitutes and their precarious existence. While the image of the brazen whore would continue to circulate, the softening of sentiment towards those young women who had been seduced led to a greater understanding of the different reasons why women ended up in prostitution.

William Hogarth, *The Laughing Audience*, 1733, etching.

6
Stage Strumpets

> The Playhouse is their place of traffick, where
> Nightly they sit to sell their rotten ware . . .
> For while he nibbles at her am'rous trap
> She gets the money: he gets the clap!
> JOHN DRYDEN's *Prologue* to Thomas Southerne's comedy *The Disappointment* (1684)

London theatres were known as places in the capital where streetwalkers could be found hanging around outside picking up passing trade. Inside, the theatres proved popular meeting-places for prostitutes, not merely to watch the entertainment, but as a site for networking and introductions to interested men. According to *The Times* on 2 November 1786, the theatre boxes at Drury Lane were 'licensed stews for the abandoned and profligate to meet and pair off'. Courtesans hired boxes for the season and were in an ideal position from which to display themselves in their latest fashionable dress. New patrons would queue outside the boxes to woo potential lovers with flatteries and gifts, as they would the actresses backstage.

Actresses were lumped together with mistresses, courtesans and whores and often had a reputation for immorality simply because of the profession they chose; their standing was automatically diminished because they displayed themselves publicly. Indeed, all thespians were seen as the dregs of London town by some critics, as *The Secret History of the Green Room* pointed out: 'That austere and illiberal prejudice which banishes from the Stage men of respectable birth and situation, almost exclusively places the origin of Actors in the lowest orders of Society.' Few players avoided tarnishing their lives with immorality, and the author believes that 'were we to dissemble the vices which stain the private life of too many Performers, the full merit would not appear of the virtuous few who escape untainted by the contagion.'[1]

The theatre had changed dramatically over the preceding years. Having thrived during the Elizabethan period, when men took the roles of the leading female characters in plays by the likes of Shakespeare, Marlowe and Webster, a particularly nasty bump erupted with the banning of plays in 1642 by the puritanical Long Parliament. Happily for theatrical audiences, the monarchy was restored in 1660, this time with a theatre-loving leader at its head. The royal patent of 1662 allowed for two theatres to operate 'serious' drama, declaring, 'we do likewise permit and give leave that all the women's parts to be acted in either of the said two Companies for the time to come may be performed by women.' In 1663 the King's Company, led by Thomas Killigrew, opened a new playhouse in Bridges Street (now Catherine Street), which was later rebuilt and renamed the Theatre Royal, Drury Lane. A licence was also granted to William Davenant, whose players became known as the Duke of York's Company and eventually established themselves in Lisle's Tennis Court in Lincoln's Inn Theatre. Non-patent theatres wangled their way round this by putting on melodramas, pantomimes, ballets and operas. Castrato Gaetano Guadagni (1728–1792) was fined £50 and threatened with the whip for performing unlicensed performances of Mattia Vento's *Artaserse* at the home of Teresa Cornelys, a socialite known for her parties. She was also Casanova's lover and had two children by him. Her masquerades for the elite at her house in Carlisle House in Soho Square were some of the biggest attractions in London.

The appearance of women on stage was a revelation to Restoration audiences and theatre managers would make the most of actresses' appearances. Their costumes were of particular importance, as they needed to show off their figures to attract audiences. In other words, single women displaying their bodies was an intentional ruse to titillate the male theatre-goer. Female dress consisted of a loose shift or chemise overlaid by a tightly laced corset made with wooden or bone stays to make the spine straight, the waist small and the breasts prominent; the chemise had a rectilinear bodice cut low to reveal as much bosom as possible; the top gown was covered in lace, brocades and satins, its skirts open at the front, sometimes caught up to reveal highly decorative petticoats underneath. By this method, female bodies might be

Unknown artist, *Theatre Royal, Drury Lane*, *c.* 1775, oil on board.

displayed to perfection. Yet being seen publicly, showing herself off on stage, did not fit in with the public's conception of a respectable woman. Ultimately, this resulted in a problem for an actress – how was she to conform to social restrictions around women in general and to society's understanding of upright behaviour if she was on public display? How were actresses supposed to experiment with new opportunities on stage in these situations when constant restraints were placed on them? Consequently, women were left wading through a mire of insults about their depravity while trying to construct their own public identity.

'Memoirs' of actresses began to be published as information for their admirers, feeding the emerging cult of celebrity. The hacks knew they were onto a money-spinner in feeding the enthusiasm of those who adored certain female players. They often criticized an actress's behaviour at the same time as expounding on sexualized fantasies made up of fabricated anecdotes about their private lives. The biographer of Eliza O'Neill (1791–1872) used the 'biography' as the opportunity to both complain about the actress's conduct and explore her sexual promiscuity. Her marital status was important to the way she was seen, since being single meant she was 'available'. This allowed her admirers to uphold their illusions that they might have a chance at becoming her lover, or at least romanticize while seeing her perform. The author asserts, 'While she continues Miss O'Neill, and an interesting unprotected female, she will find that patronage which generosity and every better bias of public regard will continue undiminished to extend her.' Once she married, the dream and the lust would collapse: 'the moment she places herself under the protection of a husband . . . the charm is over . . . she sinks into a wife.'[2] So the female libertine actress and her ability to titillate is clearly linked to her potential attainability. The woman who changed all this was Sarah Siddons, who first went on stage as a wife rather than as a single woman. This gave her gravitas in the public imagination, but limited her roles; as one critic pointed out, while the single O'Neill could carry off the character of wife and mother as well as the young unmarried female, 'This is an excellence Mrs Siddons could never attain, for on the London stage she appeared always the wife and mother . . . having passed the vale of youth.'[3]

Theatrical biographies are no more reliable than memoirs of non-theatrical courtesans, and similar caution needs to be executed in their examination.[4] The fact that actresses were women who chose to expose themselves publicly on stage placed them within the same immoral range as courtesans, and pushed the boundaries of acceptability in polite society. However, many actresses took lovers from an assortment of wealthy men and the stage was a well-established route from poverty to riches. A young woman from a lowly background might work her way up from singing and dancing in taverns to performing at one of the two top theatres in London. The fact that some of these women managed to marry into the aristocracy or otherwise above their station caused even more consternation within the upper echelons of society, as this was thought to upset the natural class hierarchy.

Even other women held antagonistic views about the libertine actress. Feminist writer Mary Ann Radcliffe was well aware that deprivation and lack of work opportunities for women forced them into prostitution, yet she also saw actresses in a negative light. Famous for her feminist work *The Female Advocate* (1799), Radcliffe warned that 'the numbers of unguarded young men, even with hearts inclined to virtue, have been happily drawn to vice' by actresses. A person need look no further than the theatre to find 'abandoned females, of all ages and degrees of profligacy'.[5] The female libertine was once again attacked for leading men astray.

The Actress and Restoration Drama

Restoration plays such as George Etherege's *The Man of Mode; or, Sir Fopling Flutter* (1676), William Wycherley's *The Country Wife* (1675) and *The Plain Dealer* (1676) (the last two both based loosely on those of Molière) offered romping female roles in which women were central to the plot. Cunning women and conniving men were often an integral part of the play and known for suggestive sexual overtones and lewd puns.

In order to cash in on the fame of leading Restoration actress Anne Oldfield (1683–1730) after her death, Edmund Curll wrote and

Depiction of Anne Oldfield in the frontispiece to *Faithful Memoirs of the Life, Amours and Performances, of . . . Mrs Anne Oldfield* (1731), written and published by Edmund Curll under the pseudonym William Egerton.

published her memoirs under the pseudonym 'William Egerton'.[6] She was born in Pall Mall and spent her life acting in London theatres. When she was young, her father mortgaged their property to buy a post in the Horse Guards but he died soon after; her family was left in difficult circumstances so she was 'put out to a seamstress' with a Mrs Wotton in King Street, Westminster. In 1699 Oldfield managed to attract the attention of Irish playwright George Farquhar, who produced some of the best Restoration comedies, including *The Constant Couple* (1699), *The Recruiting Officer* (1706) and *The Beaux' Stratagem* (1707). Farquhar had allegedly overheard her reciting lines from Francis Beaumont and John Fletcher's play *The Scornful Lady* (1616) in the back room of a tavern. She had perhaps positioned herself for exactly that purpose, to be 'discovered'. On either Farquahar's or Sir John Vanbrugh's suggestion, she was engaged by theatre manager Christopher Rich to play at the Theatre Royal in Drury Lane after being introduced by Vanbrugh. She would sometimes take roles in other theatres, but for the most part would remain at Drury Lane for the rest of her career. Her first appearance was as Candiope in John Dryden's tragicomedy *Secret Love; or, The Maiden Queen* (1667), for which she was paid fifteen shillings a week. She went on to play Lady Lurewell in Farquhar's *The Constant Couple*, but the role of Lady Betty Modish in Colley Cibber's *The Careless Husband* in 1704 was to be her signature role. The *Daily Courant* for 24 March 1721 reported that she played the role for the benefit of Mr Keene's widow, along with the company of comedians. Benefit performances originated in England around 1685 and were popular until at least 1870, usually undertaken for a charity of some kind, or to help struggling actors and their families who had fallen on hard times. Oldfield also collaborated on *The Perjured Husband* (1700) with another popular actress and playwright, Susannah Centlivre, her sometime rival for roles.

While she was pursuing a successful acting career, her personal life was to raise questions about her moral compass – but then, women taking lovers always did. Oldfield attracted the attention of Arthur Maynwaring, MP for Preston, around 1703 and they embarked on a passionate affair. He had inherited an estate after his father's death in 1693 and held a high position in political and social life, making him an attractive catch. He was a member of the Kit-Cat Club, alongside Lord Montagu, who assisted his career. While Maynwaring's friends were warning him off Oldfield, according to her titillating memoirs, she 'more and more entangled him in Cupid's Net, which was costing him dear'.[7] It certainly elevated her status, as once the Parliamentary recess began, they took a holiday at Windsor, staying in the castle in the house of the treasurer, John Sewell. Their joy was not to last, as Maynwaring died in 1712 at only 44. Rumours sprouted that he had died of venereal disease, with all fingers pointing at Oldfield as the cause. She had the sense to try and circumnavigate these accusations by ordering his surgeons, Mr Buffiere and Mr Browne, to open up her deceased lover and investigate the reason for his death, with three other doctors standing in as witnesses. This allayed the gossip, as all the men present declared he had died of consumption and there 'was not the least Symptoms of any thing Venereal'. In his spurious biography of Oldfield, Curll insisted on dragging down the reputations of his subjects, claiming that Maynwaring had indeed died of the pox. In an aside, he proclaimed that Maynwaring had confessed to him that 'he had made an unfortunate Sally in an Amour, which gave him a slight Tinat at Paris, 1698, that he was only patched up there, but afterwards, perfectly cured at London.' Since there was no cure, it is possible that venereal disease hastened his demise.

By now, Oldfield (who had taken the title 'Mrs' as did many mistresses and courtesans, as a way of salvaging their reputation) was living in Southampton Street in Covent Garden. She had evidently had a son by Maynwaring, as he left the whole of his small estate of only £3,000 to be divided equally between his sister, his child and his son's mother. Oldfield was made the executrix of his will. Their son was only seven years old at the time and £2,000 was hardly enough on which to bring him up. Gossip quickly died down and she was offered various parts in both comedy and tragedy, becoming universally admired. *The Tatler* gushed, 'There was such a Composure in her Looks, and Propriety in her Dress, that you would think it impossible she should change the Garb you one Day see her in, for anything so becoming, till you next day see her in another.'[8] She went on to play various parts, including Sylvia and Mrs Sullen in Farquhar's *The Recruiting Officer* and *The Beaux' Stratagem*, respectively. She was lauded for her performance in the main role in John Gay's *Three Hours after Marriage*, which premiered on 16 January 1717 at the Theatre Royal, Drury Lane.

Illness plagued Oldfield over a six-month period, culminating in her death. Charlotte Charke (neé Cibber, 1713–1660) remembered Oldfield in her own autobiography: their paths crossed at Charke's first performance and Oldfield's last. Oldfield was taken ill and suffered over the following seven or eight months. The *Monthly Chronicle* for October 1730 reported on 'Mrs. Anne Oldfield the celebrated actress, who died at her House in Grosvenor-Street, after a lingering illness of several Months'. Her friend Mrs Saunders had looked after her, no doubt grateful for the fact that Oldfield had helped introduce her to the stage. Oldfield was only 47 when she died, but had gained some respectability and had been living in the parish of St George's, Hanover Square, according to her will. In a testament to her popularity, she was buried in Westminster Abbey. Her corpse was first carried from her house to the Jerusalem Chamber, where it lay in state, her coffin decorated with rich Brussels lace.

Apparently, her moral status was still up for question; Curll assured his readers in the 'memoirs' that she had had only two sons, one with Maynwaring and another with Brigadier General Charles Churchill. Maliciously, he suggests (through the voice of another female character) that the cause of her death may well have been the same ailment that allegedly caused her lover's demise, 'for the Surgeons when she was opened up, made no other Report, than what had been before reported by the Physicians; and it was a Malady known by everybody to be incident to our Sex although we were Vestals'.[9] Oldfield had amassed enough money to direct her estate to pay her eldest son £5,000 every six months until he reached the age of thirty. If he died, it was to go to her younger son. To her mother, she left £60, to be paid four times a year, with various annuities for friends and relatives.

After her death, gossip sheets were at the ready to cash in on her fame. On 26 October 1730 the *Daily Journal* advertised 'A Pamphlet, intitled, Authentick Memoirs of the Life of the Celebrated Actress Mrs Anne Oldfield, containing a Genuine Account of her Transactions, from her Infancy, to the Time of her Decease'.[10] The publication was supposedly undertaken 'to prevent Encouragement being given to the Town to fictitious Stories that may be compiled and published under the Title of the life of Mrs Oldfield' and purported to stick strictly to the facts, unlike some works which include 'a Heap of Forgeries and Inconsistencies'. Edmund Curll had another hit on his hands with her 'memoirs', which sold for three half-pence per sheet.

Nearly fifty years after her death, Anne Oldfield was still the subject of news. The *London Chronicle* for 8 August 1778 included an article titled 'Memoirs of Mrs Oldfield' which described her as 'a good daughter, a good mother, and a good friend; and from the charms of her conversation, and the elegance of her manners, [she] led the *ton* for many years in the most fashionable circles'. The article criticized Curll's earlier scurrilous memoirs, declaring,

> She was not, however, free from the frailties of her sex, as General Churchill, and Mr. Maynwaring, were both happy in her affections. The Scandalous Chronicle, however, did not stop here, but gave her many more lovers; but this we are led to think arose more from her conversation, and the liberality of her heart, than from any real foundation.[11]

A friend who was living with her at the time of her death reported within the article that she had often felt so ill on stage 'that many a time when she had been playing a part to the universal applause of the audience, the tears have fallen from her cheeks with the anguish she felt from her disorder'.

Francesco Bartolozzi, after Henry William Bunbury,
Ticket to Wynnstay Theatre, 1785, engraving.

The publication of suggestive memoirs and articles indicates just how easy it was for a woman to have her name maligned. An actress had to battle for her position, not just on the stage of the theatre but as an upright woman. Some actresses simply did not care and were lucky enough to become popular and wealthy, gaining themselves some independence. Others married into money. Actress Fanny Kemble published her opinions on the flightiness of fame in *Records of a Girlhood*, referring to her aunt, actress Sarah Siddons:

> What a price she had paid for her great celebrity! – weariness, vacuity, and utter deadness of spirit . . . She had stood on a pinnacle till all things have come to look flat and dreary. Poor woman! What a fate to be condemned to, and yet how she had been envied as well as admired.

'Breeches' and 'Weeping' Roles

Throughout the eighteenth century, Drury Lane Theatre would flourish under the leadership of Colley Cibber, David Garrick and Richard Brinsley Sheridan. Their rivals at the Duke of York Company moved from Lincoln's Inn Field to the newly built Covent Garden Theatre, which opened in 1732 under the direction of John Rich. Meanwhile, a new theatre in Haymarket built by John Potter in 1720 would flourish, with Henry Fielding, Charlotte Charke and her brother Theophilus Cibber among the actors working there. Problems were created with the introduction of the Licensing Act in 1737, which created a theatrical stranglehold, restricting dramatic performances to the two 'royal' theatres, Drury Lane and Covent Garden Theatre. Thereafter, the Haymarket theatre worked under temporary licences, getting round the constrictions by putting on concerts followed by 'free' plays. Samuel Foote was granted a lease on the theatre in 1746. He first illegally performed *Othello*, then wrote his own plays to produce; his play *The Dish of Chocolate* referred to the hot drink that was sold to complement the musical entertainment while the performance was offered 'free', a contrivance needed to avoid the Licensing Act. However, in this case, the morning after the performance, the authorities locked the theatre and turned away the audience for the matinée. It took Foote's friends in high places to prevent a permanent lockdown. The Haymarket was eventually granted a licence to put on plays in the summer periods only (May to September) in 1758.

London theatregoers increasingly demanded diversity from their entertainments, including comedy, tragedy, singing and dancing. Actresses therefore had to have a range of talents at their disposal, to be able both to play comedy and make people laugh, and to produce feelings of despair and tears. The *Theatre Review* for 1758 suggested,

> I think tragedy-acting, besides several other secondary requisites, demands the following five, to wit, *genius, judgement, expression, action* and *voice.* Comedy requires other qualification, very different from those, the genius of comedy implies a feeling of circumstances of ridicule, whereas, the genius of tragedy implies a feeling of passions of a higher nature.[12]

Some actresses could play both, but usually they excelled at one or the other. Both roles exuded a degree of eroticism and emotion; one involved the audience watching overt displays of a female figure dressed as a man; the other depicted a suffering woman in pain and tears. The roles were used to express certain types of sexual behaviour and exploited the sexual expression and vulnerabilities of female performers on stage.

Comedy roles often involved actresses dressing in male attire, and actresses who played 'breeches roles' gained increased popularity. The tight-fitting stockings and short jerkins of male costumes allowed women to strut the stage and show off their shapely legs and figure. One of the most renowned breeches part was that of Sir Harry Wildair in Farquhar's *The Constant Couple*, a role made famous by tempestuous Dublin actress Peg Woffington (1720–1760). As with many other poor girls, Woffington had started off as a street singer, making her debut as Polly Peachum in John Gay's *The Beggar's Opera* when she was only ten. Her success in Dublin was followed by a triumphal debut in London in 1732, and she went on to play various roles at Drury Lane Theatre for several years, including Shakespeare's Rosalind. Her numerous lovers included Edward Bligh, 2nd Earl of Darnley, and Irish actor Charles Macklin, but her most famous affair was with actor and theatre manager David Garrick, whom she lived with for some years. She played numerous roles opposite him, including Cordelia to his King Lear. She left Garrick in 1744 and Drury Lane in 1747 and went on to play at Covent Garden Theatre, by which time she was already notorious for her amorous intrigues. Her rivals included actress Kitty

Peter van Bleeck, *Peg Woffington as Phoebe*, 1747, mezzotint.

Clive (1711–1785), who wrote plays as well as sang and acted in them; as one critic said of Clive, 'There are no characters in comedy, wherein she fails for want of feeling; but there are some that she feels beyond her means of expression; such as the Coquettes . . . but even then she is most admirable, by the art with which she makes up in humour every deficiency of that sort.'[13] The same critic bewailed the loss of Woffington from Covent Garden Theatre, which she had left after not being treated in the manner she ought to have been; 'This season is marked with a great calamity for the stage; the loss we have had of this charming actress is daily more and more felt by the public.'[14] He reckoned her the best coquette that ever appeared on stage, except for Mrs Oldfield. He hinted at the problem between Woffington and other actresses, her biggest rival being Mrs George Anne Bellamy. Of the two actresses, the critic favoured Woffington, as he declared of Bellamy's acting, 'This in Mrs. Bellamy I will only stile imitation; but in the lady whom Mr R____[Rich] has thought proper to impose on us for Mrs. Woffington's successor in all her parts, it is rank mimickry.'[15] Woffington's jealousy of Bellamy ended in a public clash on stage in 1755 during a performance of *The Rival Queens* when she stabbed her rival just offstage from the audience.[16] A couple of years later, Woffington collapsed on stage during her epilogue in *As You Like It* and never recovered enough to act again, dying three years later.

While Woffington was famous for playing her breeches roles, Charlotte Charke also made her name playing male roles both on and off the stage. Her breeches roles at Drury Lane Theatre were a hit with audiences, but more unusually, she adopted a male persona. As a child, she lived with her parents in Southampton Street West, the youngest of twelve children born to actress Katherine Shore and playwright Colley Cibber. According to her autobiography, she was

Unknown artist, *Charlotte Charke*, 1725–50, mezzotint.

sent to a famous school in Park Street, Westminster, where she learnt Latin, Italian and geography and later taught herself to garden, shoot and race horses, forsaking any domesticated roles. When she was only sixteen, she married Richard Charke, having admired his virtuosity as a violinist – she 'held [him] in great estimation' – and soon afterwards had a child.[17]

Charke's first performance was at Drury Lane Theatre (where her father was joint manager) in John Vanbrugh's *The Provok'd Wife* on 8 April 1730. She fell out with her father when he sold his share of the theatre to John Highmore rather than offer it to her or her brother Theophilus Cibber. The rift was to be a permanent one and obviously caused her great upset: she referred to this time as 'my painful separation from my once tender father'.[18] Her autobiography may have been written as a plea to ask his forgiveness and to try and re-establish their relationship. Charke and Theophilus, together with the other actors of Drury Lane, set up a rival company at the Haymarket, which was then managed by Henry Fielding. Once a settlement had been reached with the new owner, Charles Fleetwood (Highmore had sold on his share), at Drury Lane, the company went back and performed there with Charke further developing her breeches roles. She performed in various plays over her career, including Nicholas Rowe's *Jane Shore*, Lucy in George Lillo's *The London Merchant; or, George Barnwell*, Mrs Slammekin in *The Beggar's Opera*, Miss Hoyden in Vanbrugh's *The Relapse* and Fainlove in Richard Steele's *The Tender Husband*. Charlotte Charke also took the male role, Lord Place, in *Pasquin*, which, as she pointed out, 'til then had been performed by Mr Richard Yates',[19] as well as Plume in *The Recruiting Officer*, Roderigo in *Othello* and Lorenzo in Dryden's *The Spanish Friar*, among others.

The Licensing Act limited Charke's available jobs to only two theatres. Ever inventive, she set up her own puppet show at the Old Tennis Court, St James's. That same year, her faithless husband died, having previously moved to Jamaica under the pressure of massive debts, leaving Charke to bring up their daughter alone. Further crisis was to follow when she fell ill and into debt. Thanks only to the kindness and generosity of coffee-shop owners, prostitutes and her actress friends did she avoid prison. She recalled in her autobiography, 'I was surrounded by all the ladies who kept coffee houses in and about the garden, each offering money for my ransom.' Writing as a woman, she knew she would receive criticism: 'As the history is the product of a female pen, I tremble for the terrible hazard it must run in venturing into the world, as it may very possibly suffer, in many opinions, without perusing it,' but her cross-dressing alone would have been enough for some eighteenth-century readers.[20] The next acting opportunity came when she set up her own company again at New Theatre, James Street, Haymarket, in November 1742. The role of Pope Joan was apt for her, considering that Joan was allegedly the first female pope. The play was based on a revival of Elkanah Settle's *The Female Prelate* back at the Haymarket in 1745. Acting did not make her enough money to keep her going and at various times she worked as a valet, a grocer and a sausage seller. Under her own admission, none of her ventures were successful; at one time she opened a tavern, which she later had to sell at a loss.

Disguised as a man, she wooed a wealthy young heiress, fell in love and proposed. This came to nothing, as eventually she had to reveal herself. She took to cross-dressing on a more permanent basis as 'Charles Brown' when she was forced to start playing the provinces, no doubt as a disguise to escape her creditors. She lived with a woman, Mrs Brown, an actress who played in *The Spanish Friar* opposite her and who nursed her through three years of illness. Given the vulnerabilities of women travelling on their own, the pair probably thought it safer to travel as man and wife. Back in London, Charke tried her hand at novel-writing, but her success came with her autobiography. Switching back to her female self, she married John Sacheverell of Holborn at St George's chapel on 2 May 1746. Charke was determined to take up acting once again and her brother offered her roles in his company in 1755 and 1756. Now in her forties, her final performance was as Marplot in Susanna Centlivre's *The Busybody* at the Haymarket on 28 September 1759. She died in debt in cheap lodgings in the Haymarket. Nevertheless, her book of adventures had left its mark and she was one of the most remarkable women of her time.

Different actresses were famous for their individual talents: while Charke was noted for her breeches roles, her sister-in-law Susannah Cibber (neé Arne, 1714–1766) was lauded for her weeping roles. Susannah made her debut as the heroine in Henry Carey's *Amelia* in 1732 at the Little Theatre in the Haymarket and quickly fell into the role of performer, becoming known for her exquisite singing voice. A few years later she was appearing in some of her best dramatic roles as the lead in Aaron Hill's *Zara* in 1736 and various Shakespeare tragedies. One critic remarked on the prowess of the actress and

Caricature of Theophilus Cibber discovering William Sloper with Susannah Maria Cibber (neé Arne): 'A late unfortunate adventure at York', etching from the *London Magazine,* vol. XXXIX (1770).

singer, declaring, 'Nature has bestowed on her an agreeable figure, a bewitching voice, and above all, an exquisite feeling.' Particularly he praised her dramatic roles, 'when passions are to be expressed, then she speaks to the eye, the ear, and through both to the heart.'[21] She seldom appeared in comedy.

Interconnections, both professional and familial, were common in the theatrical profession: Susannah had married Theophilus Cibber, an actor and company manager, Charlotte's brother and the son of Colley Cibber, but he turned out to be an abusive and profligate man. A scandal erupted after her husband sued her lover, William Sloper, for alleged adultery, claiming damages to the tune of £5,000.[22] Even the theatre world had its limits of acceptability and Susannah was forced to leave the stage in 1739. The affair appears to have been set up by Theophilus Cibber in order to make some money from Sloper, who was his lodger. Theophilus was in full knowledge of the sexual machinations going on under his own roof and had ignored the matter, as Sloper was paying the rent for all three of them.[23] The disbelief of the jury was expressed in the meagre compensation awarded to Theophilus Cibber. A pamphlet came out outlining the trial, which was to cause all three of them much embarrassment. However, Susannah's public was more forgiving and she eventually returned to the stage in 1742 to sing arias in Handel's *Messiah*, regaining her former position and acting and singing until her death. The public regarded her as the wronged wife, and she pleased her audiences in her role as Desdemona in *Othello* in 1742. Adopting the victim helped her career: she took up more and more tragic weeping roles, to great acclaim.

Actresses were able to transgress the boundaries of class in their ability to copy the fashions and manners of the elite and could therefore find acceptance among classes above their own. While actresses from the lower classes might initially struggle for recognition, the possibility existed for them to move above their station, using the theatre as a springboard to wealth and greater independence.

From Rags to Riches

Many a poor girl made the shift from selling oranges to life on the stage. Elevation to fame opened the door to meeting a wealthy potential suitor, someone who would either keep her or marry her. Lavinia Fenton (1708–1760) was one such woman and was celebrated in a biography, *The Life of Lavinia Berwick, alias Fenton alias Polly Peachum*, which was perhaps one of the earliest biographies to spring up depicting the life of a female stage player. She was born illegitimate – her father was probably the lieutenant of a man-of-war – but took her mother's husband's name, Fenton. With her boarding-school education, wit and good looks, she attracted many admirers and may have taken lovers to help her financially.[24]

Fenton started her career as a singer on the street near her mother's coffee-house in Charing Cross, and made her way up the ranks of the theatre, debuting at the Haymarket in March 1726 in the role of Serina/Monimia in Thomas Otway's tragedy *The Orphan; or, The Unhappy Marriage.* She also performed in a benefit performance playing Cherry Boniface in *The Beaux' Stratagem.* At some stage, John Rich spotted her in one of her roles and invited her to play Polly Peachum in Gay's *The Beggar's Opera* at the Theatre Royal, based at Lincoln's Inn Fields, where she debuted the role on 29 January 1728. The role was to make her an overnight sensation and public adoration quickly followed. Fenton was showered with poems and songs were written about her. Her salary doubled and she went on to play a variety of

Charles Jervas, *Lavinia Fenton as Polly Peachum in John Gay's 'The Beggar's Opera'*, 18th century, oil on canvas.

roles, including in comedies, straight plays and Shakespeare, such as Leanthe in George Farquhar's *Love and a Bottle*, Mrs Squeamish in William Wycherley's *The Country Wife*, Alida in John Fletcher's *The Pilgrim* and Ophelia in *Hamlet*.

Broadsheets cashed in on her popularity. *The Whole Life of Polly Peachum* was advertised as 'shewing how she jumpt from an Orange Girl to an Actress on the Stage and Lady of Fortune'. According to this narrative, her father was a mercer and a liveryman of the City of London. He fell into debt after investing in the South Sea Bubble, and Fenton was obliged to shift for herself. The broadsheet may have changed her background, as so often happened when hacks filled in missing biographical details, but most agreed that the role that shot her to stardom was that of Polly Peachum.[25]

As with other actresses and courtesans, images of Fenton were made and circulated in London, which contributed to the spread of her fame. Hogarth painted Fenton as Polly Peachum and admirers eagerly bought pictures of her. John Gay remarked, 'There is a Mezzo-tinto Print publish'd to day of Polly, the Heroine of the Beggar's Opera, who was before unknown, and is now in so high vogue, that I am in

William Hogarth, *The Beggar's Opera, Act III*, 1790, engraving.

doubt, whether her fame does not surpass that of the Opera itself.'[26] Domestic items such as clothes screens and painted folding fans with her image on them were available for sale.[27] Her increased fame meant Fenton had her choice of men. The poet Edward Young wrote to Thomas Tickell, 'Polly a Wench that acts in the Beggars Opera . . . 'tis said, has raised her Price from one Guinea to 100, tho' she cannot be a greater whore than she was before.'[28]

At the peak of her success, she absconded from the theatre to become the mistress of Charles Powlett (sometimes called Paulet, 3rd Duke of Bolton, 1685–1754), who looked after her for the next 28 years. In a comment to Jonathan Swift, John Gay declared, 'The Duke of Bolton, I hear, has run away with Polly Peachum, having settled £400 a year on her during pleasure, and upon disagreement £200 a year.'[29] She made her last performance as Polly on 19 April 1728, but she had to wait another 23 years before she could wed her lover. On the death of his wife, the duke finally married Fenton at Aix-en-Provence. She had borne him three sons, Charles, Percy and Horatio Armand, who had careers in the church, the navy and the army respectively. Despite the duke being 23 years older than her, it was apparently a love match.

C. Grignion and P. C. Canot, after S. Wale, *The Foundling Hospital, Holborn*, 1749, engraving.

He was obviously a caring man, as he became a governor of London's Foundling Hospital for abandoned children when it was set up by sea captain Thomas Coram in 1739. On his death, he left her all his wealth and she was the sole executor of his will. She died at her home at Westcombe House, Greenwich, on 24 January 1760 and was buried at St Alfege Church on 3 February. A road near where she had lived was named in her honour, Peachum Road, after her title role. The clergyman Joseph Warton, who had married the couple all those years before, said of her, 'She was very accomplished; was a most agreeable companion; had much wit and strong good sense, and a just taste in polite literature. Her person was agreeable and well-made; though she could not be called a beauty.'[30] Even without scintillating looks, if she were lucky, a female London libertine could end up with a life of security.

The Best Catch: Harriot Mellon and the Banker

The position of every performer was precarious, even dangerous, though not through any fault of her own or the acting business, but

Sir William Beechey, *Harriot Mellon, Duchess of St Albans*, 1817–18, oil on canvas.

a result of public opinion. For this reason actresses were denied any social status in society. Women skirted round this issue by marrying wealthy men. By bucking the boundaries of what was expected of them, they could provide themselves with the security they desired, but they did not escape criticism. Harriot Mellon (1777–1837) was castigated for using her position as an actress to manipulate herself into a wealthy marriage – but then, this was what every actress aspired to. Her acting position at the Drury Lane Theatre placed her before Thomas Coutts (1735–1822), an elderly banker who fell in love with her. Mellon was perhaps one of the most fortunate (or, some might say, astute) actresses in the business as she not only managed to bag herself a very wealthy man, but later married into a title.

Mellon started off as a child actor, following her mother and father into the theatre. Her early entrance into the theatre was no doubt due to the connections of her parents. Her mother, Sarah Mellon, was Irish and worked as a dresser and wardrobe mistress and her father was Lieutenant Mather Mellon of the Madras infantry, but it is unlikely the pair ever married. Sarah took up with Thomas Entwhistle, the leader of the orchestra in Kena's company of strolling players, where she worked, and later they were both employed by Bibby's theatre company. Harriot's debut came when she was around nine years old, in a theatre barn in Ulverstone, Lancashire, on 16 October 1787. The role was Little Pickle in the farce *The Spoiled Child.* Harriot joined Stanton's theatre company in the Midlands, where she played Beatrice, Celia, Lydia Languish and Letitia Hardy. Her breakthrough came when Richard Brinsley Sheridan saw her working there and engaged her for his production of *The Rivals* on 31 January 1795 at the Drury Lane Theatre, where she again played Lydia Languish. It was here that the eighteen-year-old Harriot attracted the attention of Thomas Coutts. Their affair lasted for the next ten years, during which time she continued to perform a wide variety of roles, while her position became increasingly secure.

Actresses had to have good memories, as they had to learn many different roles for the various plays. Productions were quick to change in order to keep pulling in audiences. Frequently players were called upon to fill in for other actors at short notice. *The Oracle* newspaper for Friday, 25 November 1796, noted that Miss Mellon was playing in a farce, *The Apprentice*. The following week, the same newspaper advertised her as playing again in different roles in various plays alongside some more famous theatrical names, Mr Barrymore, Charles Kemble, Miss Farren and Miss de Camp, in *The Force of Ridicule*;[31] the *Morning Post* also carried notices of her performance in *Who's the Dupe?* at the Theatre Royal, Drury Lane; again *The Oracle* informed the public of her role in *Twelfth Night*; and the *True Briton* commented on her playing Berinthia in *Trip to Scarborough* on 1 July 1799. With the demands of ever-changing roles, versatility was a requirement of any actress keen to maintain a position in London's theatres.

While some actresses were acclaimed for their acting prowess, Mellon never gained great accolades. However, she was competent, amiable and would willingly take over lead roles when others fell ill and go back to her secondary roles without a fuss. Another actress, Anne Mathews, who later published her own diary, described Mellon as 'a young, glowing beauty, endued with great natural powers of mind, talents and vivacity, but . . . an insuperable rusticity of air and manners'.[32] In her breeches role of Albina Mandeville, her figure was said to surpass even that of Mrs Jordan. In 1805 she played Volante in John Tobin's *Honeymoon*, Angelica in *The Constant Couple*, Viletta in *She Would and She Would Not* and Dorcu in *The Mock Doctor*.

Although later Mellon became somewhat portly, she had great vitality. Most unkindly, one source portrayed her as having a very healthy appetite, as opposed to the fashion of eating like a bird. Although she was receiving 3*s* 6*d* per week for her job of 'lady of all-work on the boards', he commented,

> these scanty resources were not sufficient to withstand the cravings of an empty stomach, and the great appetite of a coarse strong growing girl with a delicate wardrobe, whose capacity in the consumption of culinary comforts was really extraordinary, for if a pound of chuck stakes [*sic*] had been laid before her it shortly disappeared.[33]

Others spoke of her more warmly; Sir Walter Scott found her 'a kind, friendly woman, without either affectation or insolence in the display of her wealth'. As with many actresses, her portraits were painted by well-known artists such as Romney, Beechey and Masquerier, among others. Because of her affair with one of the richest men in London, she became the butt of vitriolic gossip.

Presumably she now felt safe enough to give up acting, and her final performance was on 7 February 1815 as Audrey in *As You Like It*. By this time, she was making the princely sum of £12 a week and could support herself. It seems surprising that so many actresses gave up their jobs at the height of their fame and it is hard to see why they would trust a man to keep them forever; once away from their public for any length of time, they would find it difficult to get back their popularity. They must have seen other actresses who had been offered the same position of security with annuities promised, only to be abandoned when their keeper became bored with them or infatuated with another woman. If deserted, they would be left with nothing. Luckily, once his first wife died in 1815, Coutts quickly married Mellon at St Pancras church on 12 April, proving his devotion to her. He was now eighty; she was 38. After seven years together, Coutts died on 24 February 1822, leaving his whole fortune to Harriot, including his partnership in Coutts bank. Harriot was now a very wealthy woman and attracted other suitors while throwing luxurious parties at her town house in the Kings Road, but proved herself an astute businesswoman with an ability to make wise investments. She was generous to Coutts's three daughters despite their wealthy marriages, and provided them with £10,000 a year each. At 49, she soon found her second husband, a man 23 years her junior: William Aubrey de Vere Beauclerk, 9th Duke of St Albans (1801–1849) whom she married on 16 June 1827. On top of the fortune Coutts had left her, she had now gained a title, and became the Duchess of St Albans.

Harriot's life story was the topic of one of the rash of scurrilous memoirs of supposedly disreputable women that flooded London's marketplace. Harriot had at least made herself famous enough to gain a place among the list of other actresses and mistresses who were rich enough not to care. *The Secret Memoirs of Harriot Pumpkin* was published in 1825, the same year Harriette Wilson's autobiographical memoir came out. Both books carried the same typeface and style of frontispiece, so most probably emanated from the same printer, John Stockdale. The author was well aware of Wilson's memoirs and was no doubt cashing in on the earlier enterprise, declaring, 'The public have been recently amused with the memoirs of Mother Bang, of Harriette Wilson – and why not those of Harriott Pumpkin whose prowess in deception was of a much more flagrant nature than either.' So that readers were under no illusion as to who was being written about, the author noted, 'Pumpkin, according to Naturalists, [is] a spurious kind of melon.' Disingenuously, the author admits,

> In all probability, there will be some of you amongst my readers, who, upon the perusal of these Memoirs, will say, – 'the Author has been too severe upon the conduct of his Heroine; he should have displayed more gallantry – glossed over many of her frailties, and not make use of so many coarse epithets by way of reproach.' To this charge I reply, my design is to lay before my young friends the wickedness and mal-practices of the last century, in order to render them the more detestable in this, and to paint in vivid colours the crimes of ingratitude, vindictiveness, and dissimulation, which, either separate or together, bear the strongest symptoms of depravity.[34]

Specifically, the age difference was an issue for the press and criticism was levelled at Mellon for marrying such an older man: 'when a woman of twenty-nine sells herself to age and ugliness of seventy-nine, I decidedly arrange the sale under the title of prostitution.' Contrarily, the author declared the age gap as something not too unusual, declaring, 'It is as natural for old women to look after young men, as it is for old men to wish for young women.'[35] Harriot was accused of false modesty and using her wiles to outwit men for their money: 'These ladies have made no secret of their profession, while Mrs. Pumpkin was more skilled in the ways of the world, and in the secret of committing unblushing errors under false pretences, so as to swindle folks of a good report, without a particle of pretence to it.'[36]

Coutts had allegedly made Harriot an offer of an annuity through a mutual friend, declaring, 'the insult I offer has Ten Thousand charms and one thousand by way of a bonus on every one of your future birthdays.'[37] If this is true, while Harriot would have been aware that Mrs Coutts was still alive and Thomas had three daughters from this earlier marriage, it is understandable that she grabbed at the chance of financial security. Nonetheless, she was obliged to try and defend her reputation. According to the memoirs, 'Miss Pumpkin has a lawyer to threaten anyone that even suspected her chastity.'[38] Although unreliable, this is possibly true, as she now had the financial means to strike back.

Such 'memoirs' often took the chance to attack the person they were writing about, accusing them of being mean. In Harriot's case, the author of the memoirs accused her of refusing to give money to her sick nephew and allowing an old couple she had known from childhood to starve to death. A long list of treacherous accusations followed – she had slighted her stepson-in-law, she had thrown out a companion from her house and sacked two doctors who looked after Coutts. It seems the author had a grudge against her. Indeed, the allegations that she was neglecting Coutt's daughters was untrue, as she remained close to them, providing them with financial security while alive and leaving them money when she died.

Allegedly, her second husband, the young Duke of St Albans, was riddled with debt, and Harriot was willing to pay it off for him. The author accuses Harriot of drinking Madeira and soda like a fish, screaming at her servants, even throwing a 'Ripstone Pipin' [apple] at the butler, hitting him 'smack between the eyes, and dropped him as flat as a turbot'.[39] It would seem Mellon could put away her fair share of wine, the couple drinking together, 'but with more reserve than she had done for some years before; a bottle or two she was always equal to, and she well knew how to influence his blood to a certain standard, which rendered amatory advances as a matter of course'.[40] The author suggested she was apt at the game of seduction, 'an able veteran in the field of Venus, and from long experience knew every manoeuvre to attract, and hold in firm grasp those advantages arising from her own ingenuity and acknowledged tact'. The result was inevitable, with the added incentive of aphrodisiacs;

> no game cock was ever higher fed for battle; everything that could inflame the mind was provided and applied; any jaunts in the open air, shell fish and warm cordials, Curacoa, and Martinique Noyao, to warm the stomach, everything that could create desire was copiously administered, in order to produce the desired effect.[41]

When Harriot died on 6 August 1837, at her home, 80 Piccadilly, she left her vast fortune to Coutt's granddaughter, Angela, thereby giving another young woman her freedom and independence. According to the *Morning Herald*, her fortune amounted to £1.8 million, much of which Angela spent on philanthropic works, including a home in which to redeem prostitutes.

Advertisements were carried at the back of similar books to advertise other actresses and courtesans' memoirs. *The Life and Adventures of the Celebrated Lady Barrymore, alias Mary Ann Pierce-Fanny Norton-Jenny Go-lightly Kick-the-Chrystal, and Peg of the Clink*, was interspersed with numerous and amusing anecdotes of 'Living Characters of Distinction' and seasoned with 'Delectable Sings, Rich Morceaus, &c.' It is probable that many of these women knew each other and would have mingled on the same circuit. According to Julia Johnstone's memoirs, Harriette Wilson attempted to raise a loan from Mellon, so they must have known each other; Johnstone asserted 'she [Harriette Wilson] tried to borrow money from Mrs Coutts, whose liberality is so very extensive.'[42] Such libertine women were frequently financially protective and generous to one another, aware of the delicate balance most had to make in life.

Lauded actresses demand high salaries, but in such a precarious profession, they had to find a way to safely secure some of their money in case of illness or pregnancy. While benefit nights were performed as a way of providing for the less fortunate, sometimes the proceeds went to one person. Elizabeth Barry was one of the first to take advantage of benefit nights, whereby the proceeds of the evening were given to a particular performer. Sarah Siddons ensured that her contract provided for two benefit nights per season, which considerably raised her own annual income. Often, though, the benefit night was in the form of one charity or another, perhaps the widow of an actor and his bereft children. Despite the fascination with the torrid lifestyles of these celebrities, there was a move to professionalize the theatre and 'civilize' it, so that by 1827 Siddons could safely say, 'the profession is for the most part rather above than below the middle standard.'[43] This increased respectability meant that women were earning more money from their profession.

The number of women involved in London play production, aside from actresses, was substantially increasing. By 1798 and 1832 more than forty female playwrights had their work produced on public or private stages. Actresses also turned to playwriting to supplement their income. One of the first women to write plays and adapt them was Eliza Haywood (*c.* 1693–25 February 1756), born Elizabeth Fowler. She first started in acting in Dublin in 1715 and made what she calls an 'unfortunate' marriage, describing herself as a widow in 1717 when she moved to Lincoln's Inn Fields in London. Although Pope provided

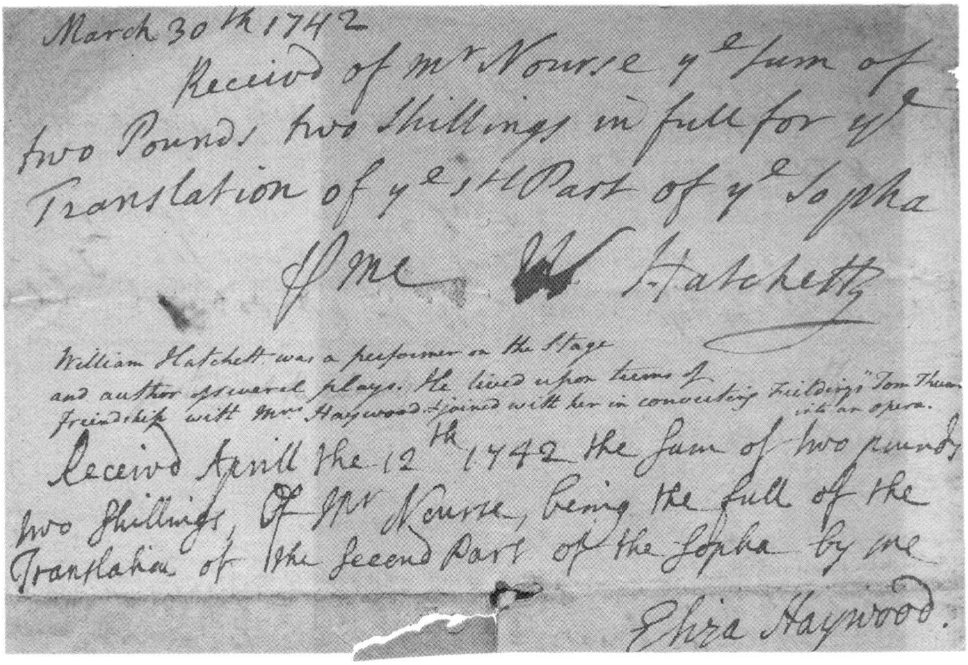
March 30th 1742
Receiv'd of Mr Nourse ye sum of
two Pounds two Shillings in full for ye
Translation of ye 1st Part of ye Sopha
⅌ me W: Hatchett

William Hatchett was a performer on the Stage
and author of several plays. He lived upon terms of
friendship with Mrs Haywood & joined with her in converting Fieldings "Tom Thumb"
into an opera.

Receiv'd Aprill the 12th 1742 the sum of two pounds
two Shillings, Of Mr Nourse, being the full of the
Translation of the second Part of the Sopha by me
Eliza Haywood.

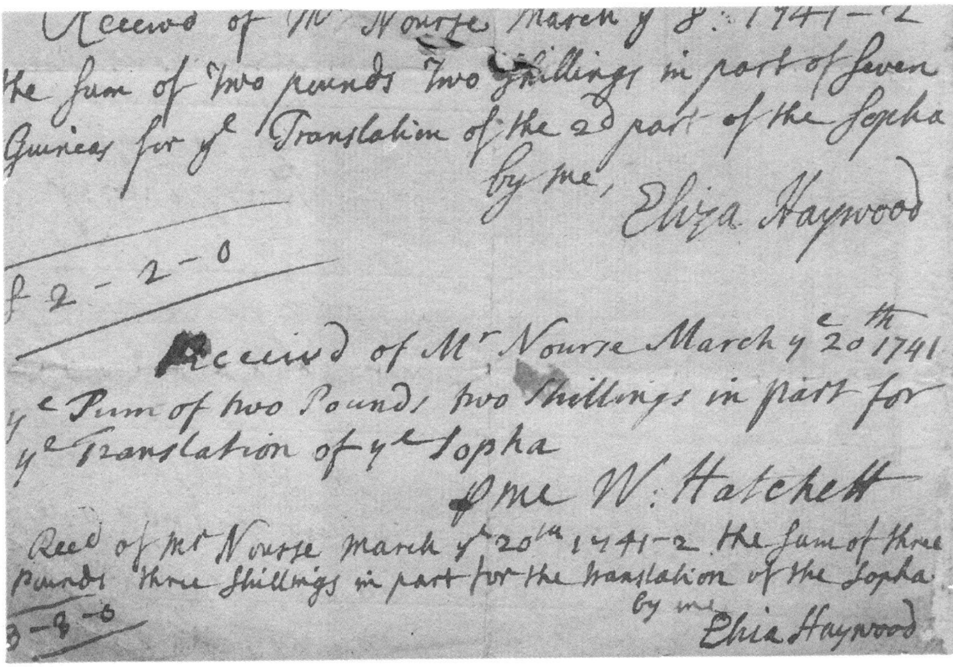
Receiv'd of Mr Nourse March ye 8: 1741–2
the sum of two pounds two Shillings in part of seven
Guineas for ye Translation of the 2d part of the Sopha
by me, Eliza Haywood

£ 2 - 2 - 0

Receiv'd of Mr Nourse March ye 20th 1741
ye sum of two Pounds two Shillings in part for
ye Translation of ye Sopha
⅌ me W: Hatchett

Recd of Mr Nourse March ye 20th 1741-2 the sum of three
pounds three Shillings in part for the translation of the Sopha
by me
Eliza Haywood

3 - 3 - 0

Receipts for payments to Eliza Haywood and William Hatchett.

a somewhat scandalous picture of her with her two children tugging at her waist, it is possible she was deserted by her husband. She met up with actor and playwright William Hatchett around 1728 and collaborated with him both in their stage career and in their writing. Together they adapted Henry Fielding's *The Tragedy of Tragedies*. She rewrote a play for John Rich, *The Fair Captive*, and also wrote her first play, *A Wife to Be Let*, in 1723, all the while still acting. Probably in an attempt to gain royal patronage, she wrote the tragedy *Frederick, Duke of Brunswick-Lunenburgh* to honour Frederick, Prince of Wales. She had success both with her plays and acting at the Haymarket Theatre, notably with the Fielding adaptation.

What is less known is the fact that Haywood worked on translating French pornography to make money. A small sheet of paper in the William Andrews Clark Memorial Library, UCLA, shows a record of payment received by Eliza Haywood and William Hatchett for their work translating Crébillon's *Le Sopha* into English for the publisher John Nourse. The sheet is written on both sides and receipts are signed by both Haywood and Hatchett. In her own hand, she confirms: 'Received of Mr Norse March of 8 1741–2 the sum of Two pounds Two Shillings in part of Seven Guineas for the Translation of 2nd part of the Sopha by me, Eliza Haywood.' Haywood was evidently paid as she went along, as a further inscription shows she received a further sum on 20 March 'of three pounds three shillings in part for the translation of the Sopha by me Eliza Haywood'.[44] Hatchett was also paid in part, receiving the sum of £2 2*s* for the translation on the same day. They were given a further sum on 30 March, £2 2*s* seemingly being the regular amount. They also translated the second part of *Le Sopha* in April.

Once again, we see a merging of the respectable with the less respectable aspects of life for those attached to the theatre. Women had to walk a tightrope in order to stay popular and unmaligned as well as financially secure. Drop into disrepute and the labels of 'whore' and 'slut' were bandied about, which could ruin an actress's career. Equally, taking rich lovers might raise the esteem in which she was held by other men, but lower it in the eyes of 'respectable' theatregoers. Biographies might also raise a female libertine's status, showing gay abandonment and a happy-go-lucky air. However, the more scurrilous of these memoirs might tarnish her reputation, a blow from which she would be lucky to recover.

Beau Brummell in his youth, frontispiece to Captain Jesse, *The Life of George Brummell* (1886), vol. I.

7
Libertines and Their Fashions

Worthy Sir, London, farewell, and all thy vain Delights,
That burry our Days, and Drown our Nights.
Adieu, Fair Miss, and all your tempting Airs,
With Freedom now I can disdain your Snares;
No study'd smile, or Kind inviting look,
Shall please my Eye, or draw me to your Hook;
Nor shall the Charms of beauty, join'd with Wine,
Rob me of Reason that is more Divine.
Truth I'll pursue, and rural Pleasures court.

NED WARD, 'The Young Libertine's Answer to His Uncle'

This poem paints a picture of the female libertine as a scheming, wanton debauchee, hell-bent on destroying all men. Women are to be desired, but the desire must be fought if a man is not to be duped. Satires showed women as tempting and delectable, but they were issued with a warning to men. Other types of literature, including poems, plays and novels, lauded the libertine woman as fun-loving, witty, pretty, free with her affections and just the woman to spend some time with. Just as there were all sorts of depictions of female libertines, there were also various descriptions of their male counterparts. Male libertines were satirized as effeminate fops, lady-lovers or excessive indulgers of vice in a 'manly' fashion.

New names sprang up for female and male libertines. One such picture of an immodest hussy was to be found in the character of the Town-Miss, a modern name given to women otherwise known as whores and strumpets. She was defined as 'a certain Help-meet for

A rake getting measured up for the latest fashion: after William Hogarth, *A Rake's Progress, Plate 1*, 1735, hand-coloured aquatint with etching.

a Gentleman, instead of a Wife; Serving either for the prevention of the Sin of Marrying, or else as a little Side Pillow, to render the Yoke of Matrimony more easie'. These descriptions were given supposedly to 'expose the Fopperies of some vain Self-conceited Pretenders to Gentility, and some good Breeding'.[1] Her male counterpart was the Town-Gallant, who came in for equal amounts of criticism. He was singled out as being 'a Bundle of Vanity, composed of Ignorance and Pride, Folly, and Debauchery; a filthy Huffing thing, three parts Fop and the rest Hector; A kind of Walking Mercers Shop, that shews one snuff to day, and another tomorrow, and is valuable just according to the price of his Suit'.[2] The Young Rake was a particular type of callous youth, 'not able to guide himself; expos'd to the World and Fortune, from which the weakness of his Childhood prefer'd him'. Instead of avoiding temptation, he seeks it out: 'He longs to be acquainted with the Vices of Fashion; and Sins to his Understanding.' He believes his youth is the proper time to satiate his lust, he dislikes religion, but 'knows not why', and his friendship is 'bought by a bottle' but lost before it is drunk.[3]

Despite their foibles, both female and male libertines were often the ones to lead London fashion. Their portraits were splashed in memoirs, newspaper reports and ladies' and gentlemen's magazines, as well as scandal sheets and trial reports. As we have seen, female libertines such as Fanny Murray and Kitty Fisher made their names by having poems written about them and artists painting them; to a large extent, they fashioned their own images by dictating how they were portrayed. These women were celebrities of their day and led new crazes and trends in terms of the clothes they wore, their choice of headgear and their elaborate hairstyles. They knew the best places to 'be seen' or fashionable places to go such as Vauxhall and Ranelagh Gardens, the theatre, operas or in the royal court. Male libertines like Sir Francis Dashwood and John Wilkes created private spaces for libertines' enjoyment in erotic gardens and at clubs such as the Beefsteak club and

Elaborate hairdos: James Gillray, *The Whore's Last Shift*, 1779, hand-coloured etching.

meetings of 'hell-fire' societies. Others, such as Beau Brummell, set fashion trends with brightly coloured waistcoats and dandyish dress, as did macaronis with their fancy walking sticks and enormous wigs.

Certain fashions and styles linked groups of people together. The pamphlet *Whipping-Tom; or, A Rod for a Proud Lady* satirized women who took snuff, drank tea and walked about in red riding cloaks.[4] Hoop petticoats were all the rage in London, a fashionable style of dress whereby a hoop encircles the petticoat in order to make the dress stand out. Some of the hoops were so large that they swept teacups from tables. Indeed, the hoop petticoat was the butt of many satirists and cartoons, yet women were prepared to continue to define their autonomy by wearing them. Despite the various jibes, women supposedly used the hoop as a form of protection from men; *The Spectator* declared in 1711 that they were an invention that 'serves to keep men at a decent distance'. A *London Magazine* article of 1741 entitled 'The Modern Hoop Petticoat' explained, 'Hoops have observ'd in their Favour, that they serv'd to keep men at a proper Distance, and a Lady within that Circle, seem'd to govern in a spacious Verge sacred to herself.' This might simply have served to tease men more by keeping them at bay, no doubt true for the libertine women who set fashions to satisfy themselves and to be outlandish. Hoops were certainly unpopular with men, who complained that they were receiving injuries: 'one with the stiff Ribbs of her Petticoat breaks your Shins, while others attacking you in the Rear, bang your Hams and the Calves of your Legs. But is it the *Ladies* Fault, if *you* have fore [*sic*] Shins and weak Hams?'[5] The fashion for the hoop lasted throughout the century, peaking in the 1750s, and was copied all over Europe.

Insinuations were often made that the fashionable set was adulterous and criticism was aimed at them for conducting their affairs in public, notably in parks and gardens of London. *The Bon Ton* magazine remarked with glee,

> With those ladies who frequent Kensington Gardens, green grass muslin gowns are quite the ton; and from the number of stars and garters continually seen among the bushes, we are led to believe the gentlemen are there full dressed. Wonder as it may appear, we are assured not one article of Crim. Con. [adultery] has transpired in the Beau Monde for more than a week past.

Hoop petticoats: James Gillray, *Enter Cowslip, with a Bowl of Cream*, 1779, hand-coloured etching.

John Collet, *Tight Lacing; or, Fashion before Ease*, 18th century, oil on canvas.

Readers wanted details of what fashionable women of the town were wearing: 'Striped silk stockings, and white stockings with coloured clocks have become quite the *ton*, with such ladies as have good legs to sport, or are desirous of sporting them.'[6] Indeed, women's undergarments were the source of much discussion. Newspapers endlessly warned women about the damage caused by their underwear, most notably their lacing and stays. *The Times* for 2 October 1788 wrote,

> As a warning to young ladies who wear small stays, and lace them into an orange and a half, let it be known, that a young lady, blessed with every pleasing feature and accomplishment, a few days since, fainted twice, in a small circle of friends in the city, before the real cause could be ascertained. A physician being sent for, immediately discovered that she was exhausted by pain and want of nourishment; after unlacing and recovering his patient, she confessed that for three days she had taken no food from the difficulty she felt of giving it room in the stomach.[7]

For the libertine woman, displaying the bosom was common. The heroine of Henry Fielding's novel *Shamela*, when trying to make an impression on a man, admitted that she 'pulled down my stays, to show as much as I could of my bosom'.

Courtesans were extravagant in their appearance. Dress was intended to enhance their looks and fill men with desire. Harriette Wilson knew the importance of elegance and fashion. Everything French was admired. When at the opera she saw her sister sitting in the next box 'dressed in the foreign style', accompanied by three counts, and 'Beckendorf was half mad for her and wanted to marry her.'[8] When 'on show', courtesans dressed to the nines: one evening, Harriette's sister Fanny appeared 'unusually lovely, dressed in a pale pink crape [*sic*] dress, which set off her rosy, white, delicate skin, to the greatest advantage; and with her unadorned bright auburn curls'. Meanwhile Julia Johnstone, her rival, was set to gain all the attention: 'This evening Julia, I suppose with a view to outshine us all, wore a dress of white silvered lama on gauze, and a Turkish turban of bright blue, fringed with gold.' Jewellery would signal the worth of a woman and was often mentioned:

> Amy wore a yellow satin dress, fastened round the waist with a gold band. Her profuse raven locks [black hair was popular] were entirely unadorned, and her neck, arms and fingers were covered with glittering jewels of every colour. My own evening dresses were invariably composed of rich, figured, white French gauze over white satin; and I never wore any ornaments in my hair, of which I was not a little proud; but my earrings were of unusual length, and consisted of diamonds, rubies and turquoise stones.[9]

Harriette recognized style when she saw it, even in men. No one could 'find fault with the taste of all those who for years had made it a rule to copy the cut of Brummell's coat, the shape of his hat, or the tie of his neckcloth: for all this was in the very best possible style'.[10] His legs must be properly covered. Harriette told Lord Molyneux, 'white silk stockings always win my heart, no matter who wears them.'[11]

Male authors complained about gossiping ladies and their concentration on fashion and appearances, particularly their criticism of other women's figures:

Thomas Rowlandson, *An Old Ewe Drest Lamb Fashion*, 1810, hand-coloured etching.

> It is really disgusting to hear the young ladies in high and middle life, who after a few common-place words upon the weather, cannot say half a dozen words upon anything but dress; – 'what a horrid figure Miss Long-waist cut at the ball last evening.' 'Oh true, my dear, I noticed her, she looked like the monuments with a carrotty wig.' Then the question was 'did you see that horrid lump of human frailty, Miss Mill-post?' 'True, my dear, what legs, when she joined in the quadrille, her pink shoes looked like a butcher's night-cap on a loaf of sugar,' &c. &c.[12]

The author goes on to slate adornment and finery and condemn uncleanliness and sluttish ways, and blamed parents for failing to cultivate their daughters properly. He complains,

> I have often seen a fine curled head – and dirty stockings; gowns trimmed with lace and fringe – over unclean body linen; and a fine dressy young lady, who could not step out without a gentle brush over of rouge, silks, and expensive paraphernalia, who, when they got married, became filthy slatterns.[13]

Coquettes and Macaronis

Fashionable libertines were often mocked in newspapers, magazines and pamphlets. Everyone from coquettes to macaronis was explored and their typical characteristics summed up and criticized. The female libertine who played the coquette set up a balancing act, simultaneously displaying modesty and lechery. Yet the coquette was denigrated in print, accused of being 'a woman who spreads all her Artillery; puts on every ingaging [*sic*] Air; to make a Lover only; to make the Man an Ass'. She is essentially jealous by nature, as nothing upsets her more than hearing another woman praised, or seeing her in a new fashion first. She spreads her favours equally; 'She Smiles on one, Winks on t'other, and Drinks to the Third; the Fourth she Admires his Air; the Fifth for his Dress, and the Sixth for his Talent in Poetry, etc.' She is ever complaining of the Vapours, 'but she never has the Spleen so effectually, as when a Man Addresses a Lady in her Company'.[14] This type of commentary, in which women are described as attractive but crafty and calculating, lasted throughout the century.

The image of the coquette can be seen in plays, operas, novels, poems and prints. *The Coquet's Surrender; or, the Humorous Punster* was a comedy performed at the Haymarket, 1732; another comedy, *The Coquette; or, the Mistakes of the Heart*, was an adaptation of Eliza Haywood's *History of Miss Betsy Thoughtless*, written by Robert Hitchcock. Even pornography took a coquette as its heroine, as in *Sublime of Flagellation*; published by the pornographer George Peacock; it was written as 'letters from Lady Termagant Flaybum, of Birch-Grove, to Lady Harriet Tickletail, of Bumfiddle-Hall', and introduced readers to 'La coquette chatie'.[15] Often an article expounded upon how women could get their own way using flattery and flirtation. However, some of the coquette books were hardly racy at all, merely sketching out lives of certain coquettes to show how their behaviour led to their undoing. One of these was *The Nunnery for Coquettes*, which noted in its preface for 20 October 1770, 'Coquettry is so prevalent and fashionable in the female world, that it calls aloud for public censure: and the fatal consequences of it to both sexes are so great and numerous, that they cannot be too strongly displayed.'[16] The book purported to be a 'gentle satire' whose purpose was to prevent women from following the fashion for coquetry, 'to point out to the Ladies the danger and folly of persevering in the present polite, but fatal plan of conduct, so generally followed by the most beautiful of their sex'.[17] It asserted that women follow 'courses', as if they have a design or plan of action. The author threatens to expose those women who continue with coquetry:

> In fine, such of those Ladies who repair to the Nunnery and repent, will have their real names concealed; but if they pursue the same wicked courses hereafter, they may rely upon it, that in the next edition of this work, not a letter of their rank or title will be suppressed.[18]

Increase in consumption of luxury items was seen as evidence of corruption and decay, notably of the class system, as people everywhere appeared to be climbing out of their allotted stations in life: 'Luxury of every kind hath risen to such a height, from various causes, that almost every station of life seems to have moved from its primitive state.' Labourers previously happy with a pint of beer now demand wine to drink: 'The artizan and mechanic, who formerly thought themselves perfectly happy over a pot of home-brewed, now consider malt liquor beneath them, and scarce pass an evening without quaffing the juice of the grape, or Ashley's staple commodity.' Increasing wealth also affected women's self-esteem and was considered the cause of the development of coquetry to a fine art, with women elevating themselves while men became underdogs:

> Nor has this ambitious frenzy made less havock in the female world; on the contrary, being blended with the natural vanity of every sex, every women with a tolerable face fancies herself a goddess or an angel, and considers it as beneath her divinity to think of man but as a slave, forced to obey, and destined to wear her chains.[19]

Women were no longer satisfied with men of their own class, but were expecting to marry up, preferring to aim for a duke or a marquis. Indeed, this appears to have happened with some frequency; 'A tradesman's daughter, who, probably, has not five hundred pounds to her fortune, will fancy herself qualified to marry a member of parliament at least.'[20] Her mother sends her to a boarding-school, which her father can ill afford, and shows her off at Ranelagh: 'A few rounds of this mill of folly turns the girl's brains: She sees lady Betty Idle coquet it with lord Dimple; she resolves to imitate that sweet creature and longs for an opportunity to be en famille with a nobleman.'[21]

The invention of new titles for those committing scandalous behaviour became common: 'Puppies' and 'Puppyesses' became affected words to describe the character of certain adulterous men and women given to having affairs. The *Covent Garden Magazine* for January 1773 declared, 'Marcaronioism is now dwindled to so contemptible a state, that the very dogs bark at the puppies as they walk.'[22] The *Bon Ton* was happy to make a mockery of anyone who carried the slightest whiff of scandal, admitting that their aim was not 'to confine our biography solely to those PUPPIES and PUPPIESSES who are distinguished merely by finery and frippery; and we are justly regarded as the diminutives of human nature' but to '"shoot folly" of every species'.[23] Adultery, warned the author, could lead to venereal disease. The affair of one couple where the lady was already married ended with the gentleman catching the pox 'in the soft Wars of Venus', acquiring 'Paphian wounds' in the process – presumably the disease having eaten away at his body.[24]

Unknown artist, *The Jelly-House Maccaroni*, 1772, mezzotint.

These early satires progressed into similar jocular broadsheets that contained lists of popular figures of the day, mocking their mannerisms and appearance. In a sheet entitled 'Characters of Gentlemen that have put in to The Ladies Invention' (presumably alluding to the way women were calling the tune to which the men danced), one is referred to as The Ladies Lap-Dog; another makes a reference to an infamous case describing a Dutch merchant of 'the Italian humour' (homosexual) known as the Queen of Sheba, who was frightened enough to flee to Germany after seeing the fate of Captain Rigby. Rigby's trial for sodomy was a cause célèbre; he was tried at a court martial but acquitted. However, a member of the Society for the Reformation of Manners pursued the case and worked on a plan to entrap him using a servant named Minton. He was sentenced and, after a stint in prison, fled to France.[25] Homosexual behaviour was always fair game for attack.

Even men might be accused of being coquettes, as seen in David Garrick's play *The Male Coquette* (1758) performed at Drury Lane Theatre. It was intended 'to expose a Set Of People, (the Daffodils) whom the Author thinks more prejudicial to the Community, than the various Characters of Bucks, Bloods, Flashes and Fribbles, which have by Turns infested the Town, and been justly ridicul'd upon the Stage'.[26] A daffodil was an effeminate, a precious young man, and points to the macaroni types swanning about London. The epistolary novelist Jane Timbury took up the epithet in *The Male Coquette; or, The History of the Hon. Edward Astell* (1770), which first appeared anonymously but was republished in 1778 under her own name.[27]

One of the first glimpses of the London macaroni can be seen in *The Macaroni Jester and Pantheon of Wit* (1730). His fashion was one of his identifying characteristics: 'His Coat is very short, and long-waisted, with a Flyflap cut, leaving only Pocket-Room enough for a Handkerchief and Snuff-Box. The Sleeves are very low on the Arm, and Button close round the Wrist.' His breeches must be made of black soy (or Paduasoy, a luxurious strong corded or grosgrain silk textile) with buttons as large as the head of a blanket pin. 'He must wear white, or speckled Stockings; Shoes buckled almost to the Toe, and just high enough behind to get his Heel in. His Hair must be full of Powder and Pomatum, and the Curls pasted close above the Ear.'[28] Typically he also carried an oversized sword and a tassled walking stick.

This craze in dress peaked in the early 1770s. The term 'macaroni' was adopted by elite gentlemen who had been influenced by their Grand Tour and was in reference to the pasta dish they had encountered on their travels. Because of their affected politeness and overstated dress, they became a frequent object of ridicule. One of the main objections was that macaronis looked effeminate and fake and stood in direct opposition to everything that was manly. Their adoption of Continental manners and dress was derided and they were criticized in numerous satires: macaronis were reputed to drink only milk and to avoid roast beef, ale and smoking. This was no man of public virtue and sober vigilance, but a flimsy man of flippant air and dress. The *Macaroni and Theatrical Magazine; or, Monthly Register*, a journal that flourished from 1772 until 1773, described in its first issue, 'The word Macaroni then changed its meaning to that of a person who exceeded the ordinary bounds of fashion; and is now justly used as a term of reproach to all ranks of people, indifferently, who fall into this absurdity.'

Caricatures such as those made by James Bretherton and Matthew and Mary Darly took a satirical poke at the macaroni. However, while macaronis were considered decadent and effeminate, historians have argued that they were also an evolution of the modern self-made

Unknown artist, *The Fly Catching Macaroni*, 1772, hand-coloured etching.

man.[29] To be captured in one of the Darlys' set of images contributed to a man's notoriety; *The Fly-Catching Macaroni* and *The Simpling Macaroni* depicted Joseph Banks and Daniel Solander, respectively, who had both just returned from one of Captain Cook's voyages in 1771. Unlike the more satirical prints, these demonstrated the individual personalities of each man. By 1778 images of the decayed macaroni showed him as an old man and accompanied a poem:

> Alas! What Misfortunes attend
> The Man of a *liberal* Mind!
> How poor are his Thanks at the End,
> From base and ungrateful Mankind![30]

The macaronis would soon die out, but not before they had been seen around London in all the fashionable places.

Fashionable Places of Assignation

The Pantheon in London opened during this macaroni period in 1772 and became famous for its masquerade balls. Its elegant public rooms were considered the archetypal space for the fashionable libertine.

Isaac Cruikshank, *Preparing for a Masquerade*, 1802, etching and engraving.

Attendees paid an entrance fee and came dressed up in fancy costumes. Women came as milkmaids, shepherdesses or queens, men as kings or dominos, in unisex costumes comprised of a black silk gown, mask and tricorn hat. Those attending knew that masquerades were seen as places of moral laxity and as long as their disguise was kept up, sexual dalliances could take place undetected.

Masquerades, though not new, were increasingly plentiful as a method of entertaining the rich during the eighteenth century. As early as 1725, ditties and tales of masked sexual encounters were puffed up by journalists such as Ned Ward in *The Amorous Bugbears; or, The Humours of a Masquerade*:[31]

> But now, new vitious [*sic*] Projects we Devise,
> And make our wanton Courtships in Disguise,
> That neither sex their Quality need own,
> But mutually indulge their Lusts unknown.[32]

The tale gives readers an insight into the goings-on at these sorts of gatherings as they follow a group of male friends determined to gain entry into a masquerade. The men have heard about 'so dazzling an Entertainment' and excitedly plan to attend dressed up as a Turk, a Venetian, a Scottish Highlander, the winged Mercury and a Dominican monk.[33] Pondering on their preposterous dress, the narrator jokingly suggests that 'instead of forwarding intrigues and heightening Debauchery according to the World's Opinion, they were spitefully intended by the Enemies of Generation [those against sex], to fright both Sexes into a mutual Aversion to each other'.[34] Despite any reservations about their disguises he might have, his description of the scene on entering the revelries is one of wonderment. The excesses on show leave him awed and give an idea of what some of the masquerades looked like; gaming tables beckon punters and 'the dimensions of the Room and the Sides of it adorn'd with such Beautiful Pyramids of fine Fruits and Sweetmeats' were enough to have 'tempted Eve all over again'.[35] Tapers illuminate the room and music wafts all around them. However, the illusion is ruined by all the ugly faces before him and the feigned voices they are all affecting. With typical sarcasm, the narrator rejoins, 'I could not forbear thinking I was drop'd into Hell, through some Newcastle Cole-Pit, and was accidentally tumbl'd among a Legion of Devils that were keeping Holliday.' More aptly, once over the initial sight, with some glee, he recognizes 'that all the Vices and Follies in the Universe were promiscuously huddl'd together in this sinful Repository'.[36] In the gallery of these Grand Assembly Rooms, a set of musicians 'Fiddling and Tooting' gamely play on above the noise, encouraging everyone to dance – Green-sleeves, Pudding-Pies, Bobbing-Joan and the Belsize Minuet. Women are swirling around 'industrious to win Hearts by the putting of their Bubbies, the wriggle of their Bums, and the activity of their Pettitoes'.[37] The usual descent into excessive drinking and sexual encounters follows until the narrator and his companions leave in the early hours of the following morning.

Masquerades evidently worked as a sort of dating service where couples could try each other out, and if they enjoyed themselves, form a more binding agreement. However, the disguises at these events often made finding a person again somewhat difficult. Therefore, a man might advertise to find a woman he had met incognito at such venues in newspapers' lonely hearts-style columns. One clipping from an unspecified newspaper, printed in London on 1 March 1754, was from a man who wanted to find a mistress:

> If the Lady that was at the last Masquerade, dress'd in a white Domino, trimm'd with Purple, a Hat of the same, tall, and genteel in Person, will be so obliging as to favour the Gentleman who ask'd her to dance, but was refused, with a Line when and where he may have the Pleasure of seeing her, by directing for C.G. at the Cocoa-Tree in Pall-Mall, he intends to propose something greatly to her Advantage, and hopes it will meet with her Approbation.

He had obviously had some sort of connection with this woman and thought this was a good way to find her and set up a viable ongoing relationship beneficial to them both. In way of enticement, he offered 'A Coach and Six, and 7000 *l.* per Annum, at her Service if she don't think the Gentleman too old.'[38]

While masquerades were places where debauchery, adultery and secret assignation could go uncontested, more diversions were on offer than ever before in London. As well as the sober entertainments of theatre and concerts, which were so central to the hub of the city, taverns were the most obvious picking-up places for men and women. Disreputable taverns where working men and whores mingled proliferated, the worst being full of low-life characters and not for those wanting a polite drink. Billingsgate contained a boozing-den 'in a narrow lane, as a bury-vault, which stunk of stale sprats, piss and sir-reverence'.[39] More gentrified taverns attracted gentlemen, who might hold their all-male society meetings there, and certain coffee-houses acted as a rendezvous for men to discuss everything from politics and antiquities to gossip and sex.

Coffee-houses had become important places for political debate, but could also be used as places for fashionable meet-ups. First evident in London from 1670 to 1685, they were growing in numbers, with around 3,000 open in England by 1675. While coffee-houses may have been enjoyed by men and various all-male societies as a place to debate their arguments and show off their erudition, satirists seized on the opportunity to do them down. Many thought them a 'nursery for training up the smaller fry of virtuosi in confident tattling, or a cabal of kittling [carping] critics that have only learned to spit and mew'.[40] Coffee was seen as detrimental to a man's libido: in *The Women's Petition Against Coffee* (1674), supposedly an address on behalf of 'several Thousands of Buxome Good-Women, Languishing in Extremity of Want', a 'Well-willer' complains of 'The Grand Inconvenience accruing to their Sex from the Excessive Use of that Drying and Enfeebling Liquor' jocularly presented to 'the Right Honorable the keepers of the Liberty of Venus'. Coffee-drinking men were seen as able performers prior to the introduction of coffee, but had now become bereft of 'the true old English vigour', 'our Gallants being so Frenchified [meaning weak and unmanly] that they have become meer Cocksparrows'. Taking a swipe at foreigners was a common trait and there was a general acceptance that French men were fops and milksops. Now, English men were 'not able to stand to it [get an erection], and in the very first Charge fall down flat before us'. This disaster of mass impotence was attributed to a surfeit of coffee, the anonymous author declared, 'For the continental sipping of this pitiful drink is enough to bewitch Men of two and twenty, and tie up the Codpice-point without a Charm.' Men had become lethargic and unfit for action, 'their Ammunition wanting; peradventure they Present, but cannot give Fire'. The final threat is that husbands 'run the hazard of being Cuckol'd by Dildo's'.[41] This 'Women's Petition'

George Moutard Woodward, 'Georgian gentlemen smoking, drinking and reading newspapers in a coffee shop', 1798, aquatint with etching.

may have been a satirical attack in the war between coffee-houses and taverns. With coffee-houses fast becoming the main place to go, taverns were in competition for customers.

Various entertainment locations embraced Londoners' fascination with Roman and Greek ruins and interior decorations reflected the love of the ancient world. One pub landlord kitted out his garden with a mural in the style of Roman ruins; a poem, given as written by 'J. M.', described the sight on casually landing at Mr Hall's the Hoop and Bunch of Grapes at Battersea, and seeing 'the fine Alteration of his Garden, together with the delightful View of some antient [*sic*] Roman Ruins, well worthy the Observation of the Curious, and inferior to none of its Kind in England; the Painting being done by one of the best of the Hands in Europe':[42]

> Great God of Poets, and of Musick King,
> Let me with Calliope Rhetorick sing;
> Let the Grandeur of an Eden shew,
> A second Paradise entirely new;

Her Umbrias green, do form th'safe Retreat,
From blust'rous Winds, and Sol's more scorching Heat;
His fiery Beams but dart a noble Glade,
And gild with Golden Hue the pleasant Shade;
There gentle Zephyrs cool the sultry Air,
And winged Singsters please the nicest Ear.
View well the Prospect from each charming Grove,
'Twill Admiration raise, and kindle Love;
Inspir'e by both, you then may justly own,
The like ne'er seen before, nor never known;
Ruinous Fabricks, moul'ring Walls they raise,
Grand in their Ruin, well deserving Praise;
There fallen Columns and Pilasters lay,
Mix'd with each other, on the Maiden Clay;
And in the Entrance, caset a graceful View,
A Building standing, on her Relics too;
Between the shatter'd Sculptures stand
The sacred Urns of Kings that rule the Land.

This incorporation of antiquities into fashionable decor had emerged from various gentlemen's obsessions with ancient Greece and Rome. The Grand Tour, on which gentlemen visited the sites and ruins of Roman and Greek temples, was clearly an influence. Men such as Francis Dashwood and his friends formed the Dilettanti club in 1732 and the Divan club in 1744 for friends who had travelled to Italy and Turkey. These societies funded trips abroad to measure and draw ruined temples and buildings in order to map out parts of the ancient world. The residence of Sir William Hamilton, a diplomat in Naples, was one of the ports of call made by many youths during their Grand Tours, where they would observe his collection of vases and erotica found in Pompeii. Hamilton would write about the strange religious practices he came across, such as the worship of Priapus by Neapolitan women who wanted to become pregnant (whom he incidentally believed would be impregnated by their priest). Hamilton influenced Richard Payne Knight's erotic book *The Worship of Priapus*, with its spectacular rude etchings of Greek and Roman ruins in the guise of disembodied phalluses.[43] These findings of the ancient world trickled down the social ladder to become common knowledge to the public and became part of the fashion, even in taverns.

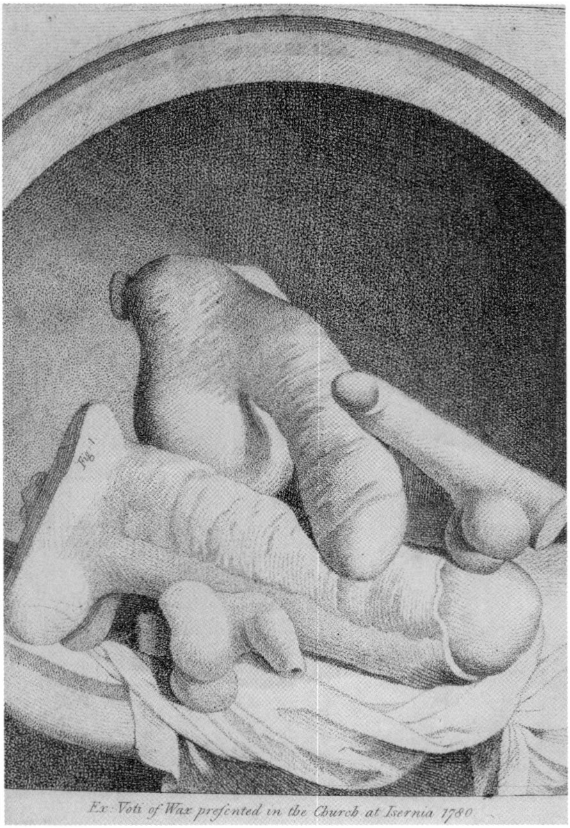

Votive wax phalluses, frontispiece to R. P. Knight, *An Account of the Remains of the Worship of Priapus* (1786).

Various clubs and societies pulled together men and women who had similar interests, but many of them tended to be sex-specific. Some all-male clubs concentrated on conversation, smoking and getting drunk. Many of them involved the libertine or at least liberal man with open attitudes towards sex. The all-male Kit-Cat Club, which initially met informally after the accession of William III, was a private aristocratic circle with political (Whig leaning) and literary aspirations. It flourished in the late 1690s and early 1700s and had approximately thirty or forty members. The club grew out of a friendship between bookseller and publisher Jacob Tonson the Elder and a London pastry-cook, Christopher Cat. Tonson was heavily involved in the literary set – he published the works of John Dryden – and he encouraged Cat to hold meetings with the Earl of Dorset and other literary folk at his establishment, the Cat and Fiddle on Gray's Inn Lane. The lure was the quality of Cat's mutton pies.[44] The club seemed to be playful rather than lewd, with an emphasis on food and drink. However, the

Drunken party with men smoking, sleeping and falling to the floor: William Hogarth, *A Midnight Modern Conversation*, 1733, etching and engraving.

members were often labelled libertines and criticized for their whoring. Thomas Wharton had a satire written about him and his sexual laxity, and kept a mistress for many years during both his marriages; his second wife, 22-year-old Lucy Loftus, was said to be as sexually free as her husband. Similarly, another member, Charles Montagu, 1st Earl of Halifax, had an affair with Catherine Barton, who kept house for him after his wife died. While gossip abounded, their affair did not seem to be an impediment to her later marriage to politician John Conduitt. The club had specific glasses made for toasting the reigning beauties of the day, among them the seven-year-old Mary Pierrepont (later Lady Mary Wortley Montagu), the daughters of John Churchill, 1st Duke of Marlborough, and Barton, a Kit-Cat toast of 1698. The group eventually moved to the Fountain tavern on the Strand. Invariably one of the pleasures of these clubs was imbibing much liquor and singing songs, although they were also supporters of the theatre and playwrights. The Kit-Cats helped to build the Queen's Theatre at the Haymarket, which opened in April 1705, each donating £100.

The clubs with the most outrageous sexual philandering invariably involved the elite rake Sir Francis Dashwood, mentioned above. Of all his clubs, the 'Knights of St Francis' or the 'Monks of Medmenham' was the most debauched. For the meetings, Dashwood organized regular revels with women brought down from Covent Garden brothels run by bawd Charlotte Hayes. Libertines John Wilkes and Fanny Murray were involved in the latter two clubs, as were other women. Paintings of Lady Mary Montagu and Fanny Murray dressed in Turkish garb hang in Dashwood's West Wycombe estate; both were honorary members of the Divan Club. Walpole recorded that the intention of the Monks of Medmenham was to 'meet to drink, tho the rule is pleasure, & each is to do whatever he pleases in his own cell, into which they may carry women'.[45] He also alluded to their worship of Bacchus and Venus. But perhaps the worst behaviour was seen in the Man-Hunters Club, whose members, a group of young men involved in the legal profession in Chancery Lane, took it upon themselves to do all sorts of evil pranks. This group of young rakes frequented a tavern at the back of Lincoln's Inn Fields near the Tennis Court Playhouse and their idea of fun was to hide in parks, then jump out and frighten passers-by and beat them up. They were bawdy, obscene drunks who committed 'monstrous inhumanities' on innocent strangers. They boasted about their sexual prowess:

> One would pluck out an Alphabetical Pocket-Book, where he had Register'd the Names of all the Loose Ladies that ever had oblig'd him, since his first knowledge of the pleasing difference between a Woman's Honour and a Cart-Wheel, having fairly enter'd his whole Catalogue of Punks from Madam Althea down to Oyster Moll.[46]

Another would boast of the collection of personal items he had filched from his conquests, such as fans, rings, pendants and necklaces. They delighted in aggravating London whores, knocking up their houses at night, breaking bawdy-house windows and generally wreaking havoc.

Various fashionable crazes emerged to continue for the entertainment of Londoners. An interest in female fighting proved something of a sexual turn-on. Reports of female wrestlers were described in a letter to *The Spectator* in 1711 by a female reader: 'From ten in the evening until four in the morning they tumble about wildly, pummelling and scratching each other and destroying both the property and clothes of each other.'[47] This interest seems to have continued through the century, as the *Bon Ton* reported in an article entitled 'Female Pugilism'. A fight had been arranged between the wife of a publican and a virgin, to take place on Monday, 21 February, in Camberwell. The focus was on the lack of clothing the women were wearing, presumably the better to get hold of each other's flesh. It was reported that 'these fair ones were nearly in buff' when they met on the field for the fight. After only 22 minutes, combat was over.[48] These fights were sources of entertainment; another incident is reported as having taken place at the Adelphi on the previous Saturday, where one woman gave 'her antagonist several severe body blows in the stomach and other parts of the body'. One of the combatants was socked in the face so hard that it 'closed her peepers'.[49] Few entertainments involved such violence between women.

London libertinism was reflected in the fashions of the day. Town-misses, coquettes, macaronis and dandies paraded at popular venues in their brocaded dresses, brightly coloured waistcoats and silk stockings. For those on the town, the entertainments on offer were plentiful, with masquerades, clubs, coffee-houses and taverns allowing for meetings of minds and bodies alike. Indulgence in luxury items saw movement of people beyond their allotted station seemingly making society more fluid. However, with the liberal sexual attitudes of some came mocking criticism, although none of this would affect the fashionable libertines, who continued to dance, drink and indulge in a life of gay abandonment.

8
Mad About the Boy

Much wine has pass'd, with grave Discourse
Of who fucks whom and who does worse . . .
And nightly now, beneath their shade
Are Buggeries, Rapes and Incests made . . .
Great Ladies, Chambermaids and Drudges
The Rag Picker and the Heiress trudges.
Carmen, Divines, Great Lords and Taylors
Prentices, Poets, Pimps and Jaylers,
Footmen, fine Fopps do here arrive
And here – promiscuously – they swive.

Earl of Rochester, *A Ramble in St James's Park*, 1672

During the court of Charles II, admiration of a pretty male youth was accepted as normal. Courtier John Wilmot, 2nd Earl of Rochester, was well known as a notorious libertine and he openly expressed his love of boys in his poems. He declared, 'There's a sweet, soft page of mine/ Does the trick worth forty wenches.'[1] The king valued him enough to make him his Gentleman of the Bedchamber in March 1666. His male-orientated verses therefore did not appear to affect his social standing, possibly because he played the sexual role he was supposed to play. So long as a man was publicly seen to take a wife and enjoy women, he could fulfil his position at court. Rochester eloped with heiress Elizabeth Mallet, eventually marrying her in January 1667, and made her Countess of Rochester. Apart from his wife, Nell Gwyn may have been his lover before she became mistress to Charles II. However, his main association with homosexuality was his writings rather than his actual behaviour.

Jacob Huysmans, *John Wilmot, 2nd Earl of Rochester*, 1665–70, oil on canvas.

Sodomy was discreetly tolerated in court circles and even took place outside the main palace in St James's Park in London. Rochester's poem *A Ramble in St James's Park* (1672), quoted above, suggests that the park had gained a reputation for buggery and open-air sexual encounters.[2] While his raucous poems were accepted as good fun, he overstepped acceptable boundaries with his play *Sodom; or, The Quintessence of Debauchery*, written in 1684. The authorities felt impelled to take action and hastily censored the work. The objection was mainly a result of its overt references to sodomy, and there can be little doubt that restrictions were creeping in to prevent sodomy becoming more widespread.

A change had begun to occur in how sodomites were seen and treated. While buggery had been a capital offence since Henry VIII's time, not much had been done in law to punish transgressors on a regular basis. During the first few decades of the eighteenth century, there was an increase in the use of the pillory against sodomites.[3] However, elite transgressors found punishments easier to avoid. Various rumours circulated against Lord James Stanhope and Lord Sunderland, yet neither of them were ever arrested or tried for sodomy.[4] Jonathan Swift had cast aspersions on Stanhope's sexuality; and similar allegations were made about the Earl of Sutherland when in 1718 it was reported that Thomas Kinnersley had conspired with William Moore to 'charge the Earl of Sunderland with an attempt to commit Sodomy on the said Moore, in order to extort great Sums from the Earl'.[5] Whether this was the case or not, the mud stuck.

Broadside sheets decrying sodomites were increasingly available, most which could be brought for a few pence. John Dunton's poem *The*

Unknown artist, *St James's Park and the Mall*, *c*. 1745, oil on canvas.

He-Strumpets: A Satyr on the Sodomite-Club (1707) insisted that men were seeking out sodomites because so many prostitutes had the clap:

> All Cracks are found so full of Ails,
> A *New Society* prevails,
> Call'd *S[o]d[om]ites*; Men worse than Goats,
> Who dress themselves in Petticoats,
> To Whore as *O[s]born* did with *O[a]tes*.[6]

Gossipy publications were used to expose men's affairs, such as the pamphlets on the sodomite Captain Edward Rigby.[7] William Roose's *Love Letters between a Certain Late Nobleman and the Famous Mister Wilson* (1723) described how a nobleman seduced Wilson and offered him a large amount of money to keep quiet.[8] Although this is thought to be a fictional account,[9] blackmail against sodomites was common in the eighteenth century and the punishments were harsh enough for homosexuals to warrant covering up their activities.[10]

The love lives of Lord John Hervey, William Beckford and Lord Byron demonstrate how attitudes to male passions changed over time. During the earlier time of Lord Hervey, there was a more louche attitudes towards men having love affairs with other men; by the time William Beckford came on the scene, persecution of homosexuals meant that Beckford had to escape into self-exile; the more cautious Lord Byron took the decision to pursue his love of boys only when abroad, but continue public affairs with women. Indeed, Byron was responsible for creating his own wild masculinized image. No longer would the free love between men be acceptable if kept quiet enough, as it had been with Hervey, but men now had to go to foreign countries to indulge their sexual predilections for fear of severe punishments.

The Effeminate Courtier

Courtier Lord John Hervey (1696–1743), 2nd Baron Hervey, provides a glimpse of the life of an effeminate bisexual man in the heterosexual court of George II (although it was rumoured that his predecessor, Queen Anne, also had an unusually close affection for her lady-in-waiting Sarah Churchill). Hervey had affairs with Anne Vane and Stephen Fox and was seen as an ambiguous figure in society. This did not stop him from being a favourite of Queen Caroline in his post as vice-chamberlain to the royal household.

Taking Hervey as an example, we can see that not all men who had love affairs with men were persecuted. In Hervey's case, they were more or less ignored, but this seems to be because he kept his feelings undercover to all but his closest friends. Lady Mary Wortley Montagu, poet and gossip, was a close friend (and possible lover) of Hervey's and had an inkling of his true orientation. Of Hervey, she infamously said, 'This world consists of men, women and Herveys,' thereby acknowledging the sexual difference of the man.[11] His friendship with Lady Mary was tested when he wrote passionate letters to Francesco Algarotti, with whom they were both in love. According to his biographer Robert Halsband, Hervey's personality was satirized by Henry Fielding in the dedication to 'Miss Fanny' prefixing *Shamela*.[12] Indeed, his foppish appearance, general weakness and rigid diet proved a source of ridicule to his detractors. He was also the object of savage satire by Alexander Pope, in whose works he figured as 'Lord Fanny', so the joke was a shared one. The quarrel is generally put down to Alexander Pope's jealousy of Hervey's friendship with Lady Mary Wortley Montagu. But there is no doubt Hervey was good looking. Pope described him as having

> A cherub's face, a reptile all the rest
> Beauty that shocks you, Parts that none will trust
> Wit that can creep, and Pride that licks the Dust.[13]

There is no doubt that Hervey was a flamboyant, colourful personality around court. Heir to the title of Lord Bristol, he was a frequent visitor at the court of the Prince and Princess of Wales at Richmond. He was intimate with the royal family and wrote about his relationship with them in his memoirs.[14]

While Hervey was attracted to both women and men, his relationship with Anne Vane around 1723 led to squabbles with Frederick, Prince of Wales, and he may have had an affair with Princess Caroline. As custom dictated at the time, Hervey was obliged to marry and provide an heir. It appears he was in love with his fiancée, since she came with no money when the couple married in 1720 and the union was against the wishes of her family. His betrothed, Mary Lepell, was a great court beauty and one of the Princess of Wales's ladies-in-waiting.

Jean-Baptiste van Loo (attrib.), *John Hervey, Baron Hervey of Ickworth*, *c.* 1740–41, oil on canvas.

In 1723 his elder half-brother Carr died, whereupon Hervey became heir apparent to the Earldom of Bristol with the courtesy title of Lord Hervey. Two years later, he was elected MP for Bury St Edmunds. Despite his initial love for his wife, who bore him six children, he would later become extremely cruel to her.

It was Hervey's homosexual relationship with Stephen Fox, MP and Lord of Ilchester, that demonstrates his true affection. While bubbling about in politics, floating in and around the court in his naturally exuberant way, Hervey was to keep his relationship with Stephen Fox private. Their affair was carried out with discretion, the true nature of their relationship known only to his intimate friends. They spent their first length of time together on a trip to Italy in 1728 and were to live together during the following decade.

Thirty-one-year-old Hervey had met 23-year-old Stephen Fox in 1727, after becoming friends with his brother Henry the previous year, and the three became close. The trio began to spend increasing amounts of time in each other's company, attending assemblies, royal receptions, chocolate-houses and dinner parties in London. Gradually, Hervey's relationship with Stephen moved up a notch and they became sexually intimate, proof of which lies in the surviving copies of the letters from Hervey's letter-book and Stephen Fox's two surviving letters to Hervey. At the end of May, after spending time with Hervey, Ste (as Hervey called him) returned from London to his home in Redlynch, Wiltshire. Hervey wrote to him about his intense feelings; 'I have thought of you and wished for you a thousand times since you went.' Though demonstrative protestations of friendship and affection were commonplace in eighteenth-century letters, these letters have a distinct difference to the letters he wrote to other friends of whom he was fond. As Hervey became increasingly politically active at court, he was at pains to remind Ste of his feelings for him: 'Though I have lived ever since I saw you in a constant hurry and a perpetual succession of different company, I don't find any change can produce so great a one in me, so to make me regret the loss of you.'[15]

In June 1727 Hervey's position was keeping him at court. He was missing Ste and chastised him for not coming to London to see him. He alluded to their sexual activities:

> the favours I received at your honour's hands are of such a nature that though the impression might wear out of my mind,

Sir Godfrey Kneller, *Lady Mary Wortley Montagu*, 1715–20, oil on canvas.

> yet they are written in such lasting characters upon every limb, that it 'tis impossible for me to look on a leg or an arm, without having my memory refreshed: I have some thoughts of exposing the marks of your polissonnerie [mischief] to move compassion, as the beggars that have been slaves at Jerusalem do the burnt crucifix upon their arms; they have remained so long I begin to think they are equally indelible.

It would seem that the gentle Ste was perhaps not so gentle in bed. Sensibly, Hervey did not sign his letters, although his handwriting might have been recognizable. This, after all, was a time when inquisitive servants might seek a bribe and corrupt politicians sought leverage with such letters which might implicate a rival.

In autumn 1727 Hervey became quite ill. By this stage, six months into his friendship with Fox, their relationship was so intimate that he discharged his wife, Mary, from her domestic duties and superimposed Stephen in his place. Now Ste was taking over the total nursing care of his lover. Hervey reported that Ste 'loved me too well not to take a part in anything that made me uneasy and do all in his power to alleviate the weight of it'. He took Hervey to recuperate, first at his home in Redlynch, and then to Bath. While there, Hervey wrote ambiguously to Lady Mary Wortley Montagu, 'I have met with several accumulated proofs since I last saw you [since Hervey had been with Ste], that confirm me more and more in that faith [his homosexuality]; and being to think it impossible I should change my religion, unless you will be so good to take my conversion into your own hands [have an affair with him].' In December, back in London, he reminded Fox of his promise to him, 'You once told me, you were never so convinced 'twas impossible for you to be happy or even easy when you were from that [which] you had resolved for the future, never to be out of long sight whenever it was avoidable.'[16] Fox went home to Redlynch, unable to indulge for too long in London life.

Meanwhile Hervey was still under the doctor's care. He reported to Fox somewhat melodramatically, '[Dr] Amyand has put fresh caustic to my cheek but the pain I am now sensible is from the caustic your absence has put to my heart.' In spring 1728 Hervey's health deteriorated and Fox rushed to nurse him. He took him to Redlynch and never left his side. Hervey wrote, 'Mr Fox never left me night or day; I saw nobody but him and servants; he went out with me whenever I

William Hogarth, *The Hervey Conversation Piece*, 1738, oil on canvas.

was able to go out, read to me at home when I had not the spirits to talk, and constantly lay in my room.'[17] During this time, their relationship deepened; once back in London, he wrote to Ste every other day. Eventually, the pair of them took off to Europe, allowing them to indulge their passions unobserved. This was to be the only length of time they spent together on their own, during which they were able to share rooms together without controversy. On their return from the Continent on 15 November 1729, Hervey could not stand the separation: 'I must see you soon; I can't live without You.'[18]

Stephen Fox eventually married in 1736. Despite his love for Hervey, Fox became closer to his wife and shared a companionable marriage. No longer so reliant on Hervey for emotional input, his relationship with Hervey waned. To compensate, Hervey struck up a new relationship, this time with Francesco Algarotti, whom he first met in 1736 and to whom he also wrote passionate love letters, although the intensity of feeling was not shared. However, Ste and Hervey were still writing to each other. In a letter written on 19 January 1734, Hervey rebuked Ste for not writing a longer letter. He insinuated that Ste had written it while drunk at eleven at night, 'so much, as not to be able to add a little to it, or at least to underline those words, which your eagerness for oysters [vulvas] might make you omit at the time of writing, & which I assure you were very material to the construction of your Letter'. Even at this late date, Hervey was still making sneering remarks about Ste's desire for women (and preference for his wife), no doubt in bitterness that he was no longer the focus of Ste's life. However, he also wrote, 'I do sure you Dear Count I love you sincerely.'[19]

Hogarth's picture *The Hervey Conversation Piece* (1738) shows Hervey to the right of centre. In it, his friend Henry Fox, later first Lord Holland, indicates an architectural plan held up by the Surveyor-General of the King's Works. On the right is Lord Charles Spencer, 3rd Duke of Marlborough, who is wearing civilian clothes in military red, indicating his rank as infantry colonel, and on the far right is Thomas Winnington, Lord of the Treasury. To the left is Stephen Fox, toppling the chair on which stands the leading scientist the Reverend John Theophilus Desaguliers. A version of this picture hung in Stephen's dining room at his home in Redlynch.

As for Hervey's own sexuality, there can be no doubt he was an ambiguous figure even in his own time, as William Pulteney, then Leader of the Opposition remarked upon it. Pulteney attacked Hervey, calling into question both his gender and his sexuality. He begins his reply to a ministerial pamphlet by pretending to have mistaken its author for a child — a public-school boy or a boarding-school girl – and then insists that when he learned that its author was Hervey, he felt reluctant to attack 'such a delicate Hermophrodite, such a pretty, little, Master-Miss'.[20] Hervey's passion for men was to continue unabated. However by the second half of the eighteenth century it was becoming more difficult for two men to have a sexual relationship without some level of persecution.

For the Love of Boys

Some people would consider William Thomas Beckford (1760–1844) a creative genius, others would class him as a pederast – in fact, he was both. He was a connoisseur of music, a convivial host who threw

George Romney, *William Beckford*, *c.* 1781–2, oil on canvas.

Richard Cosway, *William 'Kitty' Courtenay, 3rd Viscount Courtenay* (later 9th Earl of Devon), n.d., watercolour on ivory.

extravagant parties and concerts. He was also a talented writer, best known as the author of the gothic novel *Vathek* (1786). He spent much of his fortune on collecting art – but above all, he loved boys.

Not only did he frequent London on his various travels and in Parliament, but he created a wonderful architectural folly at his home at Fonthill in Wiltshire, which he would inherit from his plantation-owning father. He was probably born at his father's residence at 22 Soho Square in London, but would spend much of his childhood at the family estate in Fonthill. His father was mayor of London twice and served as an MP for London from 1754 until his death in 1770. His involvement in politics was mainly to ensure his slave-trading interests were upheld and protected by the government. When his father died, he left his fortune to his nine-year-old son, who was educated

Joshua Reynolds, *Louisa Beckford*, 1782, oil on canvas.

first at home at Fonthill, then in 1777 sent to live with his uncle in Geneva, accompanied by his tutor Reverend John Lettice. Beckford junior had no doubt already read *Arabian Nights* in his father's library, which would inspire his writings on mad sultans and lusty Easterners.

Beckford was to become the centre of a scandal that circulated in London to such an extent that he was obliged to leave England and live abroad for a while. The beginning of the affair that led to his disgrace can be traced to Beckford's visit to see the 2nd Viscount Courtenay on a three-day trip to Powderham Castle in Devon in 1779. It was here that Beckford first saw the viscount's eleven-year-old son William (1768–1835), affectionately known as 'Kitty', and became enamoured with him. Beckford himself was nineteen years old at the time but the pair formed an easy connection and soon became besotted with each other. Beckford wrote, 'Why did we experience this sudden love for each other? Did it not increase each hour and when I quitted his native castle – what expressive melancholy looks were cast after one down the long avenue . . .'[21] Beckford continued on his tour of England all the while transfixed with thoughts of young Courtenay, admitting, 'Every morning, I discovered some new recess in the rocks – some rude neglected spot where I might enjoy my reveries and think undisturbed on my dear C.'[22] London was the place his tour ended and, to his delight, Courtenay was the first one to greet him.

Beckford's mother was well aware of her son's leanings and, in order to deflect any future possibilities of accusations of homosexual pederasty, invited the daughters of George Pitt, 1st Baron Rivers, down to Fonthill in 1779. The plan backfired, as rather than falling for Maria, who was still single, Beckford fell for Louisa, who was already married to his cousin Peter. However the pair were alike in many ways. She too was without any sexual boundaries, suggesting to Beckford that she murder her husband and give her child to Beckford as his catamite (this was possibly a depraved joke, as her son was under two at the time). While this idea did not interest Beckford, he continued his emotional affair with Louisa, a relationship which their friends believed was sexual.

In London, Beckford was presented at court at St James's Palace by his uncle Sir George Howard in the first week of June 1780, during the time of the Gordon Riots, and he witnessed the anti-Catholic mob rioting in the streets. Virtuoso singing enraptured him, with the voice of opera singer Gaspare Pacchierotti ringing through the London concert halls. Beckford and his tutor Mr Lettice embarked on a Grand Tour, arriving in Venice in 1780. His desires for Kitty Courtenay were put on hold while he developed a passion for one of the Cornaro brothers, a handsome, educated boy of his own age for whom he 'suffered a strange delirium which had nearly proved fatal'.[23] Meanwhile Emma Hamilton was living in Italy, her husband an ambassador to the king and queen of Naples. As a woman well aware of the pitfalls an irregular sex life could bring, Emma wrote long letters to Beckford, warning him of potential indiscretions. She declared prophetically, 'if you fall – Gracious Heaven forbid it! – You will be as imminent for your vices as you may be for your talents and virtues' and urged him to contain himself: 'Continue to resist, and every day you will find the struggle less – the important struggle!' although it is doubtful Beckford paid her any heed.[24] According to his biographer, 'It was in 1781 that he lost his moral and sexual innocence, became an actual rather than a potential paedophile.'[25]

Back in London in September 1781, newspapers were full of reports of Beckford's coming-of-age party, held on 29 September at Fonthill that year. *The Gazetteer* and *New Daily Advertiser* reported that a great number of nobility, gentry, clergy and the Mayor and Corporation of the City entered into a great hall, 'most beautifully illuminated'. The ball opened at 10 p.m. and was followed by a feast accompanied by the finest wines. The dancing continued until four in the morning, with a huge firework display on the illuminated lawn.[26] In December 1781 the *London Courant* reported that Beckford was one of the supposedly 10,000 attendees at the previous day's meeting at Westminster Hall. The assembly included many earls and lords, who came together 'to take into consideration the present alarming Crisis of Public Affairs', to discuss the 'American War'.[27]

Beckford was in demand and was invited to all the parties in London, but was aware he must carry out his duty and marry, so he took the 21-year-old daughter of the impoverished Scottish Earl of Aboyne, Lady Margaret Gordon, as his bride in May 1783. It was at this stage that the scandal which would ruin Beckford's reputation would break. While his wife produced two children, Beckford continued to see William Courtenay, who stayed with them in 1784. The outrage that erupted was supposedly caused by 'a letter carelessly dropped by *young Mr Courtenay*'. According to diarist Joseph Farington, Beckford, on discovering it, 'went to his [Courtenay's] room, and horsewhipped him, which created a noise, and the door being opened, Courtenay was discovered in his shirt, and Beckford in some posture or other – Strange story'.[28] Whether or not the letter in question was a love letter to Louisa or to the seventeen-year-old William Courtenay, it was intercepted by the boy's uncle. It contained information damaging enough to make trouble for Beckford. If circulated in the London newspapers, it would ruin any chance of a career in politics and a peerage for Beckford. Lord Loughborough, Courtenay's uncle and a political enemy of Beckford, used the incident to hint at blackmail for sodomy, although initially no charges were laid against him. Beckford moved into his house in Wimpole Street, where he continued to see Courtenay; it is evident from his letters to Emma Hamilton that he did more than simply entertain him. He wrote, 'From the theatre I carried him to my bed. Nature, Morality and Fame are all forgotten, confused and swept away. Oh God! I wish I could die in these embraces and my soul dive down with his into eternal bliss or eternal punishment.'[29]

Brazening it out for a year in England, Beckford was eventually forced abroad to escape the unending scandal. Despite his fixation with Courtenay, Beckford's deep attachment to his young wife left him bereft on her death in childbirth in 1786 while they were in Switzerland. Beckford returned to England in January 1787, a grieving widower placing his two small children in the care of his mother. The scandal had evidently abated enough for Beckford and Courtenay (most likely Senior) to be seen in public together when they attended a dinner at Carlton House given by the Prince of Wales, accompanied by entertainment of 'the superior kind, with respect to elegance and conviviality'; both were listed as attendees in *The World* newspaper for Tuesday, 22 January 1788.[30] Because of his wealth, Beckford was able to pursue his desires, returning from Portugal with a seventeen-year-old choirboy, Gregori Franchi, whom he had met on his sojourn there in 1787. Franchi remained at Fonthill for the next 35 years. (There was a short gap when he married in Portugal in 1795, but he left his wife after the birth of a daughter and returned to England.)

A huge ball was thrown by Viscountess Dungannon in Berkeley Square, London, on 22 May 1801. It was attended by 'near three hundred fashionables', among them Beckford and Viscount Courtenay (again presumably the elder, as his beloved Kitty would only have been thirteen).[31] There is no report of any argument between them.

Beckford ended up selling many of his possessions in England to pay for his lifestyle abroad. The auction advertised a 'Magnificent, Rare, and Valuable Library of 20,000 Volumes',[32] which were to be sold by Mr Phillips at the abbey on 9 September 1823. His books included Sir William Hamilton's *Etruscan Antiquities*, Gells's *Topography of Troy*, *Specimens of Ancient Sculptures* published by the Dilettanti Society, Dugdale's *Monasticon*, Boswell's *Life of Johnson* and various memoirs, histories and travelogues, including *Lady Craven's Journey through the Crimea to Constantinople* and the *Aventuras de Gil Blas*. Auctions were also taking place on further dates to sell off his 'costly furniture', pictures, wines and 'useful furniture'.

Ideas about the aristocracy and masculinity were conjoined in the eyes of the public and came under increasing public scrutiny.[33] There existed an assumption that distinction and nobility equated to a sort of natural authority, more specifically in this case that aristocratic or wealthy homosexuals could do what they wished and get away with it. Attitudes to homosexuality were changing by the eighteenth century and increasingly men who desired boys and other men had to be seen to show their 'masculine' side.[34] While Beckford's marriage was a necessity for a man of his class and wealth, he genuinely loved his wife, and obviously sexually desired Louisa, and so appears to have been bisexual. His love of young men was part of his sexuality, which now had to be contained.

Byron's Bisexuality

Nobility always seemed to have an easier time of feeding their sexual desires and getting away with it, even if their activities were considered illegal. By the end of the eighteenth and the beginning of the nineteenth century, those looking on were increasingly unlikely to forgive behaviour they saw as sexually depraved. Consequently, male libertines with pederastic or homosexual leanings frequently had to go abroad to satisfy their desires rather than stay in the view of the British public eye. Because of his rampant sexual escapades, Byron would move to Greece so he could continue his homosexual love of youths. In a letter written to John Murray on 10 December 1822, Byron claimed that he had lived in 'three or four' different worlds during his 34 years.[35] This was probably as much a reference to his fluid sexuality as much as it was to his travels, as he was equally interested in sex with women as

George Sanders, *Lord Byron and His Page Robert Rushton*, 1807–8, oil on canvas.

with men. While travelling around Europe, particularly Italy, Greece and Turkey, he had various sexual encounters with women and boys. His many affairs with women reinforced his 'manly' persona and to a certain extent this image of masculinity helped overshadow his escapades with youths.

Byron travelled on his Grand Tour through Portugal, Spain, Malta, Greece, Albania and Turkey from 1809 to 1811. His affairs with women in Spain and Malta were more orthodox sexual relationships, but on his trips to Eastern Europe, he more commonly had sexual relationships with youths. He suggested that in Albania 'young men between 16 and 24 love boys from 12–17', so he was aware of his targets.[36] The lure of young boys was impossible for Byron to disguise, as he confessed to his mother on encountering the delicious grandsons of Ali Pasha: 'They are totally unlike our lads, have painted complexions like rouged dowagers, large black eyes & features perfectly regular. They are the prettiest little animals I ever saw.'[37]

Byron indulged his fantasies when he and his travelling companion, John Hobhouse, called into 'buggery shops' in Turkey, where they could pay for dancing boys, youths who were often taken as lovers by older men. His public-school education had introduced him to his true desires early on. Of his school friends, he confessed, 'My school friendships were with me passions (for I was always violent).'[38] Public schools were known for fostering intimate relationships between boys, with junior pupils being totally subservient to the older ones, running errands for them and enduring bullying and floggings. Such hierarchies in single-sex schools frequently gave rise to incidents of sodomy, or at least mutual masturbation or intercrural (between the thighs) sex, which might not have happened in mixed environments. No doubt some teachers at all-boys' schools took the job as they preferred the company and the opportunity of mixing with young men. In the case of Byron, his all-male boarding-school allowed his natural desire for youths to flourish. His earliest sexual relationships were with his male schoolfellows at Harrow and were a mere precursor to his activities at Cambridge; he drummed up a retinue of ardent followers who became his lovers, whom he called his 'hyacinths'. He also had a boy page called Robert Rushton who slept in a cubby-hole next to Byron's room, with sex included in his services. Lady Caroline Lamb would later tell Byron's mother that he had admitted 'that Rushton was one of those whom he had corrupted'.[39] The famous picture of them shows the pair against a rocky, tempestuous landscape about to embark in a small boat together, the young page looking at his master admiringly.

If the public-school system introduced Byron to sexual amours with boys, Cambridge positively encouraged them. For Byron, Cambridge was a thriving subculture of sodomy with its own rituals and secret codes. Here, the love of young men included patronage, enjoying entertainments and shared leisure activities – swimming, reading, singing and walking together. His biggest love was fifteen-year-old chorister John Edleston, whom he met at Cambridge in October 1805. Admiringly, Byron said, 'His voice first attracted my notice, his countenance fixed it.'[40] Comparing their sexual relationship, he admitted that they might 'put Lady E Butler and Miss Ponsonby to Blush'. The world had already acknowledged these women as celebrated sapphists, or lesbians, after they had eloped together, then later set up home in Wales. The newspapers had been full of them. Under the title 'Extraordinary Female Affection', the *Whitehall Evening Post* reiterated the full story of their being separated by their families and their escape together, saying that 'no entreaties could prevail on the Ladies to quit their sweet retreat.' This same-sex relationship between women was obviously intriguing to Byron.

Byron blamed his nanny, May Gray, for his passion for young men, stating that her persistent cruelty to him as a child left him with a fear of women (although he seems to overcome it to his advantage on many a subsequent occasion). She was a drunkard and sometimes beat him so hard that his bones ached. She had allegedly molested him when he was only nine years old, the older Byron recalling, 'My passions were developed *very* early – so early that few would believe me.'[41] Byron was introduced to yet more sexual experiences when he was seduced by Henry Edward Yelverton, Baron Grey de Ruthyn, in 1803. At the time, Grey was leading a dissipated life at Newstead Abbey, which Byron had inherited. Byron went to stay with him when he should have been at school at Harrow, and here the incident occurred. He later confessed to his half-sister Augusta (with whom he had an incestuous affair), 'I am not reconciled to Lord Grey, *and I never will*, He was once my *greatest friend*, my reasons for ceasing that Friendship are such I cannot explain, not even to you my dear sister.'[42] It seems Byron might have encouraged Grey's advances, then felt guilty afterwards and regretted it.

As an adult, his pederasty became more difficult to disguise and so he made the decision to go abroad in search of young men to fulfil his sexual desires unhindered. With persecution against homosexuality on the increase in Britain, it was simply too dangerous to continue his activities at home. Later his sojourns took Byron to Greece, ostensibly to fight in the Greek War of Independence, but also in order to indulge his penchant for young boys without fear of recrimination – the bodies of Greek youths appear to have been much easier to come by. Byron was aware of William Beckford's predilection for boys, as Beckford was at that time living in Sintra, Portugal, in exile because of the scandal of his relationship with Courtenay. Byron thought him 'the great Apostle of Paederasty' and a 'Martyr of prejudice' and then went on to spread the tantalizing bit of gossip that 'Ld. Courtney [Beckford's underage paramour] travelled the same night on the same road only one stage behind him.'[43] Clearly Beckford's reputation back home and his subsequent persecution was an important consideration to Byron in both hiding his love of boys from the public and in promoting his successful image as a lothario.

While he was in Greece during 1811, Byron's friend from Cambridge Charles Skinner Matthews sent him information on the Vere Street Coterie affair. Police had raided the White Swan tavern in Vere Street, off Bond Street, and caught various men in 'unnatural' situations together in the back parlour. As well as free consensual sex taking place between the men, it emerged that the services of male prostitutes could be bought at the tavern. Men would hang around the upper part of the house, waiting for casual customers. Trade came from all ranks; even so-called 'respectable' men were caught wallowing on the beds with 'wretches of the lowest description', an early example of 'rough trade'. A bargeman, a coal-heaver and a deaf ironsmith had taken on the names of the well-known courtesans Fanny Murray, Lucy Cooper and Kitty Fisher; also mentioned were Black-eyed Leonora, a drummer; pretty Harriet, a butcher; and Miss Sweet Lips, a country grocer. The house was kitted out with all amenities, with four beds in one room; another was fitted up as a ladies' dressing-room with a toilette, 'and every appendage of rouge', and a third room was called the chapel. Here, mock marriages took place and 'were solemnized with all the mockery of bride maids and bride men; and the nuptials were frequently consummated by two, three, or four couples, in the same room, and in the sight of each other!'[44] While in Pisa in 1821, Byron

Bishop of Clogher, Percy Jocelyn, caught in a homosexual act with a soldier: Isaac Robert Cruikshank, *The Arse Bishop Joslin and a Soldier*, 1822, hand-coloured etching.

heard the news about Percy Jocelyn, Bishop of Clogher, who had been caught with his breeches down facilitating a young guardsman called Moverly in the White Lion Tavern in the Haymarket, a tavern known for entertaining sodomites. The good bishop fled from England.

Byron found his idyll in Greece in a Capuchin monastery at the base of the Acropolis. Here he was awakened every morning by six young male 'sylphs' shouting for him to come and swim, play and flirt with them. His final affair before he died was with a fifteen-year-old Greek boy named Lukas, whom he immortalized in the poem 'On This Day I Complete My Thirty Sixth Year'.

When he was fifteen, Byron had fallen in love with Mary Chatworth, a neighbour two years older than him who was about to be married to someone else. This unconsummated passion fed his poems for years. He went on to seduce a series of local village girls, including his house servants, falling for the 'bright-eyed' Caroline, a sixteen-year-old prostitute. Much to the horror of his friends, he even contemplated marrying her when she became pregnant. Instead, he settled for dressing her in male clothes and parading her around London. He liked flouting convention, as afterwards he took up with the tempestuous married Lady Caroline Lamb, daughter of Frederick Ponsonby, 3rd Earl of Bessborough, and also liked her to dress as his page.

Byron was looking for trouble when he invited the quote 'mad, bad and dangerous to know' from the equally mad Caroline. But he was attracted to her style – she already dressed androgynously, wore men's breeches and cropped her hair short. From an early age, Caroline had been clever and bored, pushing the boundaries of her social upbringing, stealing the servants' uniforms and dressing like a boy. She was forced to conform, marrying William Lamb, the son of Lord Melbourne, making both of them miserable thereafter. On meeting Byron, she broke all rules of modest engagement and openly displayed her passion for him. Both Caroline and Byron were happy to fly in the face of morality and publicly parade their adulterous affair around London. Her long-suffering husband appeared to have put up with his wife's indiscretions, although it seems he had his own fetishes, as seen in his desire for flagellation. Byron eventually became bored with Caroline and refused to see her. Her reaction was to hang around outside his house late at night, waiting, and pounce on him when he came home. Their affair was short-lived but tempestuous, lasting only from spring to autumn of 1812. She eventually had her revenge for Byron's rebuff when she portrayed him as the satanic villain of her Gothic romance *Glenarvon* (1816). Her marriage would eventually be dissolved by a Deed of Separation in 1825.

Byron was very much part of the creation of his own mythology. His fame took off after he published the poem *Childe Harold's Pilgrimage* in 1812. The Duchess of Devonshire remarked, 'This poem appears on every table,' and Byron was the topic of nearly every conversation. He proposed to Anne Isabella Milbanke (niece of Lady Melbourne), who at first refused him but finally accepted him, and they were eventually married. She coined the term 'Byronmania' to describe the effect he was having on society. *The Corsair* went to thousands of copies the day it came out in February 1814. He was popular because of his immorality rather than despite it, his ability to have affairs with total disregard for society adding to the thrill for his admirers. Byron's marriage was perhaps a means of escaping the dogged stalking of Caroline, but also a means of diverting any possible interest in his affairs with youths. The newly married couple moved into Piccadilly Terrace in London and Byron's moods became increasingly mad. In an attempt to understand his strange behaviour, his wife searched his trunk and letter cases for evidence and found a cache of pornography – some scholars have suggested it was Sade's novels, possibly *Justine* (1791) or *Philosophy in the Bedroom* (1795).[45] The couple were to legally separate soon after, but this was probably less to do with his pornography stash and more to do with the fact that she had discovered his homosexual affairs and his incestuous relationship with his half-sister, Augusta Leigh.

Byron left England in 1816 in order to continue his affairs, both hetero- and homosexual, unabated. He dieted to control his weight and commissioned artists to have him portrayed the way he wanted to look, with his wild black hair and long white scarf. His publisher John Murray played a role in the marketing of his image, placing adverts in newspapers and creating expensive elite editions of his poems. On his trip to Italy, his affairs with women redefined his masculinity to the world back home, although when he became a *cavalier servente* (a lover of a married woman) to his new Venetian mistress, Marianna Segati, it appeared more like an act of servitude to some onlookers. Many Englishmen regarded the Italian *cavalieri serventi* to be nothing more than subservient lapdogs for bored married women.

Byron's boastings indicated his need to share with others an image of his own sexual virility. In a letter to John Murray on 2 January 1817, he wrote that he was engaging in sexual relations one to three times every day.[46] On 19 May 1818, after intimate relations with his lover Marianna had been suspended for three months, Byron told Hobhouse that he had 'a world of other harlotry' open to him.[47] He also wrote of his two hundred affairs in Venice. This image of a life surrounded by women and madness, fuelled by opium and alcohol, was as much promotional as it was real. Even in death he was eulogized as a hero on his way to fight in the Greek War of Independence, although he did not die fighting, but of a fever.

The comparisons between Hervey, Beckford and Byron show they were worlds apart. Even though Hervey was regarded as effeminate and his homosexuality may have shone through his personality, he duly married, kept his own counsel and kept his affairs with Ste Fox discreet. Homosexuality may well have been suspected, but it tended to be ignored unless there was another reason to pull a person down, such as political machinations or unfavourable use of a person's office. Those who had exhibitionist or homosexual leanings could indulge themselves without too much harm coming to them. For those such as the Earl of Rochester and John Hervey, there was always the possibility of being shunned at court, but the threat of prison did not seem to have raised too much anxiety for them. By the time of Byron, the persecution of homosexuals had become the norm and it was now necessary to cover up homosexual activities with greater care. Given Byron's extremes of personality, as well as his passion for women, he was able to use his vibrant character to show himself to be a lothario in order to cover his tracks as a pederast.

From around 1660 to approximately 1830, there was a distinct change of attitude to how men were treated regarding their inclination for sex with boys or young men – or indeed with adult men. More and more, men had to protect their image of masculinity while evading the accusations of effeminacy that were increasingly being bandied about. This meant a growing protective balance between their public and private personas.

9

Quacks, the Pox and the New Sexual Predators

> I look upon these Doughty Fellows to be no better then [*sic*] Quacks in their way; Pretenders to far greater Things then they are able to perform . . . He'll Cure you the Pox, Leprosie, and the Itch, and make you as clean as a Penny, at least in the Pocket. He hath a Water that he calls his Opthalmia . . . that will Cure even Blindness itself.
>
> ANON., *A Bold Challenge to the Whole College of Physicians*[1]

Quack doctors and dissecting surgeons conjured up unsavoury images in the popular imagination. Public opinion was often gleaned from real-life shared experiences of medics and most of the information was enough to make Londoners wary. Hence the medical profession occupied a relatively low status among the professions. Many people preferred to treat themselves. All sorts of medical potions and oils were on offer for all sorts of ailments, easily available from coffee-houses, the backs of taverns and bookshops. The lower classes rarely called in a medic of any sort, as it was simply beyond their reach. Instead they might use a herbalist or a local wise woman in bad cases of illness. Apothecaries were also available for remedies and the barber-surgeon would pull rotten teeth and do minor lancings.

Quacks preyed on people's anxieties – like John Burrows, who offered vegetable cures such as Veno's vegetable syrup, John Leake's pills or Kennedy's Lisbon diet drink, two bottles a day for the bowels at half a guinea per bottle. Tom's Coffee-House in Great Russell Street, Covent Garden, also offered 'all Manners of curious Galenic Medicines, and Chymical preparations at an easy Rate'.[2] Medicines

After Robert Dighton, *The London Dentist*, *c*. 1784, hand-coloured mezzotint.

were advertised as bringing on menses, but were in fact abortifacients. One advert in *The Times* for 31 July 1788 directed 'To the Female Sex' notified that

> Mr Eastland, Surgeon, at his House, No 58 Snow-Hill continues to give his advice and assistance as usual in all *Female Complaints*, and for the cure of Disorders of a *Private Nature* proceeding from irregularities; as to moist obstinate *Obstructions*, *Weaknesses*, and *Nervous Disorders* as well as the cause that prevent *Pregnancy*, on occasion *Miscarriages*; and every other disorder peculiar to the *Sex*.

Such adverts were a regular feature of newspapers and magazines, lulling patients into a false sense of security, as many of the potions were ineffective.

Physicians' treatment was often claimed to be worse than the disease. The *Tory Tatler* for 8 December 1710 declared, 'properly speaking, the Questions should be, not what Distemper, but what Doctor did he die of.' Cartoons by Hogarth, Gillray and Rowlandson fed into these ideas, showing irreverent physicians dissecting corpses, sexually abusing their female patients and haggling over the dying. One such quack was the notorious James Graham, who operated from the Temple of Health at the Adelphi in the Strand. Emma Hart, later to become Lady Hamilton, supposedly worked as a model in James Graham's Temple of Health when she was first making her way in London. Graham claimed to cure sexual problems with his 'Celestial Bed'; couples having difficulty conceiving could hire out this contraption for £50 a night, its electric properties guaranteed to make any wife pregnant. He took the opportunity to advertise his wares in a poem full of footnotes praising his 'Imperial Pills', which 'perfectly eradicate all venereal diseases and scorbutic diseases'.[3]

Layered on top of the image of the villainous quack doctor was its opposite – the gullible doctor who was taken in by mystical occurrences that defied science. The talk of London in 1726 was the fraud effected by Mary Tofts from Godalming, who claimed to have given birth to rabbits. Various eminent physicians who had investigated the incident had believed her claims and suffered acute professional embarrassment when depositions were given against her by witnesses who had seen her hide rabbit parts in her vagina. The story was written

T. Maddocks, *Mary Tofts, the Pretended Rabbit Breeder*, 1819, engraving with watercolour.

up in various newspapers and magazines, illustrated in drawings and even depicted in some of the first graphic comic strips. The more sensible of them wrote up the account and made some cash out of it: an advertisement in London's *Evening Post* for 6 December 1726 publicized 'An Account of the Imposture of Mary Tofts, the Godalming Woman in the Directions of her pretended Deliveries and the several Strategies she employed to effect the Fraud published by Sir Nathaniel St. André, Surgeon and Anatomist to his Majesty'.[4] Sir Nathaniel had in fact thought Tofts's claim genuine at first and described how he had delivered an entire trunk of a rabbit stripped of skin himself. No doubt he published the book to highlight how cunning her pretence was, in defence of his being so easily duped. After all, he had to try and resurrect his reputation, now somewhat sullied. There was still interest in Tofts's case when it was reprinted in 1774 with an added postscript of the case of a French woman who had allegedly given birth to four toads, the account written up in an esteemed journal in Paris.

While some men tarnished the profession by operating from the backs of taverns selling useless 'medic' to the unwitting sick, part of

R. Cosway, *Emma Hart (afterwards Hamilton) as the Goddess of Health*, *c.* 1775–80, coloured etching.

the blame should be shouldered by London's Royal Society, who frequently made preposterous scientific claims. The society had been formed in 1660 when a group of 'natural philosophers' and physicians came together to discuss new scientific experiments and was granted its first charter on 15 July 1662. It began to publish regular pamphlets, its *Philosophical Transactions*, which related its findings, but its more outlandish assertions would cause mirth among some of its critics. Among many embarrassments was the false identification of certain particles that Henry Miles and Henry Baker found in ditch-water. Believing them to be tiny living animals, they related their

Thomas Rowlandson, *The Quack Doctor*, 1814, coloured aquatint.

findings in *Philosophical Transactions*, but embarrassingly for them, the objects turned out to be seeds.[5] As a result, satires emerged with blatant erotic overtones ridiculing the theories of members of the society; *Arbor Vitae; or, The Natural History of the Tree of Life* (1732) and *Frutex Vulvaria; or, Flowering Shrub* (1732) satirized the botanist Carl Linnaeus' labelling of the sexual parts of plants in allegories about the penis and the vagina; *The Torpedo* (1774) and *The Electrical Eel; or, Gymnotus Electricus* (1777) did the same, satirizing reports on experiments in electricity while raising questions about foetal formation, asking which sex was responsible for the force of life in creating a baby. All these manufactured a connection between eminent physicians and sex by usurping their claims and making fun of them in erotic verses.

Medical texts were often nothing more than pornography under the guise of science, so it is hardly surprising that the public connected medics with sex. Various books were on offer for the reading public on every sexual problem or query, from how to become pregnant to how to cure impotency. Many of them were reprints or rewritings of other medical advice books, making use of the juiciest bits. The infamous pornographer Edmund Curll sold copies of *A Treatise of the Use of Flogging in Venereal Affairs* (1718), which he had appropriated from a dissertation by a German doctor, Johann Heinrich Meibom, on the benefits

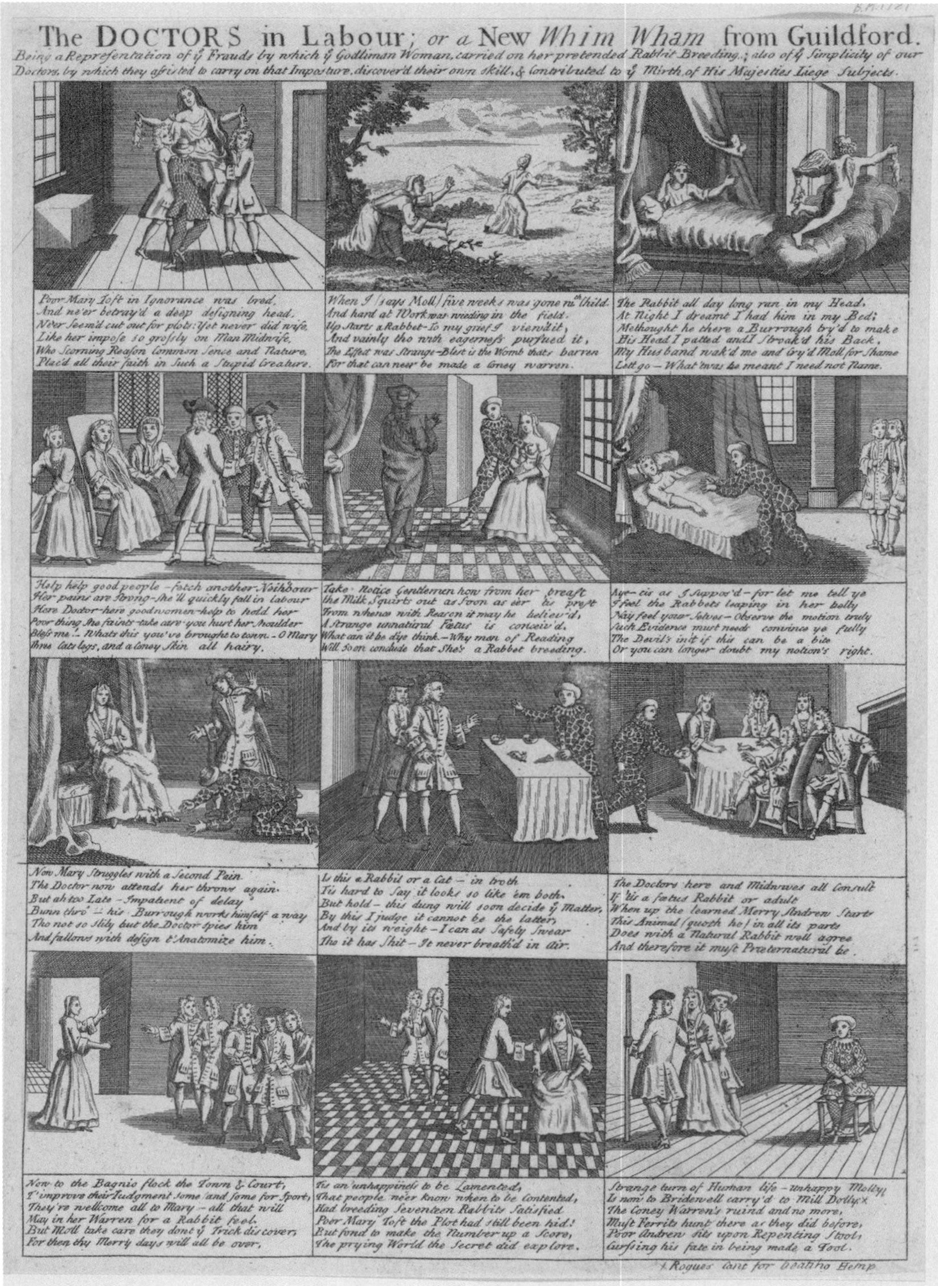

Mary Tofts's story told in graphic images: William Hogarth, *The Doctors in Labour; or, A New Whim Wham from Guildford*, 1726, engraving.

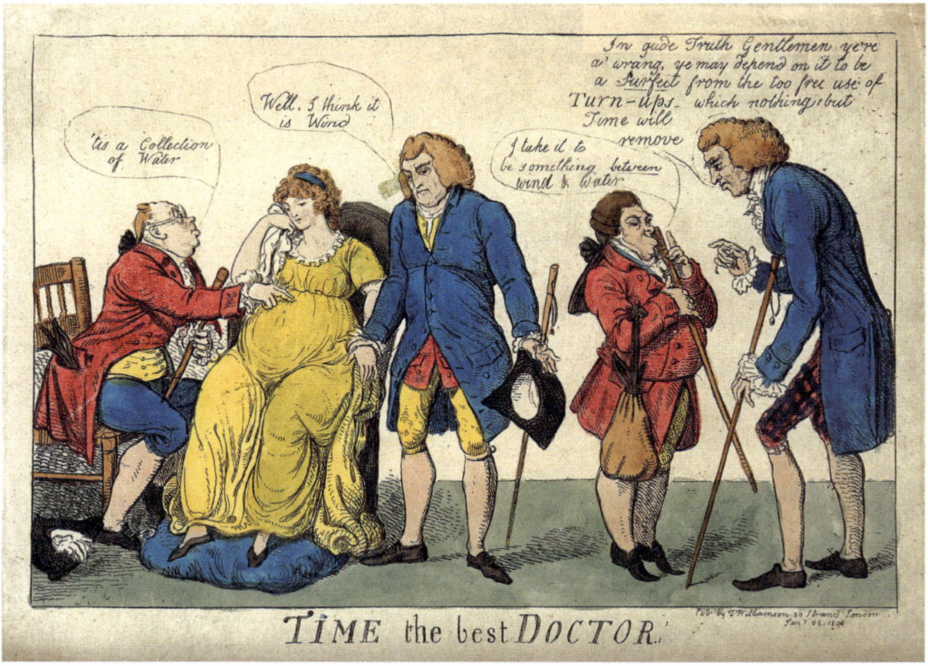

Group of physicians wrongly diagnosing the case of a pregnant woman: Isaac Cruikshank, *Time the best Doctor*, 1803, hand-coloured etching.

of flagellation as a cure for impotence.[6] Meibom remarked, 'Strokes upon the Back and Loins, as Parts appropriated for the Generating of the seed, and carrying it to the Genitals, warm and inflame those Parts, and contribute very much to the irritation of Lechery.'[7] Sex guides such as *Aristotle's Master-Piece* (1684) were rehashed and reprinted throughout the eighteenth century and would continue to prove popular.[8] Nicholas Venette's sex manual carried sexual advice with accompanying amorous illustrations. His *Tableau de l'amour conjugal* (1686) first appeared in English in 1703 as *Mysteries of Conjugal Love Reveal'd*.[9] The surgeon John Marten was prosecuted in 1709 for his *Gonosologium novum*, a book derived from Venette's *Mysteries*, but was later acquitted . . . and so the list goes on.[10] Meanwhile, European medical texts on the subjects of hysteria, masturbation and nymphomania found their way to London and underwent various translations and editions as new lines of thinking emerged in the second half of the century. Samuel D. Tissot in his *Onanism; or, A Treatise upon the Disorders produced by Masturbation* (1766) issued wild claims about the evils and dangers of masturbation, claiming that masturbation makes you blind, gives you epilepsy and convulsions and can ultimately cause death.[11] Bienville's book *Nymphomania; or, Treatise on Uterine Fury* came out in an English translation available from 1775, which discussed the problems of female over-sexualization, portraying some women as ill because of their rampant sexual desires.[12]

Many doctors were associated with lechery and accused of giving unwarranted attention to their female patients' bodies. Dramatists took up the topic with increasing interest; Edward Ravenscroft wrote a satire in 1697, *The Anatomist; or, The Sham Doctor . . . with the Loves of Mars and Venus*, which sent up doctors and the medical profession. Doctors in real life were also embarrassing themselves. Both Dr John Woodward and Dr Richard Mead lowered the general tone of their profession when they fought a duel and gave vent to their animosity to each other in an all-out pamphlet war accusing each other of sexual misconduct. Woodward had given a series of lectures in 1711 expounding his theories on medicine based on maintaining the right balance of bilious salts in the stomach. He disagreed with Mead on the treatment of smallpox, arguing that purging through vomiting was a better method. Mead and his supporters hit back with *The Life and Adventures of Don Bilioso de L'Estomac* (1719), directed at Woodward as 'Bilioso'. In the satire, they suggested that Bilioso indulged in homosexuality and referred to him as 'a Great Lover of Boys'. The pamphlet purported that he had drugged one of his patients with opium and 'attacked him from behind, and made an Evacuation in his body'.[13] These types of sexual slurs were a common phenomenon in attacking one's enemies. Meanwhile, *The Cornutor of Seventy-Five* (1748), intended 'as a Satire upon the conceited Humour of a great many Gentlemen of the faculty of Physicians . . . particularly aimed against the person of Don Ricardo, more than the rest of his Tribe', was directed at the medical profession in general, but most notably this time at Dr Richard Mead. It alleged that he bribed the university for his medical diploma, forged cases to make a point and was a plagiarist. He was accused of picking up prostitutes when young, 'a Brace or two of the most delicate Bona Robas, to solace with at Night as could be pick'd up by the most experienced Pimps of Spain and Italy'. Purportedly, his bedside manners stretched to seducing at least one of his married patients when, 'He gravely felt her Pulse, but peep'd at her snowy Busom, and fancied more than he saw. Design and Accident discovered more and more of her Charms, 'till the old Don was in a higher Fever than his Patient.' After a failed

Thomas Rowlandson, *The Anatomist*, 1811, hand-coloured etching.

attempt at sexual intercourse, his lover suggested flagellation: 'She was soon understood, and the Scheme was put in Practise with as much Severity as ever Pedant were taught a feeling, if nothing else; but all in vain.'[14] This particular public feud was based more on political enmity (Mead and his friends sided with the Tories, while Woodward and his cronies favoured the Whigs) than on any real medical arguments. Such displays of contempt between doctors were hardly likely to instil public confidence in them.

Wealthier men and women might call in top doctors; others would take to treating themselves. Doctors such as Robert James (1705–1776) wrote books extolling their own medicines, providing a catalogue of medicines and prices at the back of the book for those who wanted to purchase them. His book purported to provide 'Indications of Cure of every Secret Malady Women and Maids are liable to'.[15] Women could gain such advice from his *The Ladies Physical Dictionary* on everything from menses to greensickness, 'the whites' and barrenness. The 'whites' referred to the white discharge some women experienced and could be an indication of problems with the reproductive organs or an infection. The author reminds the reader: 'All the Medicines prescribed and recommended in this Book, are Sold only, by the Author's Appointment, at the Gentlewoman's at the Two Blue Posts in Haydon-Yard in the Minorities', pushing his 'purging pills' and 'opening powders'. Doctors refused to treat patients unless they paid up front. Customers were advised not to leave letters for the author 'unless they leave Fees with them'.

Men were told to keep their bodies healthy with regular sexual activity. The same Dr Robert James explained potential problems in his *A Medicinal Dictionary* (1743): 'too great a Retention of the Semen induces Topor and languid State of the Body, and often lays a Foundation for terrible nervous Disorder.'[16] Women were told that sperm was equally good for their sexual ailments; 'Venery both alleviates and removes various Disorders incident to Women: for the male Semen, consisting of a fine elastic Lymph, rareifies and expands not only the eggs, but also, the Blood and Juices in the Vessels of the Uterus.'[17] However, in another book, James warned, 'Those who devote themselves too much to Venus . . . may reasonably suspect that their not having Children' or infertility was due to 'Imbecility of the Genital Parts'.[18] Both sexual overindulgence and too much alcohol consumption could lead to infertility and impotence in men.

Venereal Diseases

For those with the money, a physician could be called out to treat a person infected with venereal disease in private and the whole process could be hushed up. A patient could obtain cures by post or send their maid or manservant to an apothecary for their potions. Tinctures were handed over with a pint of ale in taverns or surreptitiously pulled from under the counter in erotic bookshops. London newspapers were full of adverts in which physicians made outrageous claims for their 'cures'. Surgeon W. Rayner was among hundreds who advertised their ineffective potions and pills for venereal disease; his advertisement in London's *Daily Post* of 3 January 1727 claimed 'a speedy and safe Cure for the POX or CLAP, with all its various Symptoms, by his famous Chymical Drink, being pleasant in Taste, yet effecting in curing that dangerous Disease', to be found at the Blue Post in Preston's Yard.[19]

Prince's powder, a red precipitate of mercury, was one of the most commonly used quack remedies, mercury being one of the most evident 'cures' practised for venereal disease. White sublimate, calomel, red, white, yellow and green precipitates (oxides of mercury), natural and artificial cinnabar (mercury and sulphur) and a quick fix of sixpence-worth of quicksilver could be easily obtained, but their continual use could add up to hundreds of pounds. The medicines were expensive and out of range of the poorest in the community. Quack Dr Thomas Dover recommended several pounds of mercury as a cure for venereal disease, but also for hysteria, intestinal infection, obstruction, scrofula and infertility. In response to one advert for Leake's Patent Pills in *The Times* for 16 August 1788, a reader, Mr Henry Bateman, wrote in recommending the medicine:

> Sir, A Friend of mine had long been infected with the Venereal Disease, and insomnia that he had not been able to get out of Bed for these five years, notwithstanding he has been salivated, and every Means used by many learned Men of the Faculty, but all their endeavours were without effect . . .

He had tried Leake's Patent Pills, and 'in the course of a Month, this poor emaciated Wretch was restored to perfect Health.'

The 'cure' for venereal disease involved poisoning the patient with mercury, which was either rubbed on the sores, ingested or taken in

J. Sintelaer, 'Patients being treated for syphilis', 1709, engraving.

by a method known as fumigation. The mercury purged the system through salivation, sweating and vomiting. One doctor suggested that the best cure would see about 4 pints of saliva a day. If the treatment was bad, then the symptoms of syphilis were worse. Syphilis started with a chancre, an infectious ulcer found at the point of contact. This might then disappear, leaving the diseased person thinking they were cured. Unfortunately, it reappeared after a couple of months with a red rash on the trunk of the body and sometimes rashes on the palms of the hands and the soles of the feet. Whitish, wart-like lesions broke out in the moist areas of the body and there was a general feeling of malaise – fever, headache, sore throat and weight loss. The truly unlucky – and there were a lot of them – found themselves with tertiary syphilis. Their bodies erupted in soft, tumor-like balls of inflammation called 'gummas', and joints and skeletons degenerated, resulting in a shuffling gait. The final misery came with insanity and death.

The stigma of pox rested on the knowledge that it was sexually transmittable and therefore proved the sufferer had had sex with an infected person. But it was also a horrifically disfiguring disease and therefore difficult to hide: ulcers, pustulant sores, scabs, blotches, swelling and collapsed noses were all too evident to the would-be employer. No one wanted to buy a chicken or meat off a woman with a dripping face, or to be served ale by a waiter with open sores. Certainly, no client would touch a prostitute with such obvious symptoms. People with the pox were therefore doubly affected with both disease and unemployment.

The detrimental effects of venereal disease were highlighted by Hogarth in his depiction of the sexually promiscuous Moll Hackabout in *A Harlot's Progress* as she comes to her untimely end. On the coal shuttle lies the remnants of Moll's teeth, fallen out as a result of taking mercury on Dr Rock's advice. Dr Jean Misaubin squabbles with Rock about whose treatment is best, while ignoring their dying patient. Both are shown as money-grabbing haggling quacks, while on the floor lies an advert for the now-redundant 'Practical Scheme' for the use of the Anodyne Necklace, bought ostensibly to cure syphilis. Although originally introduced as a quack treatment for children's teething problems, the anodyne (pain-killing) necklace also professed to cure venereal disease; it sold for five shillings and appeared in many adverts around 1715 onwards. The necklace was recommended in *A Practical Scheme of the Secret Disease and Broken Constitution* as a sort of cure-all, 'for the secret disease; Broken Constitutions; Kings Evil, Gout; Rhuematism&c, the invaluable specifick Remedy and Elixir belonging to The Practical Scheme.'[20] Magazines such as the *Weekly Journal; or, The British Gazetteer* advertised the places where it could be bought:

> This Book (as also the Practical Scheme of the Secret Disease and the Gout System) is given Gratis up one Pair of Stairs at the Sign of the Anodyne necklace, without Temple-Bar: At Mrs. Garway's at the sign of the Practical Scheme at the Royal-Exchange Gate; and at Mr. Cooper's at the corner of Charles-Court in the Strand.[21]

According to *Pharmacopaeia Venerea; or, A Compleat Venereal Dispensory* (1724), written under the pseudonym of 'Anodyne Tanner', its invention was attributed to Dr Paul Chamberlen (1635–1717), a well-known male midwife whose family is supposed to have invented forceps. Chamberlen purportedly (it is most unlikely) gave the necklace his full recommendation, according to the advertisement, which quotes him as saying, 'I entirely approve of, advise, and recommend to the world, the use of two Anti-venereal Medicines; The one called by the name of the "Specific Remedy"; The other the "Diuretick Restorative Elixir for Broken and Empaired Consitutions", or for venereal disease.'[22]

Remarkably little was understood about hygiene and the spread of venereal disease. Ned Ward reported in his journal that one doctor apparently infected half of London using the same device for his 'treatment' without cleaning it between use, 'so much to the plague and terror of his patients that it is believed fallen noses will be as much in fashion about Soho and Piccadilly in little time, as scars among prize-fighters, to short snouts amongst the ladies' lapdogs'.[23] The fact that Ward alludes to the flat noses of people with gonorrhoea also shows how little was known about venereal disease, since it was syphilis that ate away at noses if left untreated. Ward also mentions the use of cantharides in attempts to cure a woman of a dangerous ulcer on her bladder. Cantharides were a preparation made from the crushed bodies of blister beetles or Spanish fly and were claimed to have an aphrodisiac affect as well as acting as an irritant that affected the body's urogenitary tract. Highly toxic overdoses led to uterine bleeding in women and priapism in men.

The Case of the Inveigling Male Midwife

For wealthy folk, new birthing methods heralded the coming of the male midwife, with his shiny steel instruments and his caring but dangerous bedside manner. His close proximity to the genitalia of their wives stirred up many husbands' anxieties. Was the man-midwife to be trusted? Concerns about this new form of childbirth expert rapidly arose in the new social whirl of the city. Nonetheless, the rise of the man-midwife moved forward unabated. Even other physicians were aghast at such developments; allowing doctors to manhandle a wife's sex organs was bound to sexually excite the obstetrician involved. Philip Thicknesse in his *Man-Midwifery Analysed* (1764) declared, 'If men midwives under these circumstances stand unmoved, they are part of the human species I am stranger to!'[24]

Increasingly male doctors were encroaching on the female bedchamber, a place previously preserved for female midwives. Women were uneasy because they had always been surrounded by other women

Thomas Rowlandson, *Medical Dispatch; or, Doctor Doubledose Killing Two Birds with One Stone*, 1812, hand-coloured etching.

in the birthing chamber and horror stories of obstetrical errors made by the man-midwife abounded. Nonetheless, engaging a male midwife was considered the way to go by anyone rich enough to afford one. No husband wanted to see his wife attended by a mere female midwife who had no official medical training (the fact that they were not allowed to obtain such training was irrelevant). Thus began the case of Katherine Biker and Dr Morley, who had been engaged to attend to her after she suffered two miscarriages.

The Biker Case was to become a cause célèbre when Mr J. G. Biker took Morley to court for 'criminal conversation' (adultery) in 1741. The subsequent publication of the trial and reports in London newspapers poured fat on the fire, with the whole of London abuzz with gossip. The trial came up at London's Guildhall on Tuesday 30 June. The pamphlet *The Tryal Between J. G. Biker Plaintiff and M Morley, Doctor of Physic Defendant for Criminal Conversation with the Plaintiff's Wife* was to reinforce some of the concerns already circulating about the predatory nature of the man-midwife and male doctors attending women for 'female disorders'. By the time the trial came up, Katherine Biker was already dead and her husband was to die soon after the trial.

What had happened to them in the interim? We know from a newspaper report that Biker had died at his country house at Tottenham, 'a wealthy Refiner in Foster in Foster-Lane', in November 1741, but it does not mention the cause.[25] Maybe it was suicide or a heart attack brought on by the trial and the possible disgrace. The biggest question hanging over this case is what had happened to Katherine Biker. She had ended up in a madhouse, but how? Had her husband put her there in retaliation for her adultery? Was this a way of getting rid of her? Did she kill herself? Although the main public madhouse was Bedlam, prior to 1774, with the introduction of the first Act for Regulating Madhouses, there was no regulation of private madhouses. Stories circulated about husbands secreting unwanted wives away in madhouses and this is where Katherine spent her last days.

Katherine Biker was only seventeen when she married in 1732, the daughter of 'an eminent citizen', in something which sounded like an arranged marriage. She had miscarried several times before her husband called in Dr Morley to treat her. The charge was that Morley 'at several particular Days and Times' over the course of three months 'made an assault upon Katherine, the Plaintiff's Wife, and ravished, debauched, lay with, and carnally knew' her. Biker, the plaintiff, was demanding damages of £10,000. Katherine was described as 'young, beautiful, virtuous and affectionate' (adding to the voluptuousness of the case) and, up until this time, her husband had considered himself a happily married man. She was first attended to by a Dr Douglas after miscarrying in July or August; James Douglas (bap. 1675, d. 1742) was a known anatomist and man-midwife with a considerable practice among the upper classes. He had been involved in the Mary Tofts case (the woman who claimed to have given birth to rabbits) and had taken down the confession of her deceit.[26] It was when Morley took over as her attending doctor that the problems began. From February 1739 onwards, he allegedly seduced Katherine over some months. He became obsessed with her and it was asserted at the trial that he had 'entertained an unwarrantable Passion for his fair Patient'.[27] Despite being twelve or fourteen years older than her, he was 'resolved to indulge and gratify it at any Rate'.[28] Taking advantage of his position, he began calling on Katherine more and more, frequently for long periods of time while her husband was out. Even worse, it was alleged that the two adulterers 'met at the Royal bagnio in St James Street, and there went to bed together'. Morley was accused of 'seducing her from those Paths of Virtue' that she had been brought up to follow.

During the trial (as was so common in adultery cases), damnation of the defendant came from the domestic servants. Biker's chambermaid, Anne Peeling, attested that Morley visited the house frequently and often dined and supped with his clients. According to her, the doctor and Katherine were often 'together without other company – often in a Bed-Chamber – for several Hours together'. This was at the end of March. He came about eight in the evening, usually when Biker was out at a tavern. Biker's cook, Sarah James, and his footman, Edward Mead, both testified to the comings and goings of Morley when Mr Biker was out, and that Mrs Biker and Morley spent long periods of time together. It was asserted at the trial that Mrs Biker had been suffering depression, but the chambermaid denied this. She stated that she had been in the room on one occasion and she 'had not observed Mrs Biker's Head to be disordered'.[29] This points to the fact that she believed Katherine to be neither confused nor deranged. Was this an attempt by a loyal servant to point the finger at Biker for putting his wife in an asylum unnecessarily?

Perhaps the most damning testimony was that given by Anne Oliver, who had been staying with her sister, Mrs Bucknall, at the Royal

Bagnio in St James's Street; this bagnio was a known assignation-place for couples wanting sex. She gave evidence to say that she saw Katherine and Morley together several times:

> a Lady came with him the first and second time . . . the first time, they were in the red Room up one of the Stairs; – there is a Bed in the Room- 'twas ready Sheeted – the Witness did not know at first who the Lady was; but knew her afterwards – went to see her afterwards at Biker's House – she was Mr Biker's wife.

Oddly, she admitted going to the Bikers' residence but does not state why. There was no reason for her to visit, unless it was at Mr Biker's request, and that he then gave her money to stand as a witness. She declared that Katherine and Morley spent long times at the bagnio:

> the Defendant and the Lady staid the first time four or five Hours – he ordered the Bed to be warmed; and asked whether the Sheets were clean; – and order'd a Fire; after they were gone, the Bed was to be made again . . . the Sheets were much tumbled.[30]

Lurid detail after lurid detail emerged. The couple went back and forth for more than three weeks. The third time, on 18 April, the witness saw 'the Lady undress'd, and went to Bed – her Cloaths were by the Bedside when the Witness came in again', asking for another quilt. Morley had even made a punch, paying 16*s* 6*d* for 'the Sangree, the Fire and the House'.[31] The most damning evidence yet came with the witness's account that 'she saw something on the Sheets, that made her believe there had been Commerce between them, as between Man and Woman'. Anne Oliver was a married woman, so she knew well what she was looking at . . . semen on the linen.

The defendant's council suggested that this was a malicious action brought for revenge on Morley 'upon some Disgust which they could not account for'.[32] They claimed the alleged adultery was wholly improbable because of the defendant's character: he was said to be sober, prudent and moral. He was at the top of his profession, a father and 'happy in an agreeable Wife of his own, with whom he lived in great Amity'.[33] Sense dictated that he would be ruined if he was suspected of a passion for a sick woman. Morley's defence was that he had diagnosed Mr. Biker as being riddled 'with the foul disease', and in turn, Biker would have given it to his wife and that there was therefore no likelihood that Morley himself would risk catching it from Katherine and giving it to his own wife. Morley's threatened reputation was pitted against Mr Biker's unfaithfulness, with the defence trying to expose the latter as not the kind and loving husband he was trying to appear before the court.

The defendant's solicitors suggested that the only evidence of any worth was that of Anne Oliver, and that she had been heard through a crevice saying that she would 'make a Bargain, and receive a Bribe for her Evidence'. Efforts were made to discredit Oliver, with other witnesses called to say they had heard about the bribe. The judge conveyed his displeasure at the bribery, no doubt swaying the jury in favour of the defendant. It would seem that the jury did not believe Oliver's evidence, as they came in with a verdict for the defendant. The fact that Morley got off in this instance meant that the assertion of Philip Thicknesse seemed to have come true: as the author of *Man-Midwifery Analysed* (1764), he had stated 'That some of these Touching Gentry have been prosecuted, and severely punished for their lustful attempt, in touching their patients, is a notorious truth; that hundreds of them get off, and that many succeed, cannot be doubted.'[34]

The judgement was reported in London's *Daily Gazetteer* for Friday, 3 July 1741:

> On Tuesday last a remarkable Cause came on to be try'd by a Special Jury at Guildhall, wherein Mr Bikers was Plaintiff, and Dr Morely Defendant for a Criminal Conversation with the Plaintiff's late Wife; then the Jury, after a Hearing which lasted twelve hours, brought in a Verdict for the Defendant.

It was stated at the trial that when Mrs Biker looked back on her deeds, it was 'with Contrition and Horror', and so great was her remorse that she had expired in a madhouse on 8 May 1732.[35] No one in the trial says how Katherine Biker had ended up in a madhouse, or how she died, but the chambermaid had attested to her being of sound mind. It is probable that her husband had her committed to the asylum as revenge for her unfaithfulness (if indeed she had committed adultery), although she was suffering from depression, so it is possible she fell into a mental decline. Furthermore, if she had caught syphilis from her husband, this may have been the cause of her madness. At the time madhouses were unregulated, with one supervisor overseeing between thirty and fifty or so patients. Cruelty and ill treatment were witnessed by one bookseller, Alexander Cruden, who had been unjustly locked up in Matthew Wright's private madhouse in Bethnal Green but managed to escape. He had been chained, handcuffed and put in a strait-jacket, and asserted that if he had not managed to get away, he would have died there.[36] He was not mad, but had been put in an asylum by people desiring to shut him up and prevent his criticisms of incestuous marriages among the aristocracy. It was all too easy to commit someone to a private asylum; it was even easier for wealthy husbands to commit wayward or unwanted wives. If this was the case for Katherine Biker, she would have suffered mental and physical anguish in her last days.

Some years later Morley was on trial again in 1754 in an action brought by Richard Maddox, this time for not performing his office as a man-midwife in the delivery of Maddox's wife.[37] Morley had been hired by Maddox to deliver his wife, but when she went into labour on 29 May, he refused to attend her and she died in agony three months later. Maddox was claiming damages of £5,000. The prosecution said, 'if he [Morley] had been an honest man, he would have demanded Assistance from some other skilful Practitioner; neither could he affirm, that he wanted proper Help, for both the midwife and Apothecary were there ready to obey any orders he should give them.'[38] Nor could he plead ignorance of the danger, as he had examined Mrs Maddox earlier. She had been attended at their house in Crane Court on Fleet Street by Mrs Hopkins, a skilled midwife, who asked for Morley to be called. When he came, he was very rude to her. On examining the patient, he 'declared he was of the Opinion that Mrs. Maddox was in a dangerous Way; that if she was to be then delivered she would not live half an Hour; and therefore they must wait a more favourable Opportunity, or to that Effect'.[39]

The female midwife, Mrs Hopkins, pleaded with Morley to do something, or to stay, but he would not and 'absolutely refused'. He said he had attended the woman some four years ago and was not paid to his satisfaction, although this was refuted by Hopkins, who testified to Mr Maddox's honesty and believed there must have been a mistake. Even the attending apothecary, Mr Langley, and a friend of Maddox, Mr Flower, begged Morley to stay, as did Mr Maddox. Two hours later, the patient took a turn for the worse and Langley was sent by Hopkins to go by coach and get Morley in his house in Lincoln's Inn Fields. In the end, they called for another man-midwife, Mr Hannakin, who called for assistance from a Mr Hume, but by this time, although they stopped the bleeding, the child was dead. Hopkins, Langley and Flower all testified as to what had happened that night. Hannakin asserted that had the woman been assisted and Morley performed his duty, the dire consequences could have been averted. Mrs Maddox languished for three months, from 29 May until 30 August, from 'excessive flooding and other Injuries received, for Want of Assistance, and being delivered in due and proper Time'.[40] Much was made of the idea that Morley was 'a Physician of great Eminence'. On this occasion, Morley got his comeuppance: the jury found him guilty and damages of £1,000 were awarded – hardly enough for the lives of Maddox's wife and child.

While in the past, the process around childbirth and miscarriage had been seen as essentially women's work, increasingly with the professionalization of the medical profession, female midwives were edged out. Male physicians who had previously been kept out of the birthing chamber and most other conditions regarding gynaecological problems were now at its centre. Some historians have argued that this development was a result of the use of new instruments such as the forceps, which had been designed over a century before by the Chamberlen family and kept secret; their design had been leaked in a publication in 1733, and the instrument was then introduced on a much wider scale. One of the reasons male midwives received such a bad press was that they were mainly called out in emergency cases; although over 90 per cent of women would give birth normally, male midwives were usually summoned in times of difficult births. This mean that they were in attendance where there was more likelihood of the death of either the child or the mother occurring, or sometimes both.[41]

Male midwives were heralded by some and lamented by others. Richer women requested their own physician to be on call, or for the doctors to live at the patient's house for some months prior to the birth so that they might watch over the mother in her pregnancy. The continual presence of another man in the home only inflamed gossip. The fact that the physicians were employed mainly by 'respectable' middle- and upper-class women meant they were seen to be morally at risk, more than poor women, who were thought to have no reputation to lose. Poorer women would continue to look to female midwives in their immediate neighbourhood for assistance in 'women's matters'. Since male midwives had access to women's genitalia and parts of the body normally reserved for the husband, it is unsurprising that they came under suspicion. Mistrust was inflamed by London gossip about prominent doctors' sexual philandering and cases such as Morley's alleged adultery. While we may think it probable that Morley was guilty of sexual exploitation of Katherine Biker when she was vulnerable, and got off because of his reputation – and because he was male and upper-class – his incompetence and neglect was evident in the ensuing case of Mrs Maddox, whose death was unforgivable. As one anonymous male author railed, directing his venom at the male midwives in a petition to the Royal College of Physicians, they 'treat our wives in such a manner, as frequently ends in their destruction, and ... have such intercourse with our women, as easily shifts into indecency, from indecency into obscenity, and from obscenity into debauchery'.[42]

Thomas Gaugain and Thomas Hellyer, *Diligence and Dissipation: The Modest Girl Rejects the Illicit Addresses of Her Master*, 1797, engraving.

10
Rape on Trial

Say, what could prompt a libertine to stray
From soft persuations soul enchanting way?
Alien to mighty love; what have recourse
To savage violence and brutal force?

The Rape, a poem humbly inscribed to the Ladies (LONDON, 1768)

For women walking out in public places, particularly at night, the threat of rape was ever-present. Streetwalkers might gain some protection by going out in pairs, but invariably peeled off from each other when one of them picked up a client. These women were the most at risk, and the least likely to take up a case in court, as any woman perceived as sexually active could not expect to be heard sympathetically in cases of sexual assault. The actual prosecution of rape was wrought with difficulties and since women were excluded from the political, legal and religious institutions that determined the making of the laws on rape, it was the male definition of rape that mattered. Women's voices, more often than not, went unheard when they attended rape trials and their testimony was often undervalued, not believed or ignored.

Different classes of women might expect different levels of harassment and outcomes of prosecution would vary depending on status. Servants were at risk of being raped inside the house of their employers by the men who employed them, be it the master of the house or his sons. Young girls were particularly vulnerable. Sixteen-year-old Sarah Bishop, who had only been in London for three years, said 'she was out of place' when she was given employment as a servant by George

Carter. He waited until his wife had gone to bed, then threw the girl on the ground and put his hand over her mouth to stop her from crying out. Many of these young girls could hardly describe what was happening to them, as they did not have the language to express themselves; she could only attest that she 'felt something come from him'.[1] All too often, mistresses covered up the crime; when Bishop told her mistress about the rape, Mrs Carter was unsurprised. Seemingly used to his assaults, she declared, 'He always served all his servants so the first night they came into the house.' She gave Bishop sixpence and told her that if she proved to be with child, they would maintain it.

Many frightened young girls would accept a small financial compensation and forget the idea of any legal action. Not so Sarah Bishop – she wanted justice. Instead of simply going away unheard, she obtained a warrant, but she was obstructed by the constables and the friends of the prisoner, who forced her to tear it up and made her take four shillings and half a crown. Still unwilling to drop the case, the next morning she went to see magistrate Sir John Fielding and got another warrant. She admitted she was a poor girl with no parents or friends. When asked how much she wanted in compensation, she said six or seven guineas. Maybe because of overwhelming pressure, Bishop gave up her battle and the prisoner was acquitted. This case was typical of many of the cases that came to court. Frequently, even with overwhelming evidence, young women would be paid off with a pittance. Sadly, compensation rather than justice is the best that most poor women might expect to receive from the judicial system.

While we are led to believe that there was an increased cult of sensibility emerging in the eighteenth century, this did not lead to more sympathy for raped women. Their sexuality continued to be used against them in rape trials. It seems obvious when examining rape cases that women's testimonies and those of their witnesses (particularly if female) were not given enough attention. They were at a disadvantage from the off.[2] What we see is a London society where rape culture flourished, one which was endemic and deeply embedded by centuries of misogyny.

Rape and the Law

Rapes in industrial England accounted for only 1 per cent of the total crimes against the person in court records. Judging by the few cases in

View of New Sessions House, Old Bailey, 1775, engraving.

the Old Bailey records in London, rapes were no doubt taking place more frequently than reported, just as they are nowadays.[3] Women were reluctant to come forward, as any connection to rape affected a woman's reputation and marriage marketability. Any previous relationships would be scrutinized. Either rapes were not reported, or, if they were, did not get to court. Of the 281 people indicted for rape in London during 1700–1799, only 45 were prosecuted (including as accessories to rape).[4] There can be little doubt that there was massive underreporting because of the tough judicial system. Securing a conviction was difficult and a high level of proof was needed. As Chief Justice Sir Matthew Hale famously commented, a rape accusation is 'easily to be made and hard to be proved, and harder to be defended by the party accused, though never so innocent'. He recognized that some acquitted men were probably guilty, but the evidence was hard to find to a satisfactorily high degree.[5] As a result, between 1700 and 1750, 85 per cent of rape trials in London reported in the Sessions Papers ended in acquittal.[6]

Rapes taking place within Westminster and the nearby areas of London were mainly heard at the Old Bailey. Perpetrators were rarely convicted, but when they were, they could be executed. The crime was taken seriously by both the judges and juries, but the definition of rape was ambiguous and juries were reluctant to send a man to his death. Records for the Old Bailey in 1780–1800 show that of 41 indicted men,

Thomas Rowlandson and Augustus Pugin, *Old Bailey*, 1809, etching and aquatint.

only seven were found guilty (two of whom had raped children).[7] Juries balked at the idea of committing a man when a woman had admitted previous sexual liaisons. If a man was found guilty, he was more likely to be fined, imprisoned or publicly humiliated in the pillory, but overall there was a low conviction rate. Even then, some of the death sentences were later overturned and the perpetrator was given a pardon.

When women did speak out, it was usually with reticence – understandably given the likelihood of the defence bringing forth every possible condemnation of the victim. The court records contain cases of women such as Sarah Tate, whose rape was supposedly mitigated by the fact that she had gone for a drink with the perpetrators. As she was walking home one summer's evening between seven and eight o'clock in July 1725 after a day's haymaking in Hammersmith, she was accosted by Will West, who took her pitchfork from her and insisted she go for a drink with him to the Wheatsheaf tavern in Kensington. Although she did not want to, she went with him in order to try and retrieve her fork. His friend, John Pritchard, came in and the two of them kept her talking. West followed her out into Lobb's Field, where he fell upon her. In her testimony, she said he 'was at the point of ravishing me. He had just made an Entrance into my – my – Body; when the Prisoner came up, and seeming to be very angry with him, he went no farther at that Time.' She went with Prichard, 'he appearing to be the civiler Man' of the two, but West followed:

> he threw me down and committed a Rape upon me; and as soon as he got off the Prisoner came on and ravished me again. They made me in such a frightful Condition, you would have bless'd yourself to have seen me; the Blood gush'd out of my Nose and ran into my Mouth as I lay upon my Back; so that I had like to have been strangled with it. I was all over bloody, from Head to Foot, both within and without – I was in such an Agony! – I struggled and strove, and did all that a Woman could do, till I was quite spent.[8]

The defence called several witnesses, who deposed that Will West and Sarah Tate had been in several alehouses together, implying that she had gone willingly. However, it was John Pritchard who was indicted and it was he who was acquitted. Despite the level of violence involved, the facts that she had gone willingly with West and that she had been drinking counted against her. Tate's case was just one of many that proves on reading that a violent rape by two men had obviously occurred but would go unpunished.

In the misogynistic eighteenth-century world, women had a hard time making themselves heard, and even more trouble being believed. A woman's reputation was always at stake in rape cases and proving that her character was spotless made up part of the prosecution. Besmirching her character was an effective strategy of the defence. Virginity was often used as a sign of a woman's respectability and reputation, and the lack of it thereby proved her immorality. Simply bringing a case might have a detrimental effect on her character. Women often had to face a hostile defence lawyer while having their reputations minutely inspected. One case heard at the Old Bailey on 28 August 1678 was particularly derogatory to the innocent victim. She had been accosted in Goswell Street after she had come to London to look for work: 'the Girl seem'd to be a silly Country animal she came up to London in expectation of a place; but being disappointed was sitting at a door in the same Street, expecting the Waggoner to come by, that with him she might return to her own Countrey.'[9] In the interim, the accused came upon her accidentally as he passed the house where she sat and told her he wanted a maid. She went along with him and he showed her his rooms and what work she would need to do. Unluckily for him, his plan was halted as reportedly; 'His Wife unluckily surpriz'd them; and it is thought, suspecting some foul play, Beat the Countrey Girl out of doors' (although why she did not also throw her husband out of doors is not said). On being questioned by a constable, the prosecutor said she had received 'no uncivil usage from the Prisoner', which was a highly unlikely thing for her to have said, given she was reporting a rape. It was suggested that she pretended a rape had occurred as revenge and the defendant was found not guilty. So often there is too little to go on in these early cases, but what is evident is that women were often in vulnerable situations where men could, and did, take advantage of them.

Rape had been deemed a capital crime from early Anglo-Saxon times. If a woman was raped, the crime committed was theft of the property of her husband, father, brother or closet male kin; in other words, the taking of her body without recourse to its rightful 'owners'. Women were under the patriarchal rule of their male kin, and it was men who were compensated. An example can be seen in a case of 1745: when John Newman was found guilty of raping the wife of John Biggs, he was ordered to pay the latter five guineas in damages while being bound over never to molest her again.[10] Abduction was also dealt with as a crime against the father or husband and it was the man who was compensated for loss of his daughter's service. In some instances, in cases of 'ravishment' or rape, at a time where women had little say legally, a woman might be offered up in marriage to the abductor or rapist. By the mid-seventeenth century the accent on rape as property was shifting and it became more about assault on a woman's body. An understanding of a rape as a 'sex crime' was developing, with a woman's innocence at the heart of the matter.[11] What followed was an emphasis on consent or lack of it and hence a concentration on proof of a woman's resistance.

Evidence of resistance was key in rape cases. A woman had to prove she had struggled if she were to be believed. Sixteen-year-old Mary Powell was raped on 23 October 1782 and John Foy went to trial at the late sessions of the Old Bailey before Mr Justice Heath. Powell was described as a spinster. She had left her parents' home to live with a Mr Cox, at the Black Horse and Trumpet on the corner of

Leman-street. The alleged rapist was a customer there, a waiter who worked at Miss Brown's hotel opposite. The difficulty of Powell in speaking about the experience is obvious given her reluctance to provide precise details of the penetration. She was told by the examiner to be more specific. She stated, 'He took me in and threw me down, and put my petticoats over my mouth, and his hand over that, while he lay with me . . . He lay with me as I suppose a man lays with his wife.' She needed a lot of provoking to be more exact, as the examiner pointed out: 'You must say particularly, you must describe it, because the man's life is in hazard.' She continued: 'I felt a great deal of pain while he lay with me: he unbuttoned his breeches while he lay with me . . . He put his t----g into my body while he lay with me.'[12] Specificity of time and place were important to the examiner, who asked, 'Then you had been thrown down, and used as you have told us, had only six minutes to adjust yourself, and come into your mistres's [*sic*] presence, and she did not observe that anything had happened, how was that?'; 'You were dragged into this room I think you say my girl, and it it was a front parlour?' The question of her disarray and the lack of tidiness in her appearance was subject to scrutiny.

> You must be pretty well tumbled; your cap, and your clothes?
> My hair was up, my handkerchief was tumbled.
> And your petticoats were tumbled a little?
> It was out of the binding.
> Only out at the binding? – I am afraid you did not make much resistance?

The fact that she had not been able to either put up a good enough fight or express herself in resisting, and indeed her inability to explain the details of the penetration, were all held against her. The fact too that she had been accosted before, albeit unsuccessfully, by a Mr Kirby, also counted against her. The prosecution stated, 'I believe you charged him with it [rape], and the poor man was frightened, and I believe you made him pay for doing nothing?' She answered, 'My mistress gave me half-a-guinea, and she told me that was to pay for tumbling my gown.'[13] Paying off the victims was commonplace. Either the court did not believe her or the evidence was not strong enough, as the verdict given was not guilty. That the victims were unable to describe the sexual act in details in court was evidently held against them.

All authorities concurred with regard to the requirement of force as an essential element of the offence, but there was disagreement on whether there needed to be emission as well as penetration during a rape. The case law reflects this divergence, and ambiguities in rape law caused problems. In some instances, proof of both emission and penetration was required; in other cases, proof of only one element was required.[14] Sir Matthew Hale, in his *History of the Pleas of the Court* (1736), defined rape as 'the carnal knowledge of any woman above the age of ten years against her will, and of a woman-child under the age of ten years with or against her will'. He maintained that only proof of penetration was required to obtain a rape conviction, and it was not necessary to prove emission. Views continued to vary; after the Reverend Russen's trial in 1777, the twelve judges, sitting in London, decided that any penetration, even if it did not break the hymen, was enough, without any need for a 'spermatic injection'. Only a few years later, in Hill's case in 1781, the verdict was that penetration without emission was not rape.[15] However, if a woman could prove emission, this was prima facie evidence of penetration. Proof of ejaculation was only officially abandoned in 1823.

If a man claimed to have had consensual sex, evidence of sexual intercourse counted for nothing. Therefore it was marks of violence or proof that the woman had put up a struggle which helped her, as seen in Sarah Tate's case. William Hawkins asserted, 'Rape is an Offense in having unlawful and carnal knowledge of the Body of a Woman by Force and against her Will.'[16] It is this point that a woman had to prove – that she had resisted with all her might. The more witnesses to attest to her being dishevelled, the better – evidence of blood on her clothes or body all helped towards obtaining a conviction. If witnesses had heard her shouting or screaming, that also stood in her favour. A woman needed to produce evidence of injury, bruises, dishevelled clothing or an eyewitness to the rape. Often injuries associated with women's robust and forceful fight in resisting a man were not enough: they had to be so horrific as to make one gasp.[17]

Even as late as the nineteenth century, a major misreading of rape in medical terms was given when gynaecologist Dr. Lawson Tait declared, 'When a full-grown healthy woman makes a charge of a completely effected assault against one man, the charge ought to be presumed to be false, unless the woman was first stupefied by drugs. I am perfectly satisfied that no man can effect a felonious purpose on a woman in possession of her senses without her consent,' because, after all, 'you cannot thread a moving needle.'[18] Because of these ill-judged and nonsensical assertions, medical interventions and misjudgements in rape on women and children were often detrimental to legal trials, another case of misogynistic assumptions about women's bodies. With such stringent markers of proof necessary for convictions, accused rapists were rarely convicted, and because of the biased handling of such episodes, women knew they did not have a fair chance of convicting the rapist.

While rape was a capital offence and a man might be put to death if found guilty, attempted rape was only an indictable misdemeanour, but easier to prove. As a lesser crime, it could be prosecuted either at the Old Bailey or at the various sessions for Middlesex, the City and Westminster held more regularly. Many attempted rape cases in London might go to smaller courts. The City of London Sessions heard 77 cases of assault with intent to rape between 1740 and 1830.[19] In some cases, where a rape case had been unsuccessful, the case could be tried again as attempted rape. In one case, the father was awarded five guineas from the public fund to pursue a misdemeanour prosecution.[20] Some cases were heard at Hick's Hall (the location of the Middlesex sessions). The records of the Guildhall Justice Room's minute books for the years between 1780 and 1796 suggest that of seventeen allegations of rape or assault with intent to rape women over twelve, only one man went for trial at the Old Bailey (he was acquitted), three others were charged but not prosecuted, in four cases the magistrates dismissed the charges and nine men were not even apprehended.[21] A further hurdle that would have precluded some women or their families from bringing cases against their rapists was the cost of bringing a prosecution. Court fees might cost anything from one to five guineas or more, higher when medical evidence was called upon.

The Case of Jane Bell

In some of the early eighteenth-century cases of rape and sexual assault, there seems to be a lack of evidence produced at court. The Old Bailey Online website state that speeches by the defendant and his or her counsel and the testimony of defence witnesses were more likely to be abridged or entirely omitted, especially when the defendant was acquitted. This had the cumulative effect of making those tried at the Old Bailey seem more culpable in the proceedings than they appeared in court.

By the end of the century, the account of the trials recorded had lengthened considerably and the public received a better idea of the full evidence. It is worth examining one case in detail in order to unpick what was relevant to the court and how the evidence was sought and then interpreted; how much pressure witnesses were subjected to through interrogation; how their claims were misjudged; how ill-informed medical witnesses were; and what type of evidence was actually needed to convict a rapist. Jane Bell believed she was fourteen or fifteen years of age when 37-year-old John Briant raped her on 19 July 1797.[22]

Bell was a servant to a Mrs Pollard, who was in the milk trade. On the evening of the rape, she had been putting her mistress's cows into Green Park at nine o'clock, when a man she had never seen before came up to her. She deposed,

> he took me under his arm, he stopped my mouth; I cried out ... he carried me upon Constitution hill, and flung me down upon my back, just by the bason [the upper bason towards Hyde Park], near the rails ...; he flung me down in a hole, upon a slanting place, on the hill; then he sat down upon his knees, and loosened his small clothes; I got away from him, and he got hold of me again, and flung me down again; he took up my clothes, and entered my body.

After the rape, a couple came to her rescue and pulled him off. A passer-by who had gone to the girl's aid, John Smith, gave evidence that he had heard the girl's cries and went over to rescue her with his girlfriend Sarah Scott. The attacker then ran away, and Smith followed him: 'I took him by the collar, and brought him back to the girl; and then, by the persuasions of the girl that was with me, I took him to the girl's mistress and a constable was sent for and examined his linen.' Giving evidence, Scott said,

> the cries that I heard were shocking for any human species, almost, to bear it; I asked John Smith to go up; he rather refused it, and I went up myself, and immediately he followed me; I found the man's hands and the girl's hands spread upon

> the green grass, his hands were upon her hands, and his small clothes were down between the girl's knees; upon which, I asked him if he was not a rascal . . . I told him there were plenty of unfortunate women that he might take his pleasure with, better than a child; he immediately got up, and I laid hold of him; I collared the man, and he told me that the girl belonged to him, not to me, and then he ran away; Mr. Smith pursued after him.

That women should take the initiative in protecting other women is unsurprising. Scott was obviously a woman of some pluck to have apprehended the attacker, albeit with the reluctant support of her boyfriend. Even female witnesses had to undergo public questioning of their morality.[23] When cross-examined, Sarah Scott was asked if she was married and what she was doing with a stranger in the park at that time of night.

The idea that blood was an indication of a broken hymen, and that a broken hymen was proof that a woman was no longer a virgin, was significant in these cases, as was any evidence that indicated she had been a virgin before the rape. The apothecary who had examined Jane Bell the morning after the incident deposed, 'Upon taking up her clothes, I observed great marks of violence; she appeared to have been much tumbled upon the grass, and her clothes were coloured with the grass.'[24] Yet it seemed more important to the prosecution to uncover whether she was a virgin or not, as they wanted to know if there was evidence of any blood. While the physician admitted there was no blood, he stated that 'there appeared to be human semen upon the private parts.'

The medical men involved in giving witness after examination sometimes either gave bad advice or were ignored. The legal authorities as yet often had little grasp of the realities around the connection between the existence of hymens and virginity and followed common thought on the subject. The importance of blood as a sign of virginity had been discussed at some length by physicians and disagreement reigned between them. One book, *Rare Verities*, thought that while some doctors were in agreement that the hymen is broken after intercourse, others thought there was no such thing:

> most are of the opinion that the Virginity is altogether annihilated when this Duplication is fractured and dissipated by violence, and that when it is found perfect and intire, no penetration had been made. Also some learned Physicians are of opinion that there is no Hymen or Skin expanded containing blood in it, which divers imagine in the first Copulation, flows from the fractured expanse.[25]

The fact that both legal and medical authorities in court were unfamiliar with some of the medical discussions at the time left women even more vulnerable. Even when the apothecary in this case deposed that it appeared 'as if she had been entered for the first time', that there was the appearance of violence and that he thought it unlikely she had had any man previously, this evidence was not enough. Surgeon John Andrews, who had examined the girl on 10 August, 'found a considerable swelling, a great deal of inflammation, and a considerable discharge, arising, apparently, from an intercourse with some male person or other' and 'the parts were so diseased ... the same appearances might have arisen from violence, independent of infection'. Bell attested to having been ill with lumps, sores and ulcers around her groin two or three days after the incident. The surgeon could not confirm whether it was venereal disease or a result of violence, but was sure it was one or the other.

The evidence of Jane Bell's mistress, Sarah Pollard, helped the case. She testified to the girl's good character and verified she was a good worker and always under her care, never far away from her. She had inspected the girl after her complaints and saw 'a great deal of human nature upon her, and by the appearance of that, I thought she had been violently used'. Pollard attested, 'she was as clean and fair a girl as ever sun shone upon, for I had examined her about the course of human nature, and she did not know what I meant', adding, 'a more virtuous girl never came into a house than she was before that, and a girl that I could trust with untold gold.' Pollard attested to seeing both semen and blood coming from the girl. Despite testimonies from his friends as to his good character, the defendant was sentenced to death.

Less than a fifth of convicts sentenced to death were actually executed, but according to the list of executions at Newgate, Briant's sentence was carried out.[26] In this case at least, it would seem that the medical evidence and that of her employer, along with that of the eyewitnesses, was too strong to ignore. Despite the lack of medical understanding about hymens, medical witnesses (the apothecary and the physician) could attest to blood and semen being present. In this case, the cumulative evidence was enough to convict.

Rape of Children

The age of consent was set at twelve years old, which was also the legal age of marriage. Sexual intercourse with a girl below twelve years, if achieved with her consent, was classed only as a misdemeanour, while violation of a girl below twelve without her consent was considered a capital offence, as was rape of a girl under ten, as they were considered incapable of consenting. This meant in effect that the age of consent in practice (although not in theory) was ten, since it was only a misdemeanour if a man had 'ravished' a girl between ten and twelve years old. The age of consent was raised to thirteen only in 1875 and to sixteen in 1885 with the introduction of the Criminal Law Amendment Act. In England, rape remained a capital offence until 1840.

Of 25 Old Bailey cases involving ten- or eleven-year-old victims between 1674 and 1749, 21 ended in acquittal; the conviction rate for rapes in the same period at the Old Bailey on children aged nine and under was 17 per cent. Judges were less inclined to accept the evidence of younger children, as often the child was thought too young to understand the oath and therefore incapable of testifying. The rate of conviction went up when the victims were older: at twelve or thirteen it was 23 per cent, presumably as their evidence was considered more trustworthy.[27] A judge might decide that a victim was too young to give evidence or unable to understand enough of what was going on. There are also discrepancies of what an acceptable age might be, as some girls of the same age (say, nine or ten) were allowed to give evidence and others were not. Those under eight were usually deemed incapable of giving evidence under oath, but were directed to provide testimony as to what had happened to them.

Where a child had agreed to go with the assailant, it bore against the case. When in 1747 ten-year-old Grace Pitts went willingly with John Hunter into the room and sat upon his lap in exchange for an orange, it appears she was deemed culpable because of her agreement to follow him (though she was agreeing to an orange, not a rape).

Hunter was acquitted of the rape. There was no concept of paedophilia and these men were not necessarily seen as sexual perverts, merely opportunists. Examining the court cases, most of the perpetrators being discussed in the trials were perceived as having led immoral lives, or as having an excess of sexual desire, a lasciviousness which made them prone to rape, rather than a particular fondness for children. The rape was seen to be more to do with a man's bad character rather than any predisposition towards children per se. When marriage was permissible to girls of twelve, heterosexual sex with young women and girls was not necessarily seen as a perversion. Nor was it classed as 'against God's will' or 'against nature' as other supposed perversions were, as it was perceived as 'normal' penetrative sex.[28]

That said, the rape of a child was clearly thought of as immoral and disgusting, particularly if the child was prepubescent. It was considered a serious matter because it both meant the loss of her virginity and was a stain on the reputation of her family. Comments in court on various cases indicate the unacceptability of child rapes: Edward Coker's rape of an eleven-year-old girl in 1675 was described as 'a British act of beastliness', William Rowlandson's rape of a nine-year-old girl as 'a filthy British offence'.[29] Some cases of incest with children under ten were taken to trial, but all but one ended in acquittal; this constituted only 5 per cent of trials where girls were aged under fourteen and 3 per cent of those aged under ten.[30] Perpetrators of sexual assaults on children appear not to have been given particularly harsh sentences: when George Rouson was tried at Hick's Hall for the attempted rape of a nine-year-old child in April 1730, his sentence was to be flogged twice from Islington turnpike to the local church, then to do hard labour at Bridewell prison for a year.[31]

Many of the rape victims in London were children, as they were easy to overpower and more likely to be disbelieved. When there was not enough evidence to prove a defendant guilty, it was clear that sometimes the judges thought the accused had committed the crime and would support the victim. In the case of Edward Coker, mentioned above, in order that he might not be let off entirely, the court directed that another bill be drawn up for assault on a child (rather than rape), for which he was convicted and fined 25 marks (£16 13*s* 4*d*).[32] Even when attacks had been brutal, with medical evidence and a surgeon's testimony provided, a rapist might be acquitted; however, he might be ordered to undergo trial for the lesser crime of attempted rape and recompense (five guineas) might be given to the father of the victim so he could prosecute.[33]

Medical men of the day thought that venereal disease could be transmitted by hand, so it would not mean definitive proof of penile penetration. The perpetrator might be sent for trial for attempted rape, as there had clearly been sexual contact.[34] Typically in these cases, a female relative had inspected the child, found evidence of the disease and called in a witness to inspect the child or their clothes. Elizabeth Robinson's mother found 'something unusual in her linen' and called in a midwife to examine her daughter.[35] Even where there was proof that a child had contracted venereal disease, there was no surety of conviction. While medical texts influenced the outcome of rape trials, novels and gentlemen's magazines also influenced public perceptions of rape and thereby perpetrated and perpetuated certain ideas about it.

Rape Representation in Literature

Most fiction representing rape was written by men, and it was their view of rape which counted – what rape meant for men, what it meant for women, how it should be viewed and the ensuing 'rape culture' that pervaded society was all biased towards men's understanding of what constituted rape or sexual assault. Within this, there was a level of acceptance around sexualizing women's bodies.[36] A common trope circulated in London and other cities that women were lascivious, encouraged men to want sex and had the ability to make men mad for them. As we have seen, in a wealth of men's magazines, libertine women (and often women in general) were portrayed as cunning, enticing men into sex and lying thereafter. It was easy to blame women for sexual excesses, for false accusations and bribery in a society that saw them as sexually forward, using wiles to trick men. While libertine men were often portrayed as being of a certain rank, devoid of sexual restraint – and this included fictional rapists – in reality, gentlemen were rarely punished, as their money and connections made it difficult to prosecute them. In trial reports, most of the victims were poor women as they were the most vulnerable, and most of the assailants were working men.

The rake was often at the heart of popular novels. The whole of Samuel Richardson's book *Clarissa* (1747–8) centres around Clarissa's rape, giving an overall impression of a 'prettification of violence'.[37]

The rape plot is well enough known: the virtuous young protagonist Clarissa falls for the rake Robert Lovelace, who convinces her to run away with him and then rapes her. As she is unconscious when the act takes place, she avoids any culpability and can therefore still claim to be virtuous. She kills herself. Lovelace is contrite. It has been suggested that her refusal to consider legal action shows Richardson's rejection of the utility of the laws, yet Clarissa manages to show his guilt when her letters are exposed after her death, making his act explicit; she addresses Lovelace's viewing of her body after death in a letter to her friend, referring to his raping her while as if lifeless; 'if . . . he insists upon viewing her dead whom he once before saw in a manner dead, let his gay curiosity be satisfied.'[38] This concept of sexual intercourse (rape in this case) with a passive or unconscious woman was taken up in pornography.

No doubt Richardson would have been aware of the erotic reports of the French case of Father John-Baptist Girard and his debauching of Mary Katherine Cadière, one of his parishioners. The trial had taken place sometime between December 1729 and June 1730 and the reports of the rape explored the extremes of passivity. Cadière, referred to as the penitent as she has been confessing to her priest, Father Girard, is shown as subservient. One report describes her as she lies virtually unconscious while he has sex with her:

> finding her one Day in Bed, he shut the door and locked it, then laying himself by her Side, put one of his Arms under her, with the other uncovered her, and while he kissed her so fast, that she had not time to speak, neither at those Times when he had once breathed on her had she the Power that his Hand wandered over all, even the most secret Parts of her Body, till fainting, she was no longer sensible of what he did; but when she came to herself, she was but all too conscious of what had passed, feeling herself wet, and seeing the Posture in which he lay.[39]

This was no doubt a fictionalized account, though the case was real enough.

This theme of raping unconscious women would continue throughout the next century as London writers became increasingly knowledgeable about how to write pornography. Authors were

Clarissa fainting before Lovelace, illustration by Daniel Chodowiecki for a French edition of Samuel Richardson's *Clarissa* (1785).

Jacques Gabriel Huquier, 'Seduction of Marie Catherine Cadière by Father Jean-Baptiste Girard', *c.* 1735, engraving.

developing the elements that elicit sexual excitement. *The Autobiography of a Flea Told in a Hop Skip and a Jump* brought up the topic of incest. Julia, the protagonist, is drugged and unable to cry out, her naked body splayed out on a table, her head behind a curtain, hidden as if she has been decapitated. Monsieur Delmont rapes her dismembered, headless body, but he is unwittingly raping his own daughter. The book was supposedly published by 'The Phlebotomical Society, Cytheris' and falsely dated 1789, but was in fact published in 1887; it later turned out that the author was London lawyer Stanislas de Rhodes.[40]

However, the literary trope of women fighting for their virtue was considered a sexual turn-on for male readers in the eighteenth century. The first set of pornographic literature circulating in London to include rape scenes came over from France and was read by the educated in the original French, although it later became available in English translation. The impression given is that women feign defence but want to be overcome: for example, in *The Petit Maître* (1749), women are conveyed as enjoying a struggle. 'This is the plain Reason, why most Women refuse to surrender upon Treaty, and why they delight so much in being storm'd.'[41] These tales were common in defloration fantasies, blurring the boundaries between rape and seduction.

Gentlemen's magazines such as *The Rambler* wrote up real rape cases for the edification of their readers. The retelling of the trials in magazines was often taken verbatim from the court records. Whether this was intended to be informative, educational or titillating, or all three, it is evident that the magazine was turning rape cases into entertaining reading material. The trial of John Foy, seen above, was reported verbatim both in *The Rambler* and in the *Covent Garden Magazine*. The fact that gentlemen's magazines routinely recounted the court trials for rape taking place at the Old Bailey shows just how embedded rape culture was in London. They also delighted in depicting rape in accompanying drawings, which proves to what extent it was a focus for male readers and how publishers sold the cases as quasi-pornography.

Although incest was being investigated as an erotic theme in explicit pornographic books, it only properly took off with flagellation pornography at the end of the eighteenth century. However, the theme of incest and rape was already being explored as a means of sexual titillation in gentlemen's magazines. *The Rambler* for Saturday, 2 November 1751, carried the piece 'The History of Misella debauched by her relation', a letter allegedly from a girl 'ravished' by her cousin. She related how he took advantage of the familial ties and of the submission that he exacted as her benefactor 'to complete her ruin'.[42] The following week, she related her decline in 'Misella's description of the life of a prostitute'.[43] Her cousin continues to visit and is bent on her complete defilement; she declares, 'but I now saw with horror that

Unknown artist, 'The London beau in the country, or the dairy-house gallant', from *Covent Garden Magazine* (May 1773).

he was contriving to perpetuate his gratification, and was desirous to fit me to his purpose, by complete and radical corruption.' He eventually deserts her, fleeing with his family to Ireland and leaving her destitute. Finally, after struggling to make ends meet in honest trades such as needlework, she ends up on the street, where an elderly man invites her to a tavern and initiates her into prostitution. 'In this state I have now passed four years, the drudge of extortion and the sport of drunkenness; sometimes the property of one man, and sometimes the common prey of accidental lewdness.'

By this time, the life of prostitution was being viewed sympathetically, typically not as the fault of the woman but of her unscrupulous seducer. The narrator portrays the sordid life she has been forced into:

> If those who pass their days in plenty and fecundity, could visit for an hour the dismal receptacles to which the prostitute

> retires from her nocturnal excursions, and see the wretches that lie crowded together, mad with intemperance, ghastly with famine, nauseous with filth, and noisome with disease; it would not be easy for any degree of abhorrence to harden them against compassion, to repress the desire which they must immediately feel to rescue such numbers of human beings from a state so dreadful.

Although the fall of a prostitute through seduction was a routine tale, the seducer as family member was a new twist. By the nineteenth century, incest would become the main theme of pornography.

The Infamous Colonel Francis Charteris

One of the most famous rape cases was perpetrated by Colonel Francis Charteris (1675–1732) nicknamed 'The Rape-Master General'. It became evident he was a serial rapist long before the trial that brought him down. For many years, he had been in league with Mother Needham, who had procured young virgins for him. He also sent his servants to the country to find young girls for him for sexual purposes under the pretence of offering them a job as a servant.[44] Charteris lived in the parish of St George, Hanover Square, and his downfall came after he offered Anne Bond a job as his servant under the assumed name of Colonel Harvey. No doubt she would not have ventured into his household if she knew his real name, as his reputation preceded him.

Bond started work for Charteris on 24 October 1729 and he immediately started to connive in various ways to try and make her have sex with him, asking her to lie in his bedroom with him while pretending to be ill, offering her a snuffbox and money and bribing her with new clothes. She tried to leave, but his servants prevented her escape. Finally, he called her up to his room one day, locked the door and thrust himself upon her. During the trial, she was asked what happened; she said he had pulled up her clothes and pulled down his breeches. Being asked what followed, she stood silent, embarrassed at how to explain sexual intercourse. The question was repeated and this time she replied, 'a great deal of wet'. As with other young women, Anne Bond had difficulty explaining the rape explicitly, indicating her sexual inexperience.

George White, *Colonel Francis Charteris at His Trial*, 1730, mezzotint.

The trial took place at the Old Bailey on 26 February 1730. After Charteris's arrest and incarceration, *Fog's Weekly Journal* of 14 March 1730, well acquainted with his reputation, reported wryly: 'We hear no Rapes have been committed for three Weeks past. Colonel Francis Charteris is still in Newgate.' Many pamphlets and satires about his life were published, but the following newspaper report from the *London Journal* gave a chronological account of the events that made him infamous.

> On Thursday between twelve and one o'clock at noon, came on the tryal of Col. Francis Charters [*sic*], at the Sessions House in the Old Baily, before the Lord Chief Justice Raymond, and the Lord Chief Justice Eyre, upon an indictment for committing a rape on the body of one Anne Bond, his servant maid. The Prosecutor appeared in Court, and proved that on the 24th of October last she was hired by the Colonel to be his servant; and that she had lived with him several days before she knew who he was; and that on the 10th of November following, he sent for her up into his room to make his fire,

> when he threw her on a couch, and she crying out, he pull'd off his cap and stopp'd her mouth, and then did the crime for which he was indicted.

Several other depositions concurred with Bond's testimony, and several persons with whom she had formerly lived acted as character witnesses and attested to the fact that she was a virtuous and religious young woman.

As with all rape cases, the court had been at pains to find out if the victim had fought off her offender, and with what amount of force. Bond was asked if she made any resistance or whether she cried out for help. 'She said, she resisted as long as she was able, and that she cry'd out till the Prisoner stop'd her Mouth with his Night-Cap, but that none of the Servants came to her Assistance, for that they were so much under his Command, and so frequently addicted to his Pleasures, that they durst not interpose.'[45] He tried to soothe her but could not, upon which he decided on a different tack. He took up a horsewhip and lashed her severely, calling upon his manservant Mr Gordon to search her, alleging she had robbed him. They found a snuff box he had previously given her with a guinea in it. He then threw her out. She wandered about in some distress until she recalled she had a friend nearby, a gentlewoman, Mary Parsons, and decided to call on her and tell her what had happened and see if she could help. Parsons contacted a Mr Biss, an obviously capable man who knew how to proceed with the law, as he helped them serve an indictment against Charteris. He had witnessed the terrible condition of Bond's body and the marks left on her arms, back and neck caused by the beating. The jury took only three-quarters of an hour to bring in their verdict of guilty.

Most of this report was repeated verbatim in the *Grub-Street Journal* on 5 March 1730, which added that as soon as the jury delivered their verdict, Charteris was secured by the Keeper of Newgate. Since he had been convicted of a felony at the Old Bailey, officers went to seize all his goods and chattels at his house, but were denied admittance by the servants. He must have paid his servants exceedingly well as they defended his property. One woman fired a pistol from a window, and wounded a beadle in the breast. Eventually, they managed to gain access. Officers entered his property and seized large quantities of silver plate and household furniture, carrying it all off in carts to an empty house in Old Bond Street.[46] It was obvious that Charteris had a slew of people willing to try and protect him and defend his violent behaviour. He tried to evade further exposure when his counsel persuaded the court to read the indictment in Latin before sentence was passed, which was allowed. This meant that many people present would not have understood what was being said, or the severity of his crime. He received a sentence of death for the rape of Anne Bond on 10 November, which ultimately would not be carried out.

Malicious prosecution was a subject high on a counsel's list when attempting to defend his client from an accusation of rape. Any attempt to extract money from a man would stand against a victim. Although this was a consideration in court proceedings, in reality, there seems little evidence that this is what women did.[47] Rather, the evidence indicates that accusations of malicious prosecution or extortion were part of a defendant's deliberate strategy to undermine the victim's veracity. The court's concern seems to have outweighed the realities of the difficulties and embarrassment for a woman in bringing a case to court, not to mention the costs involved.[48] This is the tack Charteris's defence tried to take, to prove that Bond was trying to extort money from him. His servants gave witness for the defence, no doubt in fear of losing their jobs, but Bond's evidence and that of those supporting her was so strong that it helped her to win the case. Sadly, as with most aristocratic men who had committed rape or other crimes, Charteris managed to wheedle his way out of the death penalty. Despite his sentence, he was granted a royal pardon on 10 April 1730 after a campaign by his crony Lord Advocate Duncan Forbes, who was a tenant of Charteris's in Edinburgh. Though he regained much of his property, he had to pay compensation of £30,000. Anne Bond seems to have been promised an annuity, possibly the only recompense she thought she would receive. Charteris evidently spent much of his fortune on bribes to extricate himself. He died of natural causes in 1732, probably as a result of the dreadful conditions in Newgate prison. His coffin was attacked on its way to the graveyard, and it is said that dead cats were thrown into his grave. Jonathan Swift wrote about Charteris in several of his poems. He described Charteris as

> a most infamous, vile scoundrel, grown from a foot-boy, or worse, to a prodigious fortune both in England and Scotland: he had a way of insinuating himself into all Ministers under

> every change, either as pimp, flatterer, or informer. He was tried at seventy for a rape, and came off by sacrificing a great part of his fortune.[49]

He was interred in Greyfriars churchyard while an incensed mob tried to mutilate his corpse. Bond married a tavern keeper, with whom she tried to set up a business in Bloomsbury.

Various suggestions have been made for the reasons for sexual violence throughout history: one is the traditional feminist argument that rapes represent male power over helpless women; a second argues that relationships are a series of struggles and negotiations that are historically specific; a third stems from Foucault, who argued in his *Discipline and Punish* in 1975 that it is necessary to examine the transition from public violence and punishment as a spectacle seen in public whippings and hangings to violence which is secret, institutionalized and defined by the elite. Looking for the reasons for ongoing rapes and sexual assaults, other elements spring up, such as consent, age, power, class and race. All these issues would come to bear in various rape trials. However, one of the problems of examining rape trials in history is that the evidence is seen only if the culprit came to trial. The incident then has to be interpreted through the third party of the court secretary, the equivalent of the stenographer, as well as the voices of the lawyers. Also, reports were written up by men, who often had biased opinions. The misogynistic attitudes of the day were ingrained in their understanding of rape and of women. A woman's dress, whether she was modest or not, if she fought back and resisted or not, were all taken into consideration, as was her sexual reputation. Rape therefore needs to be seen in terms of gender relations, sexual politics and stigmatization rather than simply in terms of individual perpetrators. It was embedded in a misogynistic culture which pervaded eighteenth-century society. The social stigma that came with rape was attached to the woman, not the man. There was every chance that a raped woman might be subject to ostracization, as she was seen as sexually denigrated, while the rapist would boast about his conquests. There was very little difference in society's attitude to a woman who had consensual sex before marriage and a woman who had been raped. Both were considered to be despoiled.

All too frequently, men who had raped women or young girls, even when they had inflicted horrific injuries, managed to escape conviction. Where a conviction for rape could not be made, sometimes a judge felt sufficiently moved to order the defendant to be tried for attempted rape, for which it was easier to obtain a guilty verdict. The judge sometimes awarded victims' parents the money for the ensuing trial. The ambiguity of the application of the law and legal definitions of rape contributed to acquittals. However, the deep-rooted misogyny permeating society at the time no doubt prevented many women from ever attempting to take their case to court. Newspapers, gentlemen's magazines and novels reinforced overall beliefs about innate female lasciviousness and cunning – which were particularly prevalent in London. This did nothing to support a woman in bringing a case, and everything to thwart it.

11
Seduction, Abduction and Adultery

Durst veil the *real* author of the deed,
To make fair innocence more deeply bleed.
On complicated schemes of ruin bent,
Not with a single villainy content,
Plund'rer of VIRTUE, then, thy next essay,
Worthy of blackest crimes that shun the day.

RICHARD DE COURCY, *Seduction; or, The Cause of Injured Innocence Pleaded* (1782)[1]

Seduction tales of innocent young women being debauched abounded in the eighteenth century, both factual and in fiction. The distinction between seduction and rape was formed during the Augustan period (from around the last decades of the seventeenth to the middle of the eighteenth century), when seduction came to mean coercion, temptation or trickery. Consent on the part of the women marked out seduction, as opposed to resistance, which marked out rape. The model of the pathetic seduced maiden emerged with discussions about how modest young women might have ended up inadvertently losing their virginity.[2] The main considerations were around those who gave themselves to their betrothed before marriage, became pregnant and then were deserted by their paramours, and those who ran off with, or were abducted by, their lovers thereby ruining their reputations. At a time when sex before marriage was considered immoral, a woman who had been seduced and then abandoned by a man was considered shocking. Angry parents brought lawsuits in order to try and punish the men involved, but this would only usually bring financial compensation and was never entirely satisfactory in terms of appeasement or revenge.

William Hogarth, *The Denunciation (A Woman Swearing a Child to a Grave Citizen)*, *c.* 1729, oil on canvas.

A father or husband could sue abductors for taking their 'property' (the man being the 'owner' of the woman), the crime being seen as perpetrated against the male guardian rather than the woman herself. There was not much of a distinction made between cases where a woman went willingly (eloped) and those where she went unwillingly (was abducted),[3] as the result was the same in any case; requests for financial reparation, for damages for trespass and loss of her domestic services, could be made. Cases of 'seduction' (although this particular case sounds more like rape) revolved around the notion of 'trespass', as seen in *Norton v. Jason* in 1653, when a father sued a man for breaking into his house and 'assaulting' and impregnating his daughter. Chief Justice Rolle declared that the father had a case 'for the loss of her service' but not for getting her with child, as 'this is a wrong particular done to her'.[4] However, nearly all cases of seduction ended in some sort of heartbreak for those involved. Broken promises led to broken hearts, and broken marriages led to financial upset and ruined reputations.

Francis Wheatley, *Valentine Rescuing Silvia from Proteus*, from Shakespeare's *The Two Gentlemen of Verona*, Act v, Scene 4: The Outlaws' Cave, 1792, oil on canvas.

Broken Promises

Women were often seduced under the promise of marriage, and broken promises might end in trials. Mrs Sarah Holt of Hackney brought an action of £4,000 against Knox Ward in 1730 for breach of promise. It was alleged that Ward did 'allure, persuade and entice the said Sarah Holt, to permit him to pay her Visits at sundry Times, upon his Protestation of an inviolable Friendship and Love'.[5] The newspapers were quick to jump on the gossip even before the case had come to court, reporting salaciously, 'we hear that all the Letters from during the Courtship, Defendant to the Plaintiff, being nearly 300, will shortly be publish'd for the Edification of the Learned, and for the good of the Publick in general.'[6]

The case came up before the court at the Guildhall, London, on 22 February 1730. Holt's mother was called as a witness and related how Ward had paid several visits in private to her daughter. She had become suspicious: 'she grew very uneasy, being afraid that he had a Design to debauch her, and therefore kept a watchful Eye over her, being resolved to surprise them the next Time he came to the house.'[7] As usual, it was the staff who were frequently brought before the court to testify. The chambermaid, Mrs Becket, who had lived with the family for eighteen months, had frequently seen Ward come to the house and heard him speak most tenderly to Miss Holt. She had heard him say, 'if she would resolve to make him happy by marrying him, he should esteem it the greatest Blessing in this World.'[8] The porter also gave evidence, saying he had delivered letters from Ward to Miss Holt, but did not know what was in them, nor was it his business. Despite there being no evidence of him having had sex with Miss Holt (her

Thomas Rowlandson, *Guildhall, Court of King's Bench*, 1808, hand-coloured etching.

mother had been too vigilant for this), it was evident that Ward had had second thoughts. This may have been because Sarah would not consent to sex with him on a mere marriage promise, though sexual activities were not alluded to in the evidence, except for the concerns of the mother about her daughter's reputation. Mr Knox denied all charges, but Lord Chief Justice Raymond decided a breach of marriage promise was to be found as 'he certainly had injured the Lady very much in her reputation.'[9] Damages were awarded against Ward for £2,000. (This was twice as much as Maddox had been awarded for the death of his wife and child at the neglect of Dr Morley.)

Prior to the Marriage Act, canon law deemed that an exchange of promise to marry in the present tense (*per verba praesenti*) was enough to constitute a marriage; if it was a future promise of marriage (*per verba de future*), the marriage was effected on sexual intercourse, without the necessity for formalities. Cases of broken marriage promise came before the ecclesiastical court and if the promise was found to be valid, the couple were forced to marry. This changed with the passing of the Marriage Act of 1753, which introduced all sorts of formalities such as banns and licenses, the presence of an ordained priest and two witnesses, as well as the need for registration – a marriage without banns being read or a licence being obtained was void. Members of Parliament debated whether the Marriage Act would damage the chances of women to obtain retribution in cases of broken marriage promises. It was thought that women might be reluctant to go through more formal proceedings than those of ecclesiastical courts in seeking reparation. However, banns had been necessary under ecclesiastical law for centuries and it is possible that the Marriage Act simply reinforced what was already in existence.[10] With the introduction of the Marriage Act of 1753, the power of the ecclesiastical court was swept away.[11]

Even London clergymen were involved in seducing young women. Given that they were in a position of trust, this was even more scandalous. One case brought before the King's Bench on 11 December 1794 was by a father for the seduction of his nineteen-year-old daughter deemed 'of much beauty and an excellent disposition'. She had become a victim of Reverend Scoolt of St Olave's Church, Southwark, who was supposed to have been focusing his energies on burying the dead and caring for the inhabitants of the workhouse, but evidently had became distracted. He had been invited to teach the young girl after becoming acquainted with the family, and, while he repeatedly promised her marriage, he already had a wife, whom he had not seen for six years. The prosecution saw it as a blatant seduction and abandonment, a broken marriage promise, and asserted, 'after he satiated his brutal appetite, [he] became indifferent to the lady whom he had betrayed and ruined.'[12] The defence argued that the father should have known better than to have invited the reverend into his house and left him alone with his daughter, and therefore should shoulder some of the blame, though the court had sympathy for him. An alternative to financial reparations was suggested – that the case be sent to the Bishop of Southwark, who would presumably mete out a suitable punishment, although the clergyman may just have been moved to another parish, as was (and is) common in sex scandals involving clergymen. Both parties were to pay their own costs, but essentially nothing came of the court case, which shows how difficult it was to succeed in a prosecution of seduction.

Broken Hearts

If the young woman involved was in love, a deep melancholy might ensue as she was left with her reputation in tatters. Forlorn at the loss of her love, the rejection she felt and ensuing depression could lead to despair. This connection between love and madness was common enough to be talked about in everyday conversation; 'love sickness' and being 'madly in love' were not simply in the imagination of lovers or idealized conventions, but alluded to very real passions and experiences. James Boswell lamented, 'Disappointed love is one of the most frequent causes of madness, as everybody may be convinced who has curiosity and firmness sufficient to visit the receptacles of insanity [mental asylums] and contemplate human nature in ruins.'[13] Londoners believed that love could seriously affect a person's health. The last scene of Hogarth's *A Rake's Progress* contains depictions of the 'love melancholic' that so rattled Boswell, with a patient committed to Bedlam as a result of a broken heart. Physician William Battie was governor at Bethlem Hospital and then founder of St Luke's Hospital in 1751. He took a sincere interest in bettering treatment for the mentally ill and hoped that the new asylum would bring about a higher standard of care for its inmates. His attempts to discover the causes, effects and cures of madness were explored in his books, among them a *Treatise on Madness* (1758).[14] Doctors saw the evidence of love sickness:

Joseph Farington wrote in his diary (covering 1793 to his death in 1821), 'a Medical man who attended Bedlam had said that the greatest number of those who were confined were Women in Love.'[15] While he might have exaggerated the statistics of Bedlam inmates, Dr William Black in his *Dissertation on Insanity* (1810) recorded 'Love' as the fifth most common cause of admission.[16] The worst cases of thwarted love were created by libertine men who abandoned their female lovers.

One case that came to public attention was that of Mary House, who was committed to Bedlam after being cast off by her aristocratic lover. According to the doctors of Bedlam who had assessed her condition, she had a mental breakdown after the Duke of Chandos broke off their affair and subsequently discarded her. The libertine (or blackguard) lover was the Marquis Richard Plantagenet-Temple-Nugent-Brydges-Chandos-Grenville (1797–1861), styled Earl Temple from 1813 to 1822. After the affair, he was to inherit the title of 2nd Duke of Buckingham and Chandos. Educated at Eton, he became a reprobate and a womanizer. On reaching Oxford in 1815, he began an affair with Mary (known as Poll) House, and kept her for a time before casting her off. The bereft young woman was to spend the rest of her life in Bethlem Hospital as a result of their affair.

Mary House's story was taken up in *A Curious and Interesting Narrative of Poll House and the Marquis of C*******, a quasi-erotic booklet that included spurious claims common to this type of publication. It was aimed at the gossips of London, who wanted more dirt dished out on the aristocracy and their sexual dalliances. It is thought Mary or 'Poll' House was a carpenter's daughter, sometimes known as Mrs Mary Dacres, and that the marquis had set Mary up in a house in Kensington and later in Grosvenor Square. While some of the facts ring true, others were simply made up for better effect. Supposedly after a visit to his dying father, the marquis returned at the instigation of his stablehand John Stubbs and caught Mary *in flagrante* with his friend. In fact, it is highly unlikely that Mary would have risked any type of contact with other men when the marquis had placed her in her own house, and she was obviously in love with him. The narrator also gives a potted version of Mary's life after her abandonment, when she supposedly turned to a life of crime (of which I could find no record); she allegedly stole a gentleman's ring and was brought before the magistrate's court. In prison, she supposedly reacquainted herself with one of her earlier lovers who, along with his cronies, encouraged her to utter forgeries (this crime carried the death penalty). The story goes on, placing Mary among the criminal classes, where she takes up various lovers and embarks on a career as a thief. The book asserted that earlier on in her life Mary had played in *Virginia* and *Agreeable Surprise* on stage, yet there seems to be no mention of her acting career elsewhere.[17]

Mary House was indeed admitted to Bethlem Hospital on 18 February 1819, as the hospital's archives confirm. A bond exists that was produced on the delivery of Mary House to the hospital, promising to 'remove and take away the said Lunatic from the said Hospital' and clothe and bury her if necessary. The bond is signed by George King, a grocer of Fitzroy Square, Marylebone, and John House, a carpenter from Hackney Road, no doubt a close relative. A certificate of insanity had been signed on 10 February 1819, by her father, George House from Marylebone (the parish Mary had lived in all of her life), and the surgeon who had examined her. The certificate declared that House had been 'disordered in her senses nine weeks and no longer'. Her admission report states that she was a 23-year-old single woman who had been a dressmaker and milliner. Her insanity had started with diarrhoea and pains in her limbs. She was given electric shocks as a cure, to no avail, but she did reveal the cause of her illness. The report states,

> her disorder arose from the disappointment of certain hopes that she'd been taught to indulge of being elevated to very high rank by a young nobleman of the Buckingham family, and the loss of her house for £1,000 given her by the same nobleman and artfully obtained back from her by some agent of the same family.[18]

According to the ODNB, Mary was bought off by the marquis's father, but in fact it would seem his father hoodwinked Mary into returning the money and the house. This was probably an easy manoeuvre given the mental anguish she was suffering at the abandonment of the marquis. She was discharged uncured on 20 February 1820, but was recommended for the hospital's incurable ward, and returned to Bethlem on 2 March 1820, less than a fortnight later. She was given three months' leave of absence in late 1820, leaving the hospital on 2 November and returning again on 7 February 1821. After spending a further dozen years in the incurable ward, Mary died in the hospital on 8 May 1833.

Immediately after Mary's committal, the marquis married the unfortunate Mary Campbell (*d.* 1862), the daughter of an earl, no doubt in hope of gaining access to her money. He became a politician, but had spiralling debts, and later went bankrupt. In 1850 his wife had finally had enough of his constant womanizing and obtained a legal separation. His final ruination came when he had to auction off his estate at Stowe with everything in it, and he ended up living at the Great Western Hotel at Paddington.

While Bedlam's abandoned lovers floundered in madness, the hospital also operated as a potential meeting place for those looking for sexual adventures. When Ned Ward visited Bedlam in the early part of the century, he found he could mingle freely with the inmates and fellow-sightseers as he wandered around watching the mad folk play out their insanity. Though visitors often entered the premises on their own, they went out in pairs, which indicated that Bedlam was a picking-up place; Ward noted, ''Tis an Alms-House for Madmen, a Showing Room for Whores, a sure Market for Lechers, a dry Walk for Loiterers.' He even had a chat with a former student of St John's, Cambridge, who had been confined for melancholia. Mistresses of all ranks, from the 'Velvet Scarf to the Scotch-Plaid Petticoat', were available inside.[19]

Abduction: The Berkeley Affair

In cases of abduction, a father might sue for the ruination of his daughter's reputation or debauchery. In many cases, abduction had not really taken place; instead, women had absconded with their lovers of their own free will against their parents' wishes. One of these cases involved the eighteen-year old Lady Henrietta Berkeley (*c.* 1664–1706) and Lord Grey of Warke, her brother-in-law, who disappeared together in 1682. It turned out that Lord Grey had secreted Henrietta in various lodging houses to avoid detection. While he admitted to her parents that he knew her whereabouts, he refused to let them know where she was. One of the main means of retaliation open to Lady Berkeley's father was to prosecute Grey. The trial was to become the sensation of the year.

Gossip about Henrietta Berkeley's affair with her brother-in-law was evidently already circulating as early as 1681 in *The Ladies March*, which included her in a satire describing a procession of court:

Next Berkeley's Harriet greets the eye,
The females of which family,
By nature or by education,
All love the act of generation.

Henrietta was one of the eight children of Lady Elizabeth and George Berkeley, 1st Earl of Berkeley, who lived at the family home in Berkeley House, where Berkeley Square now is. She was still a minor when the affair began sometime in early 1681, and she was presumed to still be a virgin. Her mother had become suspicious in 1682, having found Henrietta writing a letter to Lord Grey, her sister Mary's husband. According to the statement given in court by Henrietta's other sister, Lady Arabella, 'My mother coming to my lady Harriett's [they all refer to Henrietta as Harriett] chamber, and seeing there a pen wet with ink, examined her where she had been writing. She in great confusion, told her she had been writing her accompts.' Her mother was not satisfied with this answer and decided to search the room. A letter was indeed discovered in which Henrietta had written to Lord Grey, declaring in writing, 'My sister Bell did not suspect our being together last night; for she did not hear the noise. Pray come again Sunday or Monday; if the last, I shall be very impatient.'[20]

H. R. Cook, after Sir Godfrey Kneller, *Lady Henrietta Berkeley*, 1810, etching.

Horrified, her mother immediately took her from their London home to the family seat at Durdans near Epsom to keep her away from Grey. Lady Berkeley was unwilling at this stage to divulge the affair to either her husband or her daughter, Lady Mary (Grey's wife), in the hope the matter might be hushed up. The unwitting Lady Mary invited Grey to visit them and Lady Berkeley had little option but to allow the visit in order to keep the affair quiet.

Henrietta's other sister, Lady Arabella, later reported to the court, 'Upon his first coming in, my lady Harriett fell upon the ground like a dead creature and my lord Grey took her up, and said, "now you see how far it is gone between us: I love nothing upon earth but her."'[21] It became evident in Arabella's evidence that a servant had been taking letters to and fro between the couple. The only recourse to Henrietta's mother at this stage was to privately urge her son-in-law to leave the house as quickly as possible. At the trial she gave evidence, 'When I first discovered this unhappy business, how my son-in-law, my lord Grey, was in love with his sister, I sent to speak with him, and I told him he had done barbarously and basely, and falsely with me, in having an intrigue with his sister-in-law.' Instead of defending the honour of the family, she declared that he had endeavoured to bring about the ruin of her daughter, and had done worse than if he had murdered her.[22]

Charles Turner, *Lord Ford Grey*, 1813, mezzotint.

George Cruikshank, *Galvanism; or, The Miraculous Recovery of the Unfortunate Miss Baily*, *c.* 1807, pen and ink and watercolour.

According to Lady Berkeley, on confronting Grey about the affair, he appeared contrite when faced with her wrath. She acknowledged, 'He fell a weeping and said, he was unfortunate' (probably thinking it was unfortunate he had been caught). He asked Lady Berkeley not to tell either his wife or her husband. He promised he would go away and not see either her or Henrietta again and would avoid them when in London. He planned to go to his house in Uppark (which incidentally is where Lord Fetherstonhaugh impregnated the young Emma Hart, later Emma Hamilton, which was to be her downfall). Lady Berkeley had entreated him to leave Henrietta alone: 'I told him, that his going on in any such way would be her utter ruin.'[23] She pressed him to go to France and to take his wife with him, which he promised to do. All the while, Henrietta had been kept in her bedroom.

In court, Lady Berkeley called on her role as a mother to point to the dreadfulness of her daughter's actions, calling Henrietta 'my wretched unkind daughter' and adding,

> I have been so kind a mother to her, and would have died rather, upon the oath I have taken, than have done this, if there

> had been any other way to reclaim her, and would have done anything to have hid her faults, and died ten times over, rather than this dishonour should have come upon my family.[24]

Whether such histrionics were over the shame of her daughter's affair with her son-in-law – sometimes referred to as incestuous in reports of the case – or her daughter's loss of chastity is difficult to establish, but both must have pained her mother. Overall, the loss of the reputation of the family was the key issue.

Henrietta's response to her mother's confrontation was much the same as Grey's. According to her mother's testimony, Henrietta fell on her knees crying and agreed that she would never see Grey again and would do anything her mother told her to do. Presented with these signs of repentance, Lady Berkeley was convinced that her daughter now regretted her actions and so she agreed not to tell Lord Berkeley. Henrietta was either unsure of her position in the family, or was trying to gain ground to best organize her escape. A few days later, she came to her mother, decided to blame Grey for her seduction and set herself up as a victim. Whether she truly believed this or was playing a part, it is difficult to surmise. She cried, 'Oh . . . he has seduced me to this . . . it is he, he is the villain that hath undone me . . . but pray do not tell my father of my faults.'[25]

Despite her mother's vigilance, once Grey left, Henrietta quickly escaped the house, aided by his servant Charnock, and followed Grey back to London, where he hid her in lodging houses and refused to tell her parents where she was. Her father immediately put up a £200 reward (around £32,000 in today's terms) for any information about his daughter's whereabouts. The *London Gazette*, advertising the reward, gave a description: 'a young lady of a fair complexion, fair haired, full breasted, and indifferent tall'. Henrietta's father then launched a lawsuit for unlawful seduction against Grey and his accomplices and the case came to trial at the King's Bench, London, on 23 November 1682, where the full details came out.

The full trial was printed and sold by John Morphew in 1716 (the sessions papers were published sometime later in 1735).[26] According to the sessions report, Grey pleaded not guilty. The prosecutor charged Grey with 'inveigling the Lady Henrietta Berkeley away, and causing her to live an ungodly and profligate life, carrying her about from place to place, and obscuring her in secret places, to the displeasure of Almighty God, the utter ruin of the young lady, the evil example to others, offending against the king's peace, his crown and dignity'. Among the accomplices charged were Robert and Anne Charnock from Aldgate, David Jones and his wife Frances from St Martins-in-the-Fields, and Rebecca Jones, a widow. All of them were accused of 'falsely, unlawfully, unjustly, and wickedly, by unlawful and impure ways and means, conspiring, contriving, practicing, and intending the final ruin and destruction of the lady Henrietta Berkeley, then a virgin unmarried'.[27] The accused was charged with aiming 'to commit whoredom, fornication, and adultery to live with Lord Grey'.[28]

At this stage of the proceedings, an unnamed clergyman gave evidence of the close relationship between Grey and his servant Charnock. He testified that they were planning Harriet's abduction together. The clergyman had spoken to Charnock: 'I suppose Mr. Forrester [Lord Grey] and she are together, for that was the talk of the town.' Charnock answered, 'I do not doubt my lord Grey carried her away with a design to debauch her.'[29] Meanwhile, Grey gave evidence to the court, making his defence the ill-treatment of Henrietta by her family; 'My lady Harriet came to me one day, about six weeks or more ago, in the court-yard at St. John's and says to me, I am used like a dog, I live the life of a slave here, I can endure it no longer; by the eternal God that made me, I will not be alive long, unless I can set myself at liberty.'[30] He denied having enticed her away and told the court it was her own decision to leave.

The attorney general summed up the case; it 'is in the nature of ravishment of a ward, for it is for taking a young lady out of the tuition and custody of her father, who is her guardian by nature, and it is apparent in the proofs, she is highly criminal in this very matter herself, in consenting to go away in such a manner, and to such an evil purpose'.[31] Henrietta denied that Grey had anything to do with her running away or that any of the named accomplices had any hand in helping her, and stated that she had left of her own free will. Lord Chief Justice Francis Pemberton felt it his duty to condemn her actions: 'You have injured your own reputation, and prostituted your body and your honour, and are not to be believed.'[32]

The court and family tried to prevent Henrietta from speaking out or explaining why she had left, obviously thinking it would make matters worse if she made any more public declarations. As the jury began to disperse, the Lord Chief Justice ordered, 'My lord Berkeley must have his daughter again,' but Henrietta retorted, 'I will not go to my father again.' To prevent being taken by her father she stated that she had married Grey's servant, the advocate William Turner. Henrietta chose to go with her new 'husband', at which her father called out, 'Hussey, you shall go with me I say.' A scuffle ensued, with swords drawn on both sides. Henrietta was taken away with Turner and both were imprisoned for their own safety. The pair were released some time later. Although all the conspirators, except for Rebecca Jones, were found guilty, no judgement against them was ever entered as the matter was compromised when other events overtook them. Grey was found to be involved in the Rye House plot of 1683, an attempt to assassinate King Charles II and his brother James, Duke of York. He was arrested but escaped from prison. Stopping to pick up the now-pregnant Henrietta, they fled with Turner to the Netherlands. He was indicted for high treason in his absence, and the trio moved on to Cleves.

The course of Henrietta's life becomes unclear from then on, but it is evident that she returned to London at some point. Grey became involved in the Monmouth Rebellion in 1685 but was later pardoned by James II, becoming 1st Earl of Tankerville. He died in Tonbridge, Kent, in 1701, having left Henrietta a life annuity of £200. She died in London in 1706, leaving behind her £370 (about £63,000 today). Her affair with her brother-in-law became the inspiration for Aphra Behn's first prose fiction, *Love Letters between a Nobleman and His Sister*, the first part of which was published in 1684.

Scandals die hard, and publishers had a keen eye for muckraking. They were attuned to digging into past scandals and regurgitating them for their readers and the trial was to resurface when John Morphew published *The Trial of Ford Lord Grey of Werk*, by then over thirty years old, and advertised it the London's *Daily Courant* on Friday, 2 November 1716. Having been pipped to the post on this publication, Edmund Curll decided to turn it into verse and make a profit from it. An advertisement for a new publication, *Love-Letters between Lord Grey and Lady Berkeley, in Verse*, appeared, price one shilling and sixpence. In July 1719 Curll published *Ode Sacred to the Memory of . . . the Countess of Berkely*, price one shilling: this was written by Thomas Newcomb, a friend of Edward Young, a poet whom Curll had published in partnership with two other publishers, Bettesworth and Pemberton, some time earlier. The poem itself makes direct reference to Henrietta:

'Oh Berkely! tho'your spreading Fame
In distant Worlds had been approv'd.
We shall no more your Triumphs name
Nor where you sought, but how you loved.'[33]

At the front of the poem, Curll had included a letter of recommendation supposedly from Young which read, 'Mr Curll, I have perus'd the Poem which you receive with this, with much Pleasure, and I believe you will find your Advantage considerable in printing it.'

A public spat broke out between Curll and Young, as Young had given no such recommendation. He was so annoyed that he put an advert in the *London Evening Post* for 29 August denying authorship. Curll responded in the *Weekly Journal or Saturday's Post* for 31 August 1717, declaring:

> It having become Fashion of late, to let our private Affairs make a Part of the publick Occurrences, I am obliged in my own Defence, to apply to you in this manner with relation to a rude and false Advertisement inserted in the Evening –Post of Saturday last . . . you sent me a Poem inclosed in a Cover, under the Title An Ode sacred to the Memory of that Truly Pious and Honourable Lady, the Countess of Berkely.[34]

Unsurprisingly given the publicity, the Berkeley affair ran in various satires, such as *A Ballad to the Tune of Cheviot Chace; or, When as King Henry Ruled This Land* (1682):

Old cunning Berkeley's daughter Hen,
They say was once a maid,
But Foster [Lord Grey] told me it was gone
Before he backed the jade.

The story would again be regurgitated in *A Collection of State Trials* in 1735.[35]

Adultery and Divorce

> Our inclinations are not in our power, nor should either of us be held answerable to the other, because nature has not made us suitable to each other.
>
> Prince Regent to the Princess of Wales (future Queen Caroline), 1796[36]

Wives and husbands would seek out love affairs, separations or divorces depending on their circumstances. Whether through an acceptance of their lack of passion for each other, or through the adultery of one or other of the parties, both amiable and acrimonious partings were not unusual. For the upper classes divorce might be attainable through an expensive Act of Parliament, but sometimes it was preferable to remain married to keep the family finances intact. Couples might obtain either a separation or divorce as a result of 'criminal conversation' (adultery) under an Act of Parliament. The aim was to punish the seducers of married women.

Many couples recognized that there was no way they could continue their marriage and divorce was the only option, though it was exceptionally rare, except for the wealthy. Only 325 divorces were granted between 1670 and 1875, all but four of them obtained by men. In order to divorce, adultery had to be proven although it was also possible in cases of impotency or barrenness if couples were prepared to make such a private issue public. Generally, although a husband could obtain a divorce from a wife on the grounds of her adultery, for a woman to make a claim against her husband was nigh impossible. Only if her husband had committed adultery and offences such as incest, bigamy, bestiality, sodomy or greatly aggravated brutality would a divorce be considered for a wife. A husband retained all rights over his wife's property and the children and he even had a right to money she earned after the separation. However, a woman could sue in the church courts for separation from bed and board (*a mensa et thoro*), but without permission to remarry. More often than not, the answer for the poor was desertion and bigamy. Common-law divorce practices such as handing back the ring or jumping backwards over a broomstick needed the consent of both parties, and they were not recognized in law.[37] Wife sales, as seen in *The Mayor of Casterbridge*, were demeaning for women: a husband might place a halter around his wife's neck and sell her at auction to the highest bidder. Although women were obviously treated as property, these sales often worked to the woman's advantage, freeing them from unhappy marriages. Adulterers were brought before English ecclesiastical courts, or bawdy courts up until the mid-eighteenth century, but they were rarely sentenced to corporal punishment.

Divorce cases that came to trial excited public attention because they involved sordid details of the lives of the rich and famous. As such, they were a source of titillating material for publishers. They came out in popular chapbooks such as *Old Bailey Sessions Papers* and the *Ordinary of Newgate's Accounts* (revelations by the chaplain of the prison), as well in increasingly embellished accounts in magazines and newspapers. During the second half of the eighteenth century, the magazine *Bon Ton* was happy to expand on the scandalous affairs taking place between people married to others. This was part of the new form of tabloid journalism, in which celebrity gossip about sexual relationships was to become common.[38] If a man or a woman had any hope of obtaining a divorce, they had to catch their spouse in 'criminal conversation' with another partner. The magazine declared,

> We ape the vices of the Haut Ton; insomuch, that adultery, incontinence, and every species of lewdness, are to the full as common and as prevalent among the city dames and city beaux, as among the titled votaries of dissipation that breathe the fashionable air of Mary le Bone or St. James's.[39]

One case of a flailing marriage which was publicly explored even before it reached the divorce courts was that of Baron Hugh Percy (1742–1817), Lord Warkworth, son of the Duke of Northumberland, and his wife, Anne. Rumours had already hit the news and the pair were lampooned. *Town and Country* magazine for June 1772 pointed to the habit of masturbation at public schools such as Eton, which Percy had attended, suggesting that Percy himself succumbed to such vices: 'The hero of these pages [Percy] fell a martyr to these juvenile practices [masturbation]; for 'ere he had attained the age of manhood, he was almost debilitated from performing the offices of that state.' There was an ingrained public belief, buttressed by medical texts, that masturbation left you impotent and depleted. In effect, they were blaming Percy for not satisfying his wife. Thereafter Percy

After John Collet, *The Unfortunate Discovery*, 1777, mezzotint.

was supposedly introduced to sex at the most celebrated brothels in London by his peers: 'These rites were not without many baneful effects; and his institution, already impaired, could scarce stand the shock of these repeated attacks.'[40] Meanwhile, Lady Anne was forgiven any dalliances she might have had as she had not had her conjugal rights bestowed upon her, her husband incapable of administering her lawful wishes, 'and yet so debauched as to quit her arms for those of prostitution'.[41]

Baron Percy's bride, then Lady Anne Crichton-Stuart, was daughter of Lord Bute and married Percy when she was only seventeen in 1766; her bridegroom was 24. He was made an officer in the British Army at an early age and was later obliged to leave her for North America on duty with his regiment to fight in the American War of Independence. If we are to believe the gossip, they both realized their mistake fairly soon into the marriage, and no children were born to them: 'His lordship finding himself treated contemptuously at home, sought solace in the arms of mercenary beauties; and her ladyship being apprised of his infidelities, it is said retaliated the compliment.'[42] While he was abroad, she went down to Southampton for the season, renting a house, Ash Park, with her sister, Lady Augusta Corbet, and Augusta's child. The court opened with an attack on Lady Percy, accusing her of being 'a very loose woman, of a lustful and wicked disposition',[43] though the case involved only one man, William Bird of Trinity College, Cambridge.

The affair between Anne Percy and Bird took place both in Southampton and at a rented house at 19 Brompton Row, Kensington. Bird had apparently rented the whole house for three and a half guineas a week from 5 March for four weeks. The case came to the divorce courts on 27 May 1778 and, according to the prosecution, the pair

Isaac Cruikshank, *The Cuckold Departs for the Hunt*, 1800, pen and black ink with watercolour.

Young women putting antlers on heads of older men, indicating cuckoldry: unknown artist, *Fellow Sufferers*, 1799, etching.

'used to sit up alone together until two, three, four, or five o'clock in the morning, during which time they often had the carnal use and knowledge of each other's bodies, that they lay in the one and same bed together'.[44] Her sister condemned her and left with her child to return to London, but would not give evidence, as she died before the trial came up.

A few servants were already employed at the rented house in Kensington: James Jaquet, Sarah Reeks and another domestic, Mary Knight. Reeks deposed that she had entered the bedchamber of Lady Percy in order to dress her and found her and Bird 'both naked in bed' – admittedly though Bird had his shirt on and Lady Percy her shift, indicating that naked sex was not necessarily on the agenda for eighteenth-century couples, even adulterous ones. Bird immediately jumped up, snatched up his clothes and left the room. Lady Percy never left the house and had no visitors except Bird, 'who generally breakfasted, dined, supped, and lay there every night'.[45] Twenty-year-old Mary Knight deposed that Lady Percy went to London on March

1776 and had no visitors except Bird, 'who slept in the house every night, except two nights, three at the most'.[46] Bird also kept lodgings at 5 Bury Street, St James's, but seemed not to use them, for Knight reckoned he was nearly always with Lady Percy. Bird and Lady Percy had adjourning bedchambers, which gave them easy access to each other's rooms. Bird's bed seemed 'scarce rumpled', as if he had not slept in it, whereas 'Lady Percy's bed was sometimes extremely tumbled.'[47] With such a wealth of evidence from the servants, the divorce was granted.

Even the elite were prone to a bit of eavesdropping to pick up gossip. According to Bishop Burnet, Lord Rochester dressed a footman as a guardsman sentinel 'and kept him all the winter long every night at the doors of such ladies as he believed might be in intrigues'.[48] Affairs of the rich and noble were more likely to gain notoriety as their sexual indiscretions were exposed for all to hear. Cases of impotence or adultery were frequently divulged in periodicals such as the *Gentleman's Magazine* and *Bon Ton*, as well as satirized in poems. Servants and maids were often key witnesses, having observed household intrigues at close quarters. Unmade beds, semen stains on sheets and even direct observation of the sexual act while peeping through key-holes of parlour doors – all would be proof of adultery, and cartoons of these observations became popular in satirical prints. While marriage was often a financial arrangement for the rich, their divorces became titillating reading material for magazine readers.

While in certain Christian circles men as well as women were expected to adhere to rules about fidelity, in practice men were rarely penalized for having sex outside marriage as severely as women were. The consequences for libertine women were also worse, as they were in an economically inferior position to men of the same status. No wonder Lady Mary Wortley Montagu grew incensed with such ridiculous double standards of morality, asking in one of her poems, 'Could'st thou submit to wear the Marriage-Chain?'

12
Royal Mistresses

> Heavens . . . to have Perdita in my arms, undrest, all loose and languishing, fit for the mighty business of love, and then lie a tame cold fighter only, as if the appointment had been given but to hear me prattle, see me gaze at her, or tell her what pretty sight it was to see the moon shine through her dancing boughs – O damn my hardened dullness.
>
> ANON., *Memoirs of Perdita* (1784)[1]

The palaces of Kensington, Buckingham, St James's, Clarence House, Hampton Court, Eltham and Lambeth were places of royal discussions and political debates, but also of intrigue. Elite men and women vied to be invited into the inner circle of the court and spread scandals during networking as a means of jockeying for position. This was where the best gossip in London emerged; the most engaging was rumours of the sexual affairs of monarchs and the royal family. There was plenty of fodder to be had, as most of the kings and princes had mistresses at some point or another, and even queens took lovers. Royal mistresses were likely to be targeted by the press – if not the most maligned, they were perhaps the most satirized. Among favourite targets for a monarch's wandering eye were actresses, courtesans and titled ladies, with many royal mistresses bearing illegitimate sons. Not all these liaisons were without troubles.

One of the most problematic affairs was that of Prince Charles (subsequently King Charles II) with Lucy Walter (*c.* 1630–1658). She and Charles were only eighteen when they met and formed a relationship which lasted for about a year over 1648–9. Lucy remained with Charles until September 1649. For safety, he had left England for

Holland after his father was beheaded, moving on to Jersey and France. John Evelyn recalled seeing her in August 1649 in France: 'I went to St. Germains [Saint-Germain-en-Laye], to kiss his Majesty's hand; in the coach, which was my Lord Wilmot's, went Mrs. Barlow [Lucy Walter], the King's mistress and mother to the Duke of Monmouth, a brown, beautiful, bold, but insipid creature.'[2] Even James II conceded that she was very handsome, and though of little wit, had some cunning. Her astuteness was to display itself in her later wrangles with Charles. Although short-lived, her union with him produced a son, James (born on 9 April 1649) who was to become Walter's bargaining tool; this presented Charles with various challenges after they had separated, though he recognized the child as his own and would create him Duke of Monmouth in 1663.

Once Charles returned to exile in the Netherlands in 1652, he considered the relationship over, but Lucy refused to accept this. In reaction, over the next four years, she chose to create various scandalous scenes, so much so that in 1656 she was given some money and a pearl necklace and shipped back to England with her children. In order to muzzle her, she was placed in the Tower as a spy, where she tried to use her young son as leverage against Charles and his advisers. Charles

After Samuel Cooper, *Lucy Barlow alias Walter*, 1802, engraving.

Simon Pietersz Verelst, *Nell Gwyn*, 17th century, oil on canvas.

wanted his son James to be with him, and after a kidnap attempt on the boy which resulted in a public fiasco, Lucy was persuaded in March 1658 to give him up to a tutor. By then she had contracted venereal disease, and after making a general confession to John Cosin (later Bishop of Durham), she died in Paris towards the end of 1658 at the age of 28 and was buried there. Lucy not only swore that a marriage to Charles had taken place but entrusted Cosin with documentary proof, which was kept in a 'black box' containing evidence that would supposedly have legitimized the Duke of Monmouth. The question of whether Charles had gone through a legitimate marriage with Lucy or not became an important matter as it would have made the Duke of Monmouth legal heir to the throne. Cosin's death in 1671 left no direct witnesses; when later the enemies of James, Duke of York, resurrected the Cosin story, there was another fruitless search for the black box. No supporting evidence was found. The political nation remained unconvinced of Monmouth's legitimacy, although in 1679, Charles went to the length of addressing the privy council to formally deny that he had ever married Lucy Walter. This became a central issue thirty years later during the exclusion crisis of 1679–82, and later in 1685 when Monmouth led a rebellion against James II. Three exclusion bills were proposed, intended to bar the king's brother from accession to the throne on the grounds that he was a Catholic, but none became law. Two polemic articles by Robert Ferguson were published in 1680 that resurrected rumours of the black box, but it was never uncovered.

After the Restoration in 1660, once Charles II was on the throne, he reopened the previously banned theatres and women were allowed to enter the profession for the first time. Comedies became popular and it was at the theatre in Lincoln's Inn Fields one night in April 1668, watching George Etherege's *She Wou'd if She Cou'd*, that Charles espied Nell Gwyn, who was sitting in the box next to him. Soon afterwards, their affair began.

Nell's background hardly gave her any reason to believe she would rise to a position of power as the king's mistress. She had begun life on 2 February 1650 as Eleanor Gwyn, the illegitimate daughter of an apple-seller, and had hardly known her father since, according to one satire, he died in a debtors' prison. In defence of his worthiness, Nell's older sister, Rose, declared that their father was a gentleman who did faithful service for Charles I and 'lost all he had in service of the late king'.[3] After her husband's death, Nell's mother returned to the place of her youth and opened a brothel in Covent Garden. Consequently, Nell's childhood was spent in that area of London, working in various lowly jobs including as a street hawker of herring, oysters, turnips and oranges. When she was around fourteen, Thomas Killigrew, then manager of the King's Company, spotted her potential and she was taken under the wing of two of Killigrew's finest actors, John Lacy and Charles Hart, who began training her up as an actress. Hart was to become her lover and her mentor and gave her the financial and emotional security she needed, as well as encouragement in her theatrical career.

Poet and playwright John Dryden described Nell as having an oval face, hazel eyes and bronze hair streaked with gold; she was evidently attractive, as Pepys called her 'pretty, witty Nell'. By 1664 she was taking small parts in short productions, up to fifty a year, and became a probationary member of Killigrew's acting troupe. Two years later she was starring in plays, shining best in comedies. She became mistress to Charles Sackville, Lord Buckhurst, with the promise of an annuity of £100 a year, but this would not last. Instead, the Duke of Buckingham suggested her as a new mistress for the king, and according to diarist Samuel Pepys, 'the King did send several times for Nelly.'[4] Pepys had seen Nell on stage on a visit to the theatre on 8 December 1666 and observed her develop both her comic and tragic roles. He liked her in the former but was less impressed with the latter; 'Nell's ... mad parts are most excellently done ... which makes it a miracle to me to think how ill she do any serious part ... just like a fool or changeling; and in a mad part doth beyond imitation almost.'[5] Pepys saw her again in 1667 on 1 May hanging about outside Drury Lane at her lodgings; 'in her smock sleeves and bodice ... she seemed a mighty pretty creature.'[6] He found her performances less inspiring when he wrote in his diary for 22 August 1667 that although he was pleased to see her, he 'was most infinitely displeased with her being put to act the Emperor's daughter; which is a great and serious part, which she do most basely'.[7] By 1669 Nell was King Charles's mistress, bearing him a son in May 1670. She returned briefly to the stage for a couple of months, after which the king gave her a house in Pall Mall and made her an allowance.

Though Nell returned to the stage in Dryden's *The Conquest of Granada* for a few months in 1670, after that performance she left the theatre for good. She gave birth to a second son, James, on 25 December 1671. King Charles provided her with a pension of £4,000 a year in 1674, rising to £5,000 in 1676, as well as various income from properties. To ensure her children's protection, she fought to obtain titles for them, gaining the title Earl of Burford for Charles; he was later to become Duke of St Albans. By the time of the death of King Charles on 6 February 1685, Nell was deeply in debt to tradesmen. Fortunately, on the urging of his dying brother to 'Let not poor Nelly starve,' King James II paid off her debts, providing her with a pension of £1,500 a year. She died of 'apoplexy' on 14 November 1687.

Perdita: Paramour to a Prince

Another monarch to compete for the title of royal mistress-keeper was the future King George IV (1762–1830). From his youth, the Prince of Wales was a womanizer and a profligate spender. His father, King George III, had tried to control his excesses when the prince was younger, but had not been successful. Sadly, the king became plagued with mental illness (more recently this has been diagnosed as possible bouts of porphyria)[8] as a consequence of which his son was made regent on 5 February 1811. Even before he became regent, the prince's affairs had become notorious, most notably with actresses Mary Robinson and Elizabeth Armistead. Later scandals erupted over his clandestine marriage to widower Maria Fitzherbert and his affairs with titled women including Lady Jersey, Lady Hertford, Lady Quentin and Lady Conyngham.

One of the first amorous encounters for the seventeen-year-old prince was at the theatre, where he became smitten with stage actress Mary Robinson née Darby (1757–1800). Born in Bristol, the daughter of a prosperous sea merchant, she was to become both a successful actress and author, if always better known for her role as mistress to the king. Her family had moved to London while she was still at school. Her father lost everything in a business venture in America and when he finally returned to England, it was with a mistress and young boy in tow. After a meeting in London with his wife, he ordered her to lodge with a clergyman's family and send Mary and her brother George to boarding school, while he returned to America. Inevitably, as his interest in his family waned, the money he sent his wife for the children's keep dried up too. Luckily, Mary's mother was an astute woman and managed to keep the family finances flowing. She had opened up a school at 5 Park Walk and the well-educated Mary was able to assist her mother there. This was to stand her in good stead in testing times later in her life when she turned to a literary career. She recalled, 'Assistants of every kind were engaged, and I was deemed worthy of an occupation that flattered my self-love, and impressed my mind with a sort of domestic consequence.'[9]

Meanwhile, in 1772 or early 1773 she met her future husband, Thomas Robinson (*fl.* 1750–1802), who claimed to be the nephew of a wealthy Welsh tailor, Thomas Harris, but in reality was his illegitimate son. Although Mary did not love him, her mother persuaded

Thomas Gainsborough, *Mrs Mary Robinson (Perdita)*, 1781, oil on canvas.

her to consider marrying him as their finances were so precarious. Her potential groom had a job as an articled clerk, appeared to be financially secure and so seemed a safe marital bet. It was only after the couple married at St Martin-in-the-Fields, Westminster, on 12 April 1773 that warning bells started ringing: Thomas ordered that the marriage should be kept secret until he received the approval of his 'uncle'. In order to keep up appearances, he insisted they kept separate households, with Mary and her mother moving into a house in Great Queen Street, Lincoln's Inn Fields, and Thomas staying at his employers' residence. Once they had been on a trip to Wales to visit his 'uncle' and revealed their marriage, the couple moved into their new home at 13 Hatton Garden.

Once back in London, Mrs Robinson began to make an impression on those around her. On her initial trip out on the town, according to her own memoirs, everyone was staring at her: 'The first time I went to Ranelagh, my habit was so singularly plain and quaker-like, that all eyes were fixed upon me.' Her hair was left unpowdered, her body without jewellery. It seems she was well aware of the fashion of the day and how to dress in order to make the most impact: 'A new face, a young person dressed with peculiar but simple elegance, was sure to attract attention at the places of public entertainment.'[10] After this she visited the Pantheon and made a similar splash wearing a simple pink satin dress trimmed with sable, amid the large hoops and feathers all the other women were wearing. Men were beginning to follow her around in order to make her acquaintance: Lord Northington, Lord Lyttleton and Captain Ayscough fluttered after her, despite her husband being in attendance. All three men called on her the next morning while her husband was out – newly married and pregnant, she was hardly conquest material, but here she was with three men fawning over her.

By now the Robinsons were frequenting all the fashionable places in the city, with some of the most eminent men in London now openly courting her. George Robert Fitzgerald declared himself to be her 'most ardent and devoted admirer' while lamenting her destiny in being wedded to a man who was incapable of fully appreciating her. Her husband was growing indolent, already ignoring her and having affairs of his own. Lord Lyttleton took it upon himself to tell her about her husband's infidelity; 'I must inform you that your husband is the most false and undeserving of that name! He has formed a connection with a woman of abandoned character; he lavishes on her those means of subsistence which you will shortly stand in need of.'[11] His declaration was no doubt to advance his own standing in her eyes, but she abhorred him. However, the evidence of her husband's infidelity was her licence to go ahead and forge her own destiny. She could now see that Thomas was louche and a loser, and the debts he had accumulated were growing with the birth of their first child. His creditors finally caught up with him and he was thrown into the Fleet prison on 3 May 1775. Still loyal at this point, Mary accompanied him to prison, meaning to pay off their creditors with the proceeds of her *Poems by Mrs Robinson*, but it sold badly. Despite this, her poems gained her a patron in Georgiana Cavendish, Duchess of Devonshire, who invited her to Devonshire House. Mary had been smart enough to send them to the duchess with this very intention. After nearly ten months of incarceration, Thomas was released and the couple took a house in Old Bond Street, and later in Newman Street, Marylebone. It was at this stage that Mary decided to take to the stage.

Mary had already met David Garrick when she was fourteen years old, having been introduced to him through a friend of her mother's. He had summoned her to visit him at the house he shared with his wife in Adelphi Terrace and had been captivated by Mary's youthful charm and beauty. By now a well-known and successful theatre producer and actor, he had promised to take her under his wing and train her as an actress but, under pressure from her husband-to-be and her mother, she had backed out of the agreement when she married. Now wanting to retrace her steps and enter the theatrical profession, she approached Garrick, who was gracious enough to give her a second chance. She debuted as Juliet at the Drury Lane Theatre on 10 December 1776 to much critical acclaim: 'Her person is genteel,' noted the *Morning Post*, 'her voice harmonious, and admitting of various modulations;– and her features, when properly animated, are striking, and expressive.'[12] She went on to play various parts including Shakespeare's Ophelia and Lady Macbeth, Araminta in Congreve's *The Old Bachelor*, Emily in Hannah Cowley's *The Runaway* and Octavia in Dryden's *All for Love*. While she could play drama, she was better in comedy roles. New parts for the 1778–9 season included Lady Plume in Richard Brinsley Sheridan's *The Camp*, Palmira in James Miller's *Mahomet*, Miss Richly in Frances Sheridan's *The Discovery* and Fidelia in William Wycherley's *The Plain Dealer*. Garrick was delighted with her and organized rehearsals for her at Drury Lane, arranging for her to play Cordelia to his King Lear for a benefit night on her behalf on 14 April 1779.[13] This meant at least she would get the takings for that evening's performance.

During the late autumn, Mary was having an affair with Sir John Lade, a sporting baronet. Though still in an unhappy marriage, the family had moved into a house rented from Mrs Isabella Mattocks, an actress at Covent Garden Theatre. The building was conveniently situated between the Hummums (public baths) and the Bedford Arms in Covent Garden near to where she was working. Her new parts were Viola in *Twelfth Night*, Perdita in *The Winter's Tale*, Rosalind in *As You Like It*, Oriana in Farquhar's *The Inconstant*, Mrs Brady in Garrick's *The Irish Widow* and the original Eliza Campley in Lady Craven's cross-dressing comedy *The Miniature Picture*. 'My popularity increasing every night that I appeared, my prospects, both fame and affluence began to brighten.'[14] Various propositions from titled men were coming her way, including from the Duke of Rutland, who offered an annuity of £600 a year to become his mistress. While she had made an impact on both libertines and the theatregoing public, it was the affair with the prince in 1779 that sent her notoriety stratospheric. It was around this time that her private life was increasingly made public.

Her nickname, Perdita, came from the part she played in *Florizel and Perdita*, Garrick's adaption of *The Winter's Tale*, when it was staged on 3 December 1779. A fellow actor commented, 'By Jove, Mrs Robinson, you will make a conquest of the prince tonight; for tonight you look handsomer than ever.'[15] Indeed, this was to be the night which would change her fortunes and she recalled her emotions in her memoirs: 'I hurried through the first scene, not without much embarrassment, owing to the fixed attention with which the Prince of Wales honoured me.'[16] She overheard him making flattering remarks about her from the royal box.

Viscount George Capel Malden, later 5th Earl of Essex (1757–1839), acted as a messenger and intermediary for the prince. Within two days of the prince watching her performance, he carried a note to her house. In reference to the part she performed in the play, the prince addressed her as 'Perdita' and signed himself 'Florizel'. He continued to write to her over the coming months and sent her a miniature painting of himself, which she wore pinned to her chest from then onwards. When she finally agreed to meet him, it was hard to decide on a private location. She recalled,

> At length an evening was fixed for this long dreaded interview . . . We [she was with Malden] waited the signal for crossing the river in a boat which had been engaged for the purpose. Heaven can witness how many conflicts my agitated heart endured at this most important moment! I admired the Prince; I felt grateful for his affection. He was the most engaging of created beings![17]

Only a few words 'of the most affectionate nature uttered by the Prince' were exchanged, but she was obviously flattered and enamoured with him. 'The graces of his person, the irresistible sweetness of his smile, the tenderness of his melodious yet manly voice, will be remembered by me till every vision of this changing scene shall be forgotten.'[18]

Although Mary was still living with her husband at the time, both of them had embarked on separate love affairs. By this time, Malden had fallen in love with her, and rumour had it that she was already having an affair with him before she began visits to the prince. By now, the public was well aware of the flirtation going on between Mary and the prince and the gossip columns were full of the couple's outings. She lamented, 'The daily prints now indulge the malice of my enemies by the most scandalous paragraphs respecting the Prince of Wales and myself. I found it was too late to stop the hourly augmenting torrent of abuse that poured upon me from all quarters.'[19] Even going shopping or to Ranelagh became troublesome as curious crowds gathered to stop and stare.

Wanting to remove her from the gaze of the public, the prince urged her to give up the stage and promised to set her up in her own establishment together with a bond for £20,000, payable when he came of age, as he was still only seventeen. She held out for nearly six months, but she knew the time had come where she would have to relinquish herself. Again, where to meet privately was an issue. Malden suggested his own residence in Dean Street, Mayfair, but this was too difficult as the prince's tutor kept too close a watch on his pupil; a visit to Buckingham Palace was then mentioned, but Mary objected as it was 'too rash'. They finally compromised on an encounter next to the royal household at Kew on the banks of the river Thames, where the prince and his brother Frederick, Duke of York, had their own apartments. The affair took place in a series of meetings at Kew and at the inn on Eel Pie Island across the Thames between June and

July 1780. On a visit to former actress and courtesan Sophia Baddeley, Mary recounted how the prince 'loved her, to the greatest degree' and related how they managed to arrange their secret rendezvous; 'Many a time had the poor dear boy got out of his bed when he was at Kew, and come to me in the middle of the night, at the inn, at Kew-bridge.' Baddeley had fallen on hard times and seeing her in this impoverished state should have alerted Robinson to her own possible penniless future. For now, in her excitement, all she could think about were her secret assignations with the prince. Apparently, his parents were so attentive to their children that they made a point of calling in on them every night when they had gone to bed. This made the rendezvous even more problematic. Mary told Baddeley, 'the dear prince got up after this, dressed himself, and with the assistance of his brother, the Duke of York, climbed over the garden-wall, after midnight, and come to me; staid some hours, and returned over the wall again, before daylight.'[20] Only his brother knew about their meetings.

Though Sheridan had kept a close watch on Mary's career and had helped develop her as an actress, there is no evidence they had an affair. When she decided to give up the stage and take up the prince's offer of an annuity, Sheridan offered 'a considerable advance to her salary' to try and persuade her to continue performing – she declined and made her last performance at Drury Lane Theatre on 31 May 1780. It is hard to understand why she would have made such a move; though the prince had asked her to give up the stage, he had only professed that it hurt his dignity to see her earning a living on the stage, not given her an ultimatum. He was so enamoured with her that he would have done anything to get at her body, so she could have refused. Her stage career would have been an aphrodisiac for many men who would have been happy to see her beauty and talent shining through her performances and watch their mistress being publicly appreciated while claiming her in private for themselves. But the prince was still only a boy, not yet eighteen years old, no doubt wanting her for himself as his plaything. Though she was still only 22, she must have known, as any woman in her position would have, that such an affair would not last. To give up her career and independence at this stage was madness.

The prince set her up in a fashionable house in Cork Street and she set about furnishing it with paintings and expensive items. Lavish dinner parties ensued with a constant round of entertainment, attending the theatre, concerts and the opera. As a leader of fashion, she was now more famous than ever before. While she received some attacks in the newspapers, others came to her defence: the *Gazetteer and New Daily Advertiser* for Friday, 21 July 1780, declared, 'Mrs Robinson has quitted the stage since the close of last season, is now become a private character; the envy of the world cannot reach her in her present situation; therefore the illiberal attacks made on her will prove altogether useless and unsuccessful.'[21]

After only a matter of months, with no warning, a letter arrived from the prince telling Mary that 'we must meet no more.' Only days before he had professed his affection for her.[22] Unable to comprehend his sudden coolness to her, she wrote to him asking what had happened, but received no reply. She only began to understand when she bumped into her rival Elizabeth Armistead and realized the prince's attention had wandered. It was evident he had taken up with her and by December 1780 had also fallen for Mrs Grace Dalrymple Elliott.[23] Left with no husband, no lover and no job, Mary's debt was increasing rapidly and, with her lavish expenditure, now amounted to £7,000. Quick to see her flailing position, she realized that the only hope of extracting some money from the prince hung on blackmail – money in exchange for the love letters he had sent her early on in their courtship. Her warning was placed in newspapers such as the *Morning Herald*: 'A certain amour is now totally at an end; and a separation has taken place *a thoro* for more than three weeks, and a settlement worthy of such as sultana is the only thing now wanting to break off all intercourse whatever.'[24] A war broke out between her and the prince and the entanglement dragged on for months.

With her estrangement of the prince, Mary was beside herself with worry, her debts mounting daily. She increasingly turned to Malden, though she claimed he was 'even poorer than myself'.[25] She was now more reliant on him than ever, especially in his role as her spokesperson to the prince. Discussions about a financial settlement continued unabated. Intermediaries were running back and forth trying to come to some compromise, the prince using his treasurer, Colonel Hotham, as his representative. The first offer from the prince was a one-off payment of £5,000 for the return of the letters, but this was little compensation for the annuity he had promised, or the career she had given up. By now it would not even cover her debts. Eventually Mary was worn down and accepted the £5,000 in exchange for the love letters from the prince – but she still held his signed bond for £20,000.

All sorts of satires and parodies were made about her, and famous artists were quick to make her the subject of their paintings. In a way of offsetting any bad publicity, she sat for several portraits by George Romney, one of which was sold as prints, and then for Gainsborough, probably a mutually beneficial publicity deal. Sir Joshua Reynolds and John Hoppner made portraits of her: her name and face were everywhere. Lover after lover followed. While on a trip to Paris, she was courted by the Duc de Chartres and had an affair with the Duc de Lauzun. On her return to London, her social life was hectic and she once again set the trends among the fashionable set. Now living in a house on Berkeley Square, she rode out in her painted carriage dressed in top-quality silks and brocades and accompanied by liveried servants. Romney's portrait was exhibited in the British Academy in April 1782, again making her the centre of public attention. Her affair with Charles Fox became the subject of much gossip and they remained on good terms after they parted – he would be responsible for finally acquiring an annuity of £500 for her from the prince in 1783. She could now see a comfortable future for herself. Lord Malden had made a settlement upon her and provided her with a house in Piccadilly as well as a a horse and carriage 'ornamented with French mantle: her cypher in a wreath of flowers; the seat cloths crimson, richly ornamented with silver fringe'.[26] Colonel Banastre Tarleton was next on the scene; although he was in massive debt, this affair was a love match that would last for the next sixteen years.

Mary's life of luxury and extravagance was called to a sudden end at the age of 26 when she suffered a massive blow to her health in the summer of 1783. Her memoirs related that 'she was attacked by a malady', supposedly due to exposure to the night air while travelling; a fever followed which confined her to bed for the next six months, a result of 'a violent rheumatism, which progressively deprived her of the use of her limbs'.[27] Subsequent complications with a miscarriage left her paralysed from the waist down. Cruel caricatures emerged, such as 'Perdita on Her Last Legs' (1784), an anonymous etching in which Perdita, with crippled legs, begs from the prince. With her stage career over, her writing flourished, and she wrote six novels, two plays, an autobiography and various essays and poems. Through her literary career, she networked with other writers and came to know Mary Wollstonecraft and became friends with Samuel Coleridge. Although she was recognized for her writing, it was her connection with royalty

'Perdita on Her Last Legs', illustration from *Rambler's Magazine*, 1 September 1784.

that lingered rather than any real appreciation by the public for her as an author.

As usual in these affairs, scurrilous fake memoirs were published in London in 1784, the same year as her own memoirs came out, the latter edited by her daughter. The former version told of her poise: 'You, who doubtless have seen her person, know that her deportment is elegant, and to sprightliness of wit, she joins a share of levity, that attracts, rather than disgusts, because it is not carried to the excess that constitutes the effectation of wantonness.'[28] While some appreciation of her was given, these 'memoirs' were obviously meant to be titillating, filled with sexual innuendoes and suggestions of her flightiness. Tales of her early amours were explored, her first with a sailor whom her father had brought home. An apparent sexual assault took place: 'Her lover took courage, and made a feint to push her on the bed as they passed by the side of it:– She have a gentle shriek, – he let her go, throwing himself upon it.'[29] The memoirs graciously said of her acting, 'If she was not remarkably excellent as an actress, she was at least so happy as never to be remarkably deficient, in any part she attempted; she seldom played without applause.'[30]

These racy memoirs were an obvious bid by the unscrupulous writer and publisher to usurp Mary's own memoirs and cash in on her fame. They did, however, relate tantalizing glimpses of her soirées:

> Her treats, or petits soupers, on these occasions were everything that was voluptuous: the entertainment was elegant; and during the repast, lively conversation and wanton attitudes were constantly practised, to inflame to the height of passion which, of all others is the most difficult to be suppressed; though by gentle repulses the moment of possession was continually procrastinated.

Her skills at flirtation were supposedly without parallel:

> The vivacity of her imagination suggested a thousand stratagems for raising amorous desire, and when disposed to yield the *last favour*, she suddenly retreated to her bed-chamber (which was previously illuminated) hung round with paintings executed with masterly skill, and calculated to suggest ideas of various modes to indulge concupiscence.[31]

Despite her disability, Robinson developed a talent for reinventing herself as needs dictated. The celebrity she had described as a 'national absurdity' gradually deteriorated as she lost her clout as fashion icon and socialite. In order to earn a living she redirected her skills to writing plays, pamphlets and several novels as well as poems for *The Oracle* (1790–93) and the *Morning Post* (1797–1800). Her collection of poems was brought out by subscription in 1791 and sold well, her second collection less so. Her feminist novels included the popular *Vancenza; or, The Dangers of Credulity* (1792), but she recognized that it 'owed its popularity to the celebrity of the author's name'.[32] This was followed by *Hubert de Severac: A Romance of the Eighteenth Century* (1796), *Angelina* (1796) and *Walsingham; or, The Pupil of Nature* (1797). More significantly, she published a feminist tract in 1799 under the pen-name Anne Frances Randall, *A Letter to the Women of England, on the Injustice of Mental Subordination*, later republished under her own name as *Thoughts on the Condition of Women, and the Injustice of*

Mental Subordination. Her last months were filled with ill health and increasing debt until she succumbed to 'dropsy in the chest', dying on 26 December 1800.[33]

Like so many other women who went before and came after her, her literary outpourings were overshadowed by her sexual affairs with royalty and members of the elite. Having placed herself under the protection of various men, she died leaving little behind, as her memoirs reported: 'A few trifling memorials as tributes of her affection, were all the property she had to bequeath: she also earnestly desired that a part of her hair might be sent to two particular persons.'[34] There was no mention of who these might be. However, she gave instructions that she was to be buried in Old Windsor churchyard, indicating she had not lost her connection to the prince. If she did leave him her hair, it is doubtful he would have treasured it; it is more likely that he would have merely cast it aside, as he did most of his mistresses.

Two Royal Marriages

Any restrictions on the prince's lubricious behaviour disappeared once his father became so mentally ill that he was deemed unfit to rule and his son was raised to Prince Regent to rule on his behalf in 1811. According to Maria Anne Fitzherbert (1756–1837), she was out in her carriage with her husband sometime around 1780 near Corney House in Chiswick when the prince pulled up his carriage to look at her. Only after a chance meeting outside the opera house in March 1784 did he begin his ardent pursuit. She was a Catholic and unwilling to have an affair; since, by then, her husband had died, he agreed to marry her. On her initial refusal of his proposal and learning she was to travel abroad, such was his passion, George threatened to end his own life by stabbing himself while in Carlton House. Concerned for his safety and state of mind, Mrs Fitzherbert agreed to marry him in her drawing room in Park Street on the evening of 15 December 1785. Though supposedly secret, Horace Walpole reported that 'all ranks' talked of the affair in February 1786.[35] The actress Sarah Siddons thought Mrs Fitzherbert a 'very ambitious and clever woman', and indeed she acquired a house from the prince in Pall Mall, near Carlton House. However, the marriage was invalid under the Royal Marriages Act of 1772, which prevented royal marriages to Catholics.[36] Whether Fitzherbert can technically be called a mistress is unimportant. The contrast of his feelings for

George IV's marriage to Maria Fitzherbert: James Gillray, *Wife & No Wife; or, A Trip to the Continent*, 1788, hand-coloured etching.

her and later, his 'official' wife Queen Caroline, would show up the extremes of the likes and dislikes of George.

Various other lovers ensued. In spring 1794 he fell for Frances Villiers, Countess of Jersey (1753–1821), who persuaded him to marry his cousin, Caroline of Brunswick, but his adoration of Mrs Fitzherbert persisted. Frightened he might die, he wrote a will at the beginning of 1796 making Mrs Fitzherbert sole beneficiary, disregarding Lady Jersey and Caroline and calling them '*base, vile & scandalous wretches*'.[37] Fitzherbert had left him but returned to him in 1800 when the Vatican declared her his real true wife, whereupon they spent the next six years in happy contentment. Again the prince's eye roved and he began an affair with Lady Hertford, treating Mrs Fitzherbert badly until she finally left him in 1811, albeit with a handsome annuity.

In between his affairs with Fitzherbert, duty demanded George IV marry Princess Caroline, to whom he took an instant dislike. On seeing her for the first time, such was his unfavourable reaction to her that he commented, 'Harris, I am not well, fetch me a brandy.' For her part, Caroline reckoned that George was 'very fat and nothing like as handsome as his portrait'.[38] By the time of his marriage in 1795, his father King George III had been declared mad and the prince was showing himself to be a complete wastrel. He was a debt-ridden, 33-year-old king in waiting, only marrying so Parliament would increase his allowance. Only days later, a scandal erupted as his new affair with Lady Elizabeth Conyngham emerged. The public was unhappy about his reaction to Caroline and the press took her side. It seems that Caroline was no slouch herself when it came to taking lovers. She had found herself an Italian and was said to be living with him in a villa by the sea in 1815. George was made king in 1820 and sued for divorce on the grounds of adultery, providing a public trial resulting in a settlement for Caroline of £50,000. His cruelty contributed to her demise when she was refused entry to Westminster Abbey at her husband's coronation ceremony on 19 July 1821. Dejected, the 53-year-old Caroline overdosed on laudanum and died on 7 August.

Two Affable Affairs: Ladies Elizabeth Conyngham and Georgiana Quentin

On his 59th birthday, 12 August 1821, the king arrived in Howth full of goose pie and Irish whiskey. After attending various public affairs, he took a four-night stay with his new mistress at Slane Castle, within the Boyne Valley of County Meath, Ireland. The castle was the seat of the Conyngham family, and Lady Conyngham (1769–1861) was set to become his mistress for years to come. By now, the king was looking towards the wives of his own courtiers as depositories for his passions. Such favouritism often created havoc in court circles, with jealousies and maliciousness coagulating in spiteful gossip. It was inevitable therefore that once Conyngham had become lover to the king, she would become a target, accused of having too much influence over him. Her detractors condemned the affair and suggested this was the only reason for her husband's promotion to his elevated position of marquess in 1816. As with other mistresses to the king, satires, cartoons, pastiches and bawdy poems came out to pillory her.

Lady Conyngham came from a wealthy background. She was born Elizabeth Denison in London on 31 July 1769 to Elizabeth née Butler and her husband Joseph Denison, a successful London business man and banker. She was the eldest of three children and was followed by a sister, Ann Maria, and a brother, William. The family was affluent enough for her to be considered marriage material for titled men and just before her 25th birthday she was married to an Irish peer, Viscount Henry Conyngham (1766–1832). Upon his father's death, he became 3rd Baron Conyngham, going on to raise the Londonderry regiment and becoming lieutenant-colonel in 1794. She became known for her sexual philandering. Before her affair with the king, she had had affairs with both John Ponsonby and Nicholas, the future Tsar of Russia.

As seen in his obsession with Fitzherbert, George liked his women plump and Conyngham was no exception. Her affair with the prince probably began around 1819, when she took over as royal mistress from Lady Hertford. The Conynghams attended Carlton House soirées and private parties at the king's secluded cottage at Windsor, with the king displaying his affection for her quite openly. Her increasing influence with the king concerned the Tories, as did his public displays of affection for her. Having hired a private box for herself at Westminster Hall for the king's coronation, she set about organizing the pages to carry his 27-foot train, all of whom were chosen from the Whig opposition. She was obviously now holding some political clout. During the coronation, observers noted that the king was constantly looking at Conyngham, winking and nodding at her. Worse still, at the most solemn part of the service, he took off his diamond brooch, looked at her and kissed it; she took off her glove and kissed a ring on her finger. Any observer would believe they were plighting their troth in public.

Lady Conyngham moved into the Brighton Pavilion, along with her husband and their children. Diarist Charles Greville noted, 'All the members of the family are continually there,' reporting that the king had said to Lady Conyngham, 'You cannot please me so much as by doing everything that you please here, everything to show that you are Mistress here.'[39] When not in London or Brighton, Lady Conyngham and the king spent their days at the Royal Lodge in Windsor, along with her family.

Her relationship with the king would last until his death in 1830. A titillating book was published about the affair, bringing it to the attention of the wider public. One clue to the real identity of the subject of *The Memoirs of the Celebrated Lady C*****m* (1820) is the picture of the Marchioness of Conyngham in the book.[40] A further clue rests

Lady Conyngham sitting on a stool with her hand on a crown: William Heath, *The Lady of the House*, 1829, hand-coloured etching.

in the name of 'Cunningham' mentioned in the quotation in the frontispiece, leaving the reader in no doubt as to whom the memoirs are referring. The 'memoirs' are, as usual, a highly fictionalized account, peppered with well-known names much in the news at the time. As was usual with aristocratic scandals, satires emerged, with cartoonists such as George Cruickshank and William Heath mocking the older plump couple together. The cuckolded Lord Conyngham was also a target but apparently did not care. One eight-page pamphlet, *Secrets of the Castle!!! The Life of the Marchioness of C_y_n_h_m*, carries a frontispiece depicting Lord and Lady Conyngham, the latter in tears, crying 'oh where, and oh where is my darling Georgy gone?' George plied her husband with various posts and titles, which no doubt helped bind the relationships of all three involved. Because of the Conynghams' royal affiliations, all of their children would make royal marriages. On his death, as proof of his dedication, the king left all his plate and jewels to her in his will, although she later returned much of it to the king's executors. She outlived all but one of her children, dying at the ripe old age of 91 on 11 October 1861.

Though Lady Conyngham would remain in George's affections until he died, he was not averse to adoring other women at the same time. Little is known about Mrs Georgiana Quentin (1783–1853), who allegedly became mistress to George IV, but she evidently caused a stir. Their affair came to the attention of the public in a salacious satire, *Memoirs of the Life of the Celebrated Mrs Q* (1822),[41] which related that Mrs Q moved into lodgings in St James's (an area known for its brothels) and became 'a professed spanker'.[42] Sensational fabrications such as these were usual in these booklets; in reality, she was a member of the nobility. Her father, James Lawrell, married her mother, Catherine Holme Sumner, in 1776, and owned Eastwick Park in Surrey until it was sold in 1809. Georgiana was their youngest daughter and most likely lived there with her parents until she moved to London with her sister in 1801. She married Lieutenant-Colonel George Augustus Quentin of the 10th Light Dragoons in 1811, and their wedding was announced in *The Times*.[43] He was called to a court martial in 1814, but it was dismissed after it became evident the charges had been trumped up by officers in his regiment. In fact, her husband was one of George IV's favourites.

Quentin was well acquainted with George IV when he was Prince Regent and king, acting as his aide-de-camp from 1811 to 1825. George

George IV sits on a sofa holding the plump and pretty 'Mrs Q' on his knee: Isaac Robert Cruikshank, *Baise-Mon-Q*, 1820, hand-coloured etching.

obviously thought highly of him, as he was created a Companion of the Order of Bath in 1815 and Knight Bachelor in 1821.[44] George was known for having affairs with his courtiers, and so it was not unusual for him to go for Quentin's wife. The couple obviously spent a great deal of time in the company of the king, as they are named at various balls and concerts held at his residences; Mrs Colonel Quentin was named as one of the guests of the King's Drawing Room at Buckingham House in 1821.[45] Sir and Lady Quentin were in constant attendance at entertainments at the king's residence at Brighton Pavilion. George was delighted with the company at the ball held there in January 1822, among them Sir and Lady Quentin and their young family. The newspapers reported Brighton Palace as a 'scene of polished hilarity' as the ball opened at nine o'clock and the young people of nobility and fashion were 'on light fantastic toe for a cheerful succession of hours'.[46] Georgiana's affair must have been going on during this time, but it seems that either Sir Quentin was not aware of it or he simply ignored it, as many other husbands would have done when garnished with the king's favours. Lady Quentin was still stepping out while at the quadrille ball and supper held by Mr Fitzherbert at the Steyne Mansion on the evening of 21 February.[47] No doubt they attended the chapel at Brighton for the King's Divine Service held on 24 February along with the king, Princess Augusta and the rest of the royal household, as they were with the king in Brighton at the time; the chapel was crowded with nobility, who were admitted by tickets, after which they all took a walk in the palace gardens. Sir and Lady Quentin had attended a concert the previous night, which had been a scene of great gaiety, with the grand suite of apartments brilliantly illuminated.[48] It was apparent that the couple were very much part of the intimate crowd surrounding the king and spent much of their time at Brighton with him.

George's taste was for older women, a penchant captured in *Peep into Windsor Castle after the Lost Mutton* (1820), a satire targeting the Prince Regent as a bloated buffoon.

> Stretched at length on a sofa, with bloated face
> He saw the 'Lost Mutton' of B___k's lost race.
> . . . Whilst over him bended, to sympathy true
> The voluptuous form of the fam'd Mrs Q.[49]

The 'Lost Mutton' referred to may well have been Isabella Anne Seymour-Conway (1759–1834), Marchioness of Hertford, another older woman of 58; Conway had begun her affair with George, then in his mid-forties, in 1807, when she was almost fifty. Quentin would only have been around forty, so a slightly younger diversion for the king.

John Hoppner, *Lady Hertford*, *c.* 1784, oil on canvas.

Discrepancies have arisen over *Memoirs of the Life of the Celebrated Mrs Q* (1822) as to whose life story they were supposed to depict. At least two sources give the protagonist as courtesan Harriette Wilson,[50] and this initially might appear to be the case, as the text refers to 'Harriet', yet the memoirs bear no resemblance to Harriette Wilson's life account.[51] Nor did Harriette Wilson ever claim to have had an affair with the king, the focus of the booklet, which is something any courtesan would have attested to in her autobiography if it were true (Harriette Wilson's autobiography came out in 1825). While Mrs Q's 'memoirs' do not fit with Georgiana's early life (as is often the case in these types of narratives), there are many references that coincide with her later life. In the tale, Harriet marries a Captain Q who fought in the Peninsular War, which fits with Georgiana's husband; the memoirs state that the protagonist of the piece was 'now in her fortieth year', which fits more with Lady Quentin; most telling is the account given of Colonel Q, who 'was tried by a court martial, on charges which were not proved, and a bloodless duel was the consequence', both real incidents which took place. Just like the Conynghams, the Quentins had become part of the king's inner circle and the lady's affair with the king was taken up in satirical booklets.

The phrasing of the text of *Memoirs of the Life of the Celebrated Mrs Q* gives some indication whence the publication came. The opening refrain laments the enforced path of the fallen woman: 'She may, if she has made a false step, return to the practice of virtue; but she can never return to the paths of honourable society.' This language is very similar to that used in *Confessions of Julia Johnstone* (another courtesan), published three years later, as Johnstone rejoins, 'the world is very uncharitable! Man may commit a hundred deviations from the path of rectitude, yet he still can return [to society] . . . But woman, when she makes one false step, can retrieve it [her reputation] not more!'[52] Complaints about the existence of a sexual double standard biased against women were common in whore biographies. However, here it is evident that the *Memoirs of the Life of the Celebrated Mrs Q* was also the work of the publisher of *Confessions of Julia Johnstone*, William Benbow. He often wrote under the pseudonym 'Edward Eglantine', as in these memoirs. Benbow had started off in the Strand around 1818 but after being accused of fraud he moved over to work with George Cannon, pumping out cheap scandal literature, including memoirs. During this time, there was a thrust towards publishing anti-Regent material after the debacle of the king's marriage with Queen Caroline. When the prince heard about the proposed publication, he attempted to prevent it, offering Benbow £200. The money was accepted by Benbow, but he went ahead and published it anyway.[53]

The portrait in the frontispiece of *Memoirs of the Life of the Celebrated Mrs Q* is taken from an original by William Blake, one of which currently hangs in the Fine Arts Museums of San Francisco. Another image in *Mrs Q and Windsor Castle* (1906) shows a colour frontispiece of Mrs Q sitting at a piano in front of Windsor Castle; this one is engraved by 'G. Maille' and dated 1821, but in fact is again by William Blake. The original portrait was undertaken by François

François Huet Villiers, *Mrs Q (Harriet Quentin)*, 1820, hand-coloured stipple.

Huet Villiers and it is suggested that Harriette Wilson sat as the model.[54]

As men of privilege and wealth it was not only acceptable but usual for kings to enjoy affairs with a series of mistresses. When kings had illegitimate children, they were expected to provide for them. These children also gave mistresses some leverage to access pensions and houses in which to bring up their offspring. Generally, women were picked from the establishment, daughters or wives of titled men, but kings were not beyond revelling with lower-class whores or women raised from poverty. Actresses came under particular scrutiny from kings since they were on display on the stage and could easily attract royal attention. However, these women were less likely to wangle a decent pension without a fight and more often had to find a husband or turn their hand to writing, as Mary Robinson did, in order to provide security for themselves in later life.

REFERENCES

Prologue: Libertines in London

1 *Clarinda; or, The Fair Libertine, A Poem* (London, 1729); this may well have been a satirical take on Aphra Behn's poem 'To the fair Clarinda': see Jennifer Frangos, 'Aphra Behn's Cunning Stunts: "To the fair Clarinda"', *Eighteenth Century*, XLV/1 (Spring 2004), pp. 21–40.

1 Rambles through London

1 Walter Besant, *London* (London, reprint 1900), p. 275.
2 Patrick Colquhoun, *Treatise on the Police of the Metropolis* (London, 1796), pp. 34–5.
3 Ibid., pp. 39, 452.
4 Liza Picard, *Dr Johnson's London* (London, 2002), pp, 36, 135.
5 *True Domestick Intelligence; or, News Both from City and Country*, 52, 5 January 1680.
6 Old Bailey Proceedings Online, 8 April 1752, trial of John Stevens (t17520408–19).
7 Edward Ward, *The Reformer: Exposing the Vices of the Age in Several Characters,* to which is added *The Rambling Rakes of London Libertines* (London, 1700), p. 33.
8 Edward Ward, *Female Policy Detected; or, The Arts of a Designing Woman Laid Open* (London, 1695), preface.
9 Ward, *Female Policy Detected* (London, 1702), p. A3.
10 Ibid., p. 6.
11 Ibid., pp. 6–7.
12 Ibid., p. 7.
13 Ibid., p. 8.
14 Ibid., p. 20.
15 Edward Ward, *A Pleasant and Profitable Discourse in Defence of Married Men, Against Peevich, Fretful, Scolding Wives* (London, 1749), p. 33. This second book may have been written later and bound together with the first in this edition.

16 Howard William Troyer, *Ned Ward of Grubstreet: A Study of Sub-Literary London in the Eighteenth Century* (Cambridge, MA, 1946), pp. 3–4.
17 Ibid.
18 Ibid., p. 34.
19 Edward Ward, *The London Spy*, ed. Paul Hyland, 4th edn [1709] (London, rpt 1993), p. 30.
20 See Julie Peakman, *Mighty Lewd Books: The Development of Pornography in Eighteenth-Century England* (London, 2003), and *Lascivious Bodies: A Sexual History of the Eighteenth Century* (London, 2004).
21 Ward, *The London Spy*, p. 34.
22 Ibid., pp. 36–8.
23 Edward Ward, *The Secret History of Clubs Particularly the Kitcat, Beef-Stake, Vertuosos, Quacks, Knights of the Golden Fleece, Florists, Beaus. &c. With Their Original Characters of the Most Noted Most Noted Members Thereof* (London, 1709), p. 38.
24 Ibid., p. 138.
25 Ibid., p. 168.
26 Ibid., p. 171.
27 Ibid., p. 228, p. 284.
28 Ibid., p. 285. Mollies are well documented by Rictor Norton in *Mother Clap's Molly-House: The Gay Subculture in England, 1700–1830* (London, 1992).
29 *The Midnight Ramble; or, The Adventures of Two Noble Females; Being a true and impartial Account of their late excursion through the Streets of London and Westminster* (London, 1754), clipping opposite p. 8.
30 Ward, *The Secret History of Clubs*, p. 303.
31 Ibid., p. 304.
32 Ned Ward, *The London Spy*, I (1707), p. 306.
33 Ibid., pp. 306, 322.
34 Ibid., p. 322.
35 Ned Ward, *The London Terraefilius; or, The Satyrical Reformer* (London, 1707), p. 15.
36 Ward, *The London Spy*, ed. Hyland, 4th edn of 1709, p. xxi.
37 James Sandbrook, *ODNB*.
38 The characters came from traditional stock roles in popular plays, alleged to be well-known figures of 'Persons of Rank and Distinction'. For example, 'Who does not know of *Dorimant*, the Son and Heir apparent of a noble *British* Peer?' The rake Dorimant was the womanizing character in George Etherege's play *The Man of Mode; or, Sir Fopling Flutter* (1676).
39 *The Midnight Ramble*, p. 18.
40 Clipping opposite p. 20 of *The Midnight Ramble*. Ink date 1731, no newspaper specified.
41 Besant, *London*, p. 287.
42 *True Domestick Intelligence; or, News Both from City and Country*, 34, 31 October 1679.
43 *Daily Post*, 9 May 1724.
44 *Daily Journal*, 3 May 1730.
45 *Public Advertiser*, 15 August 1755.

46 *Gazetteer and London Daily Advertiser,* 12 January 1759.
47 *Public Advertiser*, 6 April 1762.
48 *Gazetteer and New Daily Advertiser*, 14 September 1767; *Morning Post*, 24 August 1776.
49 Walter Besant, *London* (London, 1892), p. 477.
50 *London and Country Journal*, 19, 7 September 1739.
51 Besant, *London* (London, reprint 1900), p. 319.
52 *Daily Journal*, 17 September 1735.
53 Besant, *London* (London, reprint 1900), p. 273.
54 Colquhoun, *Treatise on the Police of the Metropolis*, p. 40.
55 *Reasons Humbly Offer'd to the Honourable House of Commons, by the Church Wardens and other Inhabitants of the City and Libertie of Westminster: Against Passing the Bill to Exempt Apothecaries from Serving Parish and Ward-Offices* (1694 or 1702).
56 Old Bailey Proceedings Online, April 1725, trial of Susan Grimes (t-17250407–66).
57 Old Bailey Proceedings Online, October 1823, trial of Eliza Mills, Caroline Williams, Edward Haynes and Sarah Collins (t-18231022–130).
58 Penelope J. Corfield, 'Walking the City Streets: The Urban Odyssey in Eighteenth-Century England', *Journal of Urban History*, 16 (1990), pp. 132–74, 4.
59 R. W. Chapman, ed., *Boswell: Life of Johnson* (Oxford, 1976), p. 608.

2 Streetwalkers

1 Anon., *The Town Mistress; or, The Street-Walker* (London, 1726), p. iii. A book of poems, price 6*d*.
2 Saunders Welch, *A Proposal to Render Effectual a Plan to Remove the Nuisance of Common Prostitutes from the Streets of this Metropolis* (London, 1758).
3 Johann Wilhelm von Archenholz, *A Picture of England* (London, 1789).
4 Anon., *The Countryman's Guide to London; or, Villainy Detected* (London, 1775[?]), pp. 32–6.
5 Anon., *A Conference About Whoring* (London, 1725), p. 4.
6 Anon., *Satan's Harvest Home; or, The Present State of Whorecraft* (London, 1749), pp. 3–4.
7 Bethlem Royal Hospital Archives, 20 June 1960, LL REF: BBBRMG202010087.
8 Bridewell and Bethlem, Minute Book, 1775–90, London Metropolitan Archives, Ms. 33131/1, LL REF: GLBRMB20100.
9 Bethlem Royal Hospital Archives, LL REF: BBBRMG202050077.
10 Bethlem Royal Hospital Archives, 19 February 1724/5, p. 48.
11 *Covent Garden Magazine; or, Amorous Repository Calculated Solely for the Entertainment of the Polite World and the Young Gentleman's Education*, II (January 1773), p. 37.
12 Ibid.
13 *Covent Garden Magazine*, II (1773), p. 26.
14 Bethlem Royal Hospital Archives, 4 July 1690, LL REF: BBBRMG202010097.

15 Bethlem Royal Hospital Archives, 9 July 1721, LL REF: BBBRMG202040498.
16 Bridewell Royal Hospital: Minutes of the Court of Governors, 26 June 1713–2 August 1722.
17 Linda E. Merians, 'The London Lock Hospital and the Lock Asylum for Women', in *The Secret Malady: Venereal Disease in Eighteenth-Century Britain and France*, ed. Merians (Lexington, KY, 1991), pp. 128–45, 128.
18 Anon., *An Account of the Institution of the Lock Asylum, for the Reception of Penitent Female Patients, when discharged from the Lock Hospital* (London, 1796), pp. 3–4.
19 Elaine A. Reynolds, *Before the Bobbies: The Night Watch and Police Reform in Metropolitan London, 1720–1830* (London, 1998), p. 24.
20 London Metropolitan Archives, LL REF: GLBRPM205000052, 15 December 1693.
21 Maureen Waller, *1700: Scenes from London Life* (London, 2001), p. 297.
22 Bridewell Royal Hospital: Minutes of the Court of Governors, 23 August 1695–2 May 1701, LL REF: BBBRMG202020383.
23 Bridewell Royal Hospital: Minutes of the Court of Governors, 26 December 1722–15 December 1737.
24 Bridewell Royal Hospital: Minutes of the Court of Governors, 26 December 1722–15 December 1737 (20 July 1722), p. 518.
25 Bridewell Royal Hospital: Minutes of the Court of Governors, 26 December 1722–15 December 1737 (21 August 1735), LL REF: BBBRMG202050385.
26 Bethlem Royal Hospital Archives, 4 July 1690, LL REF: BBBRMG202010091.
27 Anon., *The Oath of a Constable* (London, 1704).
28 *True Domestick Intelligence; or, News Both from the City and Country*, 2 January 1680.
29 Tony Henderson, *Disorderly Women in Eighteenth-Century London: Prostitution and Control in the Metropolis, 1730–1830* (London, 1999), pp. 111–12.
30 Ned Ward, *The London Spy Compleat* (London, 1703), p. 137.
31 Ibid., p. 109.
32 Bridewell Royal Hospital: Minute Books of the General Prison Committee, 11 October 1775–9 December 1790.
33 London Metropolitan Archives, LL REF: GLBRMB201000011.
34 London Metropolitan Archives, 13 May 1779, LL REF: GLBRMB201000013, www.londonlives.org.
35 London Metropolitan Archives: 6th November 1783, LL REF: GLBRMB201000022.
36 Newgate was originally built in the twelfth century but was torn down and rebuilt many times over the next few centuries. It fell victim to the Great Fire of London in 1666 and was rebuilt by Christopher Wren and extended in the 1770s; it was again gutted by fire during the Gordon Riots in 1780.
37 Bernard Mandeville, *An Enquiry into the Causes of the Frequent Executions at Tyburn* (London, 1725), pp. 2, 13.
38 Ibid., p. 20.
39 Her date of birth is given as 1677, as claimed by Captain Johnson's account of her life below, and as 1682 in this account by Paul Lorrain.

40 Paul Lorrain, *The Ordinary of Newgate: His Account of the Behaviour, Confession, and Last Speech of Deborah Churchill, That Was Executed at Tyburn, on Friday the 17th of December, 1708*, can be found in the Old Bailey sessions: Old Bailey Proceedings Online, *Ordinary of Newgate's Account*, December 1708 (OA17081217).
41 Ibid.
42 See Julie Peakman, *Whore Biographies, 1700–1825* (London, 2006–7).
43 Anon., *The Whole Life and Conversation, Birth, Parentage and Education of Deborah Churchill* (London, 1708), p. 3.
44 Lorrain, *The Ordinary of Newgate: His Account . . . of Deborah Churchill*; Anon., [Captain Johnson], *The Lives and Adventures of the German Princess (Mary Carleton), Mary Read, Anne Bonny, Joan Philips, Madam Churchill, Betty Ireland, and Ann Hereford* (1755); P. Lorrain, *The Ordinary of Newgate's Account of the Life, Conversation, Birth and Education of Thomas Ellis, and Mary Goddard, Who Were Executed at Tyburn on Wednesday the Third of March, 1708* (1708); 'Lorrain', *The whole life and conversation, birth, parentage and education of Deborah Churchill; condemn'd some time since for the barbarous murder of Mr. William Ware in Drury-Lane, and now brought down to her former Judgement. AS Also, Her Behaviour, Confessions, and last Dying-Words at the Place of Execution.1708 A true copy of the paper at large, left by Mrs Deborah Churchill, which she delivered at the place of execution to a friend of hers, to be made publick after her death* (1708); *The Whole Life and Conversation, Birth, Parentage and Education of Deborah Churchill*; A. Smith, *A Complete History of the Lives and Robberies of the Most Notorious Highwaymen*, ed. A. L. Hayward, 5th edn [1719] (London, 1926); J. L. Rayner and G. T. Crook, eds, *The Complete Newgate Calendar*, vol. II (London, 1926).
45 Lorrain, *The Ordinary of Newgate: His Account . . . of Deborah Churchill.*

3 Brazen Bawds

1 Lowell Blair, ed., *Casanova's Memoirs* (London, 1958).
2 Old Bailey Proceedings Online, 27 October 1790, trial of Maria Ann Cooke (t17901027–8).
3 Parliamentary Papers, Police Committee 1st Report, vol. II (1817), p. 152.
4 Julie Peakman, *Mighty Lewd Books: The Development of Pornography in Eighteenth-Century England* (London, 2002).
5 Richard King, *The New Cheats of London Expos'd* (London, 1780[?]), pp. 23–4.
6 Tassie Gwilliam, 'Female Fraud: Counterfeit Maidenheads in the Eighteenth Century', *Journal of the History of Sexuality*, VI/41 (1996), pp. 518–48.
7 Anon., *The Constables Hue and Cry* (London, 1700), p. 6.
8 Maureen Waller, *1700: Scenes from London Life* (London, 2000), p. 295.
9 John Cleland, *Memoirs of a Woman of Pleasure* (London, 1749), vol. II, p. 120.
10 Richard King, *The New Cheats of London Exposed; or, The Frauds and Tricks of the Town Laid Open to Both Sexes* (London, *c.* 1780). This book also covers duffers, fortune tellers, gamblers, gossips, hangers-on, jilts,

intelligencers, 'Jews', defaulters, insolvents, kidnappers, lottery, office keepers, mock auctioneers, money droppers, ring droppers, pretended friends, quacks, receivers of stolen goods, setters, 'spungers', sharpers, swindlers, smugglers, shoplifters, street robbers, trappers, way-layers and waggon hunters, pp. 16–17.

11 Newspaper tracts, British Library shelf mark 816m19.

12 William Hickey, *Memoirs of William Hickey*, Chapter 12, p. 247, at https://archive.org.

13 Old Bailey Proceedings Online, May 1693 (s16930531–1).

14 Old Bailey Proceedings Online, July 1726, trial of Margaret Clap (t17260711–54). The full tale of Mother Clap has been told by Rictor Norton in *Mother Clap's Molly-House: The Gay Subculture in England, 1700–1830* (London, 1992).

15 Old Bailey Proceedings Online, October 1728, trial of Julius Cesar Taylor (t17281016–60).

16 Anon., *The Life and Character of Moll King* (London, 1747), p. 8.

17 Ibid., p. 10.

18 Ibid., pp. 11–12, 24.

19 Ibid., p. 16.

20 There is some confusion around the date of her death. Burford suggests 1684, and John Callow 1698. According to Burford, probate of her will was granted on 29 October 1689, so, if this is correct, her death would have been earlier than 1698. See E. J. Burford and Joy Wotton, *Private Vices–Public Virtues: Bawdry in London from Elizabethan Times to the Regency* (London, 1995), pp. 77–93; E. J. Burford, *Wits, Wenches and Wantons. London Low Life: Covent Garden in the Eighteenth Century* (London, 1986) p. 245; see also John Callow's entry for Cresswell in the ODNB.

21 See Peakman, *Whore Biographies, 1700–1825* (London, 2006–7), vol. 1, on Dunton's *Shortest Way with Whore and Rogues*, pp. 1–5.

22 Melissa Mowry in *The Bawdy Politic in Stuart England, 1660–1714* (London, 2004) suggests more complicated political and economic reasons.

23 Samuel Pepys, *Diary*, 24–5 March 1668.

24 *Impartial Protestant Mercury*, 64 (November 1681).

25 'Anodyne Tanner MD', *The Life of the Late Celebrated Mrs Elizabeth Wisebourn* (London, 1721).

26 See *The Practical Scheme of Secret Injuries. And Broken Constitutions. By Fast Living, Former Ill Cures, Salivations and Mercury. With an Appendix of Gleets, And other such Weaknesses in either Sex* (London, 1719).

27 See Burford, *Wits*, pp. 42–52.

28 'Tanner', *The Life of the Late Celebrated Mrs Elizabeth Wisebourn*, p. 6. Three copies are extant in the British Library shelfmarks, 808g36; 635f11 (12); 1419k.21. The Anodyne Necklace was purported to be a cure for everything from venereal disease to children's teething.

29 *Weekly Register*, October 1730–April 1732; issue 55 (1 May 1731).

30 Anon., *Mother Needham's Elegy. Who Died the 31st of September 1730. Containing, an Account of Mother Needham's Life and Death, Manner of Lying in State, Her Funeral, and Epitaph* (London, 1730).

31 *Fog's Weekly Journal*, 28 December 1728.
32 Anon., *Drury Lane in Tears; or, The Ladies of Pleasure Mourning* (London, 1740[?], more likely 1738/9), pp. 1–8.
33 Old Bailey Proceedings Online, Ordinary Account, 17410318, 18 March 1741, includes her confession.
34 Within this confession, the Polari heard at Moll King's was taught to Webb so she could talk with her fellow criminals: 'very Rum Muns (a great Beau) Glim Star, (a Ring) upon his Feme, (Hand) Bulk the Muns forward, (Push) Slanging the Gentry Mort rumly with a sham Kinchin, that is, (Cutting well the Women big with Child), Saweer clearly, (keep a good look out), Gentleman's Loges and Tales, (Men's repeating Watches) and to Chive the Froes of their Bungs, (cut off the Women's Pockets)'. Old Bailey Proceedings Online, Ordinary Account, 17410318, 18 March 1741, includes her confession.
35 Old Bailey Proceedings Online, 13 January 1738, trial of Mary Young for theft (t17380113–18).
36 Old Bailey Proceedings Online, 12 April 1738, trial of Jane Webb for theft and larceny (t-17380412–40).
37 *Drury Lane in Tears; or, The Ladies of Pleasure* 1740[?].
38 Old Bailey Proceedings Online, 16 January 1741, trial of Mary Young, Elizabeth Davis for violent theft and highway robbery (t17410116–15).
39 Old Bailey Proceedings Online, Ordinary Account, OA17410318, 18 March 1741.

4 The Celebrated Courtesan

1 Richard King, *The New Cheats of London Exposed; or the Frauds and Tricks of the Town Laid Open to Both Sexes* (London, 1799[?]), p. 24.
2 Ibid., pp. 20–22.
3 Julie Peakman, *Whore Biographies, 1700–1825* (London, 2006), p. 452.
4 *Covent Garden Magazine*, II (1773), p. 21.
5 Anon., *Kitty Attalantis* (London, 1766), p. 9.
6 *Covent-Garden Magazine*, II (1773), p. 22.
7 Alfred Spencer, ed., *Memoirs of William Hickey* (London, 1913), p. 126.
8 Captain Charles Walker, *Authentick Memoirs of the Life, Intrigues and Adventures of the Celebrated Sally Salisbury* (London, 1723), p. 8.
9 There is another copy of *An Account of the Tryal of Sally Salisbury* in the back of the second edition of Captain Charles Walker's *Authentick Memoirs of the Life, Intrigues and Adventures of the Celebrated Sally Salisbury*, in the British Library.
10 Anon., *The Genuine History of Mrs. Sarah Prydden, usually called Sally Salisbury, and her Gallants* (1723); *The Effigies, Parentage, Education, Life, Merry Pranks and Conversation of the celebrated Mrs Sally Salisbury* (1723); *An Account of the Tryall of Sally Salisbury* (1722); *Sally Salisbury's Garland, containing four excellent new songs* (n.d.), including 'Sally Salisbury farewell to her sister'; a version of this ballad appears in *The Bleach Yard's Garland* (1775).
11 *The Genuine History of Mrs. Sarah Prydden*, p. 2.
12 Ibid., p. 4.

13 Ibid., pp. 11–15.
14 Ibid., p. 22
15 Ibid., p. 29.
16 *Original Weekly Journal* (London), Saturday, 12 September 1719.
17 *The Genuine History of Mrs. Sarah Prydden*, pp. 30–31.
18 Ibid., pp. 39–41; Also see *Annals of Newgate* (London, 1776), a repeat of the trial, pp. 163–9.
19 Robert Halsband, ed., Mary Wortley Montagu, *Complete Letters* (Oxford, 1965–7), vol. II, pp. 15, 20.
20 For examples see *British Journal* (London), 21 (722), Saturday, 9 February 1723; *Daily Journal*, 639 (London), Friday, 8 February 1723; and *Post Boy*, 5231 (London), Tuesday, 29 January 1723. Newspapers gave her alias as Sally Prettyn or Pretteyn.
21 *British Journal*, 21, Saturday, 9 February 1723.
22 *Evening Post*, 2119, Saturday, 23 February 1723.
23 *Daily Journal*, 656, Thursday, 28 February 1723.
24 Anon., *Select Trials for Murderers, Robberies, Rapes, Sodomy, Coining, Frauds and Other Offences at the Sessions-House in the Old Bailey*, vol. I: *1720–24* (London, 1734), pp. 317–22.
25 The whole of the trial is recorded ibid., pp. 317–22; p. 320.
26 *London Journal*, 195, Saturday, 20 April 1723.
27 *Daily Journal*, 705, Friday, 26 April 1723.
28 *Daily Post,* Thursday, 25 April 1723.
29 *Evening Post,* Saturday, 27 April 1723.
30 *Daily Journal*, Thursday, 9 May 1723.
31 *British Journal*, Saturday, 11 May 1723.
32 *Daily Journal*, Friday, 1 March 1723.
33 *London Journal*, Saturday, 9 March 1723.
34 *Daily Journal*, Saturday, 16 March 1723.
35 *Daily Journal*, Tuesday, 5 November 1723.
36 *Daily Journal*, Tuesday, 11 February 1724.
37 *London Journal*, 8/15 February 1724.
38 John Mason Good, *A Dissertation on the Diseases of Prisons and Poor Houses* (London, 1795), p. 25.
39 *Daily Journal*, Thursday, 13 February 1724.
40 *London Journal*, Saturday, 22 February 1724.
41 *The Genuine History of Mrs. Sarah Prydden*, p. 41.
42 *Weekly Oracle; or, Universal Library*, Saturday, 1 February 1735.
43 *General Evening Post*, Tuesday, 27 May 1740.
44 Anon., *Characters of the Present and Most Celebrated Courtezans* (London, 1780), p. 127.
45 Ibid., p. 131.
46 Ibid., pp. 136–7.
47 He graduated in 1773, so it had to be before then.
48 Parish Register Baptisms, Westminster, St Anne's, Soho, 10 June 1741, Westminster Registry Office.
49 Martin Postle, *Sir Joshua Reynolds* (Cambridge, 1995), p. 3.
50 Anon., *The Uncommon Adventures of Miss Kitty Fisher* (London, 1759); *Kitty's Stream; or, The Noblemen Turned Fisher-Men: A Comic Satire*

(London, 1759); *Horse and Away to St. James's Park; or, A Trip for the Noontide Air Who Rides Fastest, Miss Kitty Fisher or her Gay Gallant* (London, 1760); *A Sketch of the Present Times and the Time to Come: In an Address to Kitty Fisher* (London, 1762).

51 Jacques Casanova de Seingalt, *Memoirs of Casanova* (London, privately printed for the Navarre Society, 1921–3), vol. II, p. 222.

52 *The Sun* (London), 2449, Monday, 28 July 1800.

53 *Town and Country Magazine,* September 1771.

54 *Horse and Away to St. James's Park.*

55 *Universal Magazine* quoted in Grace E. Thompson, *The Cyprian: The Life of a Covent Garden Lady* (London, 1932), p. 122.

56 *The Public Advertiser*, 24, 27, 28 and 30 March 1759.

57 *Public Advertiser*, 8503, Wednesday, 3 February 1762.

58 Thompson, *The Cyprian*, pp. 118–25.

59 *Memoirs of Casanova*, vol. II, pp. 228–9.

60 Cindy McCreery, *ODNB*.

61 Parish register, Westminster, St George's, Hanover Square, 4 December 1766.

62 There is contention over the date and place of her death. From the dates given in the *ODNB*, she was about 26 when she died but Bleackley states she was 29. According to the editor of Casanova's memoirs printed for the Navarre Society in 1921–3, she died in Bath: Horace Bleackley, *Ladies Frail and Fair: Sketches of the Demi-Monde during the Eighteenth Century* (London, 1909); *Memoirs of Casanova*, vol. II, p. 223.

63 Bleackley, *Ladies Fair and Frail.*

5 Public Opinion: The Way with Whores

1 *Farringdon Without. At a Meeting of the Alderman and Common Council of this Ward, at the Inquest Room in Saint Andrew's Church-Yard, on Wednesday, 11 December 1799* (London, 1799).

2 Penelope Corfield, 'Vauxhall, Sex and Entertainment: London's Pioneering Urban Pleasure Garden', *History and Social Action Publications* (London, 2012).

3 James Boswell, Diary, 10 May 1763.

4 Old Bailey Proceedings Online, 5 December 1718, trials of John Bowes and Hugh Ryly (t17181205–24); and 30 August 1727, trials of John Painter and John Green (t17270830–53).

5 Daniel Defoe, *Some Considerations Upon Street-Walkers* (London, 1726), p. 2.

6 Ibid., p. 5.

7 Ibid., p. 7.

8 Ibid., pp. 4–5.

9 John Robert Moore, *Defoe in the Pillory* (Bloomington, IN, 1939); Maximillian E. Novak, *Daniel Defoe, Master of Fictions: His Life and Ideas* (Oxford, 2001).

10 Dunton would write, 'Mr. Daniel Defoe is a man of good parts, and very clear sense: His conversation is brisk and ingenious enough. The World is well satisfied that he is enterprizing and bold; but, alas! Had

his prudence only weighed a few grains more, he'd certainly have writ his *Shortest Way* a little more at length.' Theodore Merryman Hatfield, 'The True Secret History of Mr John Dunton', PhD thesis, Harvard University (1926), p. 169.

11 Peter Murray Hill, *Two Augustan Booksellers: John Dunton and Edmund Curll* (Lawrence, KS, 1958), p. 3.

12 Jennine Hurl-Eamon, 'Policing Male Heterosexuality: The Reformation of Manners Societies' Campaign against the Brothels in Westminster, 1690–1720', *Journal of Social History*, XXXVII/4 (Summer 2004), p. 1021.

13 J. Woodward, *A Rebuke to the Sin of Uncleanliness*, 'By a Minister of the Church of England' (London, 1740), p. 17.

14 Defoe, *Some Considerations Upon Street-Walkers*, title-page: 'With A Proposal for lessening the present Number of them. In Two Letters to a Member of Parliament. To which is added, A letter from One of those unhappy Persons, when in Newgate, and who was afterwards executed, for picking a Gentleman's Pocket, to Mrs. – in Great P-Ney Street.'

15 William Hawkins, *Treatise of the Pleas of the Crown* (London, 1716: reprinted 1973), p. 61; Randolph Trumbach found that 76 per cent of cases were caught inside bawdy houses, p. 93.

16 MJ/SR2275R 22, 5 July 1716 quoted in Hurl-Eamon, 'Policing Male Heterosexuality', p. 1022.

17 Anon., *A Representation of the State of the Societies for Reformation of Manners, Humbly Offered to His Majesty* (London, 1715), pp. 11–12.

18 Anon., *The Eight and Twentieth Account of the Progress made in the Cities of London and Westminster by the Societies for Promoting a Reformation of Manners* (London, 1722), p. 3.

19 John Dunton, *Life and Errors* (London, 1705), p. 15.

20 John Dunton's *Bumography* is a skit on the fashionable women of Tunbridge Wells, with their 'treacherous Smiles' and 'Dissembling Tears'. It mocks their 'High Top-Knots, Ridiculous Furbelows, Perpetual Washings, Curlings, Powdering, Various Garbs . . ., Affected Postures, tempting Smiles, and Amorous Glances'; *Bumography; or, A Touch at the Lady's Tail. Being a Lampoon (privately) dispers'd at Tunbridge-Wells, in the Year 1707, by a Water-Drinker* (London, 1707), p. iii.

21 Ibid., p. ii.

22 Stephen Parks, *John Dunton and the English Book Trade* (London, 1976), p. 1.

23 Bernard Mandeville, *A Modest Defence of Publick Stews; or, An Essay upon Whoring* (London, 1724), p. ii.

24 See remark H ibid.

25 Daniel Defoe, *Moll Flanders* (London, 1721), p. 403.

26 *Memoirs of the Celebrated Miss Fanny M_______* [Murray] (London, 1759); *Genuine Memoirs of the Celebrated Miss Nancy Dawson* (London, 1760); *The Uncommon Adventures of Miss Kitty Fisher* (London, 1759): These are all discussed in more detail in Julie Peakman, *Whore Biographies, 1700–1825* (London, 2006).

27 See Sean Shesgreen, ed., *Engravings by Hogarth* (New York, 1973).

28 W. Speck, 'The Harlot's Progress in Eighteenth-Century England', *British Journal of Eighteenth-Century Studies*, III/2 (1980), pp. 127–39.

29 Susan Staves, 'British Seduced Maidens', *American Society for Eighteenth-Century Studies*, XIV/2 (Winter 1980–81), pp. 109–34.
30 Speck, 'The Harlot's Progress', pp. 136–7.
31 On the books that year were many nobles and religious authorities, including the earls of Ailesbury, Clarendon, Cardigan, Dartmouth, Exeter, Harcourt, Hopetoun and Macclesfield; the dukes of Buccleogh, Marlborough and Northumberland; the Marquis of Buckingham; the Bishops of Bath and Wells, Durham, Exeter, Ely, Hereford, Lincoln and Oxford; and the Archbishops of Canterbury and York, as well as many members of parliament. *Report of the Committee of the Society For Carrying Into Effect His Majesty's Proclamation Against Vice and Immorality for the Year 1799* (London, 1800). This report states it was first established in 1789.
32 Ibid.
33 Ibid., p. 10.
34 *Statement and Propositions from the Society for Giving Effect to His Majesty's Proclamation Against Vice and Immorality, Delivered to the Magistrates, At Their Meeting Held at the St. Alban's Tavern, on Wednesday the 5th of May, 1790* (London, 1790).
35 *Report of the Committee of the Society For Carrying Into Effect His Majesty's Proclamation Against Vice and Immorality for the Year 1799*, p. 11.
36 Ibid., p. 13.

6 Stage Strumpets

1 Anon., *The Secret History of the Green Rooms, Containing Authentic and Entertaining Memoirs of the Actors and Actresses in the Three Royal Theatres* (London, 1790), pp. iii–iv.
2 Charles Inigo Jones, *Memoirs of Miss O'Neill, Containing Her Public Character, Private Life and Dramatic Progress* (London, 1816), p. 97.
3 Ibid., p. 93.
4 Thomas Postlewait has found theatrical autobiographies to be equally unreliable; Thomas Postlewait, 'Autobiography and Theatre History', in *Interpreting the Theatrical Past: Essays in the Historiography of Performance*, ed. T. Postlewait and Bruce A. McConachie (Iowa City, IA, 1989), pp. 248–72.
5 Mary Anne Radcliffe, *The Female Advocate; or, An Attempt to Recover the Rights of Women from Male Usurpation* (London, 1799), pp. 42–3.
6 'William Egerton' [Edmund Curll], *Faithful Memoirs of the Life and Performance of that Justly celebrated and most Eminent Actress of Her Time, Mrs Anne Oldfield* (London, 1731), p. 6, selling for 3*s* 6*d*.
7 Ibid., p. 6.
8 *The Tatler*, IV/212, p. 59.
9 Egerton, *Faithful Memoirs of . . . Mrs Anne Oldfield.*
10 *Daily Journal*, 3059, 26 October 1730.
11 *London Chronicle*, 8 August 1778.
12 Anon., *The Theatrical Review for the Year 1757 and Begining of 1758 containing Critical Remarks on the Principal Performers of the Two Theatres* (London, 1758), p. 43.

13 Ibid., p. 18.
14 Ibid., p. 35.
15 Ibid., pp. 15, 38.
16 This may have been a theatrical anecdote as there is little mention of it in the London newspapers.
17 Charlotte Charke, *A Narrative of the Life of Mrs. Charlotte Charke* (London, 1755), p. 47.
18 Ibid., p. 15.
19 Ibid., p. 63.
20 Ibid., p. 11.
21 *The Theatrical Review for The Year 1757 and Begining of 1758*, p. 15.
22 For further information see Julie Peakman, *Amatory Pleasures* (London, 2016), p. 51.
23 Anon., *The Tryals of the Two Causes between Theophilus Cibber Gent and Plaintiff William Sloper* (London, 1710), p. 2.
24 Anon., *The Life of Lavinia Berwick, alias Fenton alias Polly Peachum* (London, 1728), p. 20.
25 Anon., *The Whole Life of Polly Peachum* (London, 1730[?]).
26 C. F. Burgess, ed., *Letters of John Gay* (Oxford, 1966), pp. 72–3.
27 The same was true of many well-known actresses of the day. Eighteen of Barry's portraits were exhibited at the Royal Academy between 1780 and 1797, attesting to her lure. The most famous portrait was undertaken by Reynolds, a painting of her as a tragic muse, a pose which she later struck at lectures.
28 R. E. Tickell, ed., *Thomas Tickell and the Eighteenth-Century Poets* (London, 1931), pp. 144–5.
29 Charles Eglington, 'Lavinia Fenton', in *The Theatre: A Monthly Review of the Drama, Music and the Fine Arts* (October 1892).
30 J. Warton, ed., *The Works of Alexander Pope* (London, 1797), vol. IX, p. 100.
31 See Notices in the *Oracle*, 25 November 1796, 29 November 1796.
32 Diary of Mrs Anne Matthews (1837), otherwise known as Anne Jackson.
33 Anon., *The Secret Memoirs of Harriot Pumpkin [Mellon], A Celebrated Actress; From Her Infancy to Her Seduction of, and Subsequent Marriage to a Banker* (London, 1825), p. 7.
34 Ibid.
35 Ibid., p. 91.
36 Ibid., pp. 2–3.
37 Ibid., p. 19.
38 Ibid., p. 24.
39 Ibid., p. 76.
40 Ibid., p. 92.
41 Ibid., p. 93.
42 Julia Johnstone, *Confessions of Julia Johnstone* (London, 1825), p. 157.
43 Quoted in K. Straub, *Sexual Suspects: Eighteenth-Century Players and Sexual Ideology* (Princeton, NJ, 2006), p. 11.
44 William Andrews Clark Library, Miscellaneous Folder Record ID:3733803.

7 Libertines and Their Fashions

1 Anon., *The Character of a Town-Miss* (London, 1680).
2 Anon., *The Character of a Town-Gallant* (London, 1675), p. 2.
3 Anon., *Hickelty Pickelty; or, a medly of characters adapted to the age. Relating to different persons and persuasions, viz. a Presbyterian; or, a female hypocrite. A beau. A Whig. A Lawyer's Clerk; or, A Pot-Poet. An Attorney. A Detractor. A Bowling-Green. A Surgeon. A Player. A Tavern. A Coquet. A Pinner's-Hall Text-Driver. An unsanctify'd Dun; or, A cruel Creditor. A Bayliff's Follower. The Exchange. Will's Coffee-House. A Wit. A Flatterer. A High-Flyer. A Drunkard. A Prison. A Courtier. A handsom Bar-Keeper. A young Rake. A Whore-Master. A Pretender to Learning. A Tobacconist. An upstart Sherriff; or, A Country-Justice. A Sceptick in Religion. A Stock-Jobber* (London, 1708), p. 13.
4 Anon., *Whipping-Tom; or, A Rod for a Proud Lady* (London, 1722), p. 25.
5 'Jack Lovelass', *The Hoop-Petticoat Vindicated in Answer to the Enormous Abomination of the Hoop-Petticoat,* (London, 1745), p. 19.
6 *Bon Ton*, I (1791), p. 38.
7 *The Times*, 2 October 1788, pp. 3–4.
8 Harriette Wilson, *The Memoirs of Harriette Wilson*, 'Written by Herself', p. 41, at www.gutenberg.org.
9 Ibid., pp. 245–6.
10 Ibid., pp. 47–8.
11 Ibid., p. 209.
12 *The Secret Memoirs of Harriott Pumpkin* (London, 1825), pp. 80–81.
13 Ibid., p. 83.
14 *Hickelty Pickelty*, p. 8.
15 *The Coquet's Surrender; or, the Humerous Punster* (London, 1732); *The Country Coquet; or, Miss in her breeches. A ballad opera . . . 'By a Young Lady'* (London, 1755): *The Coquette; or, The Mistakes of the heart. A comedy, etc.* [An adaptation of Eliza Haywood's 'History of Miss Betsy Thoughtless by R. Hitchcock (Bath, 1777); *Sublime of Flagellation (London, c. 1780s or '90s); The New England Coquette: From the History of the Celebrated Eliza Wharton* (London, 1802); Ralph Bennet Forbes, *Account of the Capture of the Schooner Coquette* (London, 1807); *The Paradise of Coquettes; A Poem. In nine parts, by Thomas Brown* (London, 1814).
16 *The Nunnery for Coquettes* (London, 1771), p. v.
17 Ibid., pp. v–vii.
18 Ibid., p. vii.
19 Ibid., p. 2.
20 Ibid., p. 3.
21 Ibid., p. 4.
22 *Covent Garden Magazine*, II (1773), p. 37.
23 'The Puppy and Puppyess, of March', *Bon Ton*, I (11 April 1791), pp. 3–4, 43.
24 *Bon Ton*, I, 11 April 1791, p. 43.
25 *The Character of a Town-Gallant* and *The Character of a Town-Miss*. See Rictor Norton's website for details of case of Captain Edward Rigby: www.rictornorton.co.uk.

26 David Garrick, *The Male-Coquette; or, Seventeen Hundred and Fifty-Seven* (Dublin, 1758), frontispiece.
27 Jane Timbury, *The Male Coquette; or, The History of the Hon Edward Astell* (London, 1770).
28 *The Macaroni Jester and Pantheon of Wit* (London, 1730), p. 6.
29 Amelia Rauser, 'Hair, Authenticity, and the Self-Made Macaroni', *Eighteenth-Century Studies*, XXXVIII/1 (Fall 2004), pp. 101–17.
30 Christopher Anstey, *Liberality; or, The Decayed Macaroni* (London, 1788).
31 Ned Ward, *The Amorous Bugbears; or, The Humours of a Masquerade* (London, 1725).
32 Title page, ibid.
33 Ibid., p. 4.
34 Ibid., p. 10.
35 Ibid., p. 15.
36 Ibid., p. 17.
37 Ibid., pp. 20–21.
38 *The Midnight Ramble; or, The Adventures of Two Noble Females; Being a true and impartial Account of their late excursion through the Streets of London and Westminster* (London, 1754). Newspaper clipping pasted inside, opposite p. 19.
39 Ward, *The Amorous Bugbears.*
40 See Antony Wild, *Coffee: A Dark History* (New York, 2005), p. 90; *The Character of a Coffee-House, 1673 AD*, quoted in Fordham University blog, https://sourcebooks.fordham.edu/mod/1670coffee.asp, accessed 7 February 2023.
41 *The Women's Petition Against Coffee* (London, 1674), pp. 3–6.
42 Newspaper clipping pasted inside *The Midnight Ramble.*
43 Julie Peakman, *Mighty Lewd Books: The Development of Pornography in Eighteenth-Century England* (London, 2002).
44 Ned Ward, *The London Spy* (London, reprint 1993).
45 For a fuller description of Dashwood's clubs, see Julie Peakman, *Lascivious Bodies: A Sexual History of the Eighteenth Century* (London, 2004), chapter 5: 'Horace Walpole's Journals of Visits to Country Seats', *Walpole Society*, XVI (1927–8), pp. 50–51.
46 Ned Ward, *The Secret History of Clubs* (London, 1709), pp. 107–8.
47 Iwan Bloch, *Sex Life in England* (London, 1935), pp. 214–15.
48 *Bon Ton*, I (1791), p. 40.
49 Ibid.

8 Mad About the Boy

1 This 'Song' of Rochester's is quoted in Gregory Woods, *A History of Gay Literature: The Male Tradition* (New Haven, CT, 1998), p. 126.
2 'To swive' meaning 'to have sexual intercourse with'. This quote of lines 1–32 has been abridged here. The full version of 'A Ramble in St James's Park' can be found at Toronto university's website: https://rpo.library.utoronto.ca/poems/ramble-st-jamess-park, accessed 7 February 2023.
3 Peter Bartlett, 'Sodomites in the Pillory in Eighteenth-Century London', *Social and Legal Studies*, VI/4 (1997), pp. 553–72.

4 Randolph Trumbach, 'Sodomy Transformed: Aristocratic Libertinage, Public Reputation and the Gender Revolution of the Eighteenth Century', *Journal of Homosexuality*, XIX/3 (1990), pp. 105–24.
5 Thomas Salmon, *The Chronical Historian* (London, 1723), p. 380.
6 Titus Oates had been expelled from the Navy accused of sodomy. He was a renegade Anglican priest who accused the Catholic Church of a 'Popish Plot' to assassinate Charles II; he would have been known to readers. Rictor Norton, ed., 'The He-Strumpets, 1707–10', in *Homosexuality in Eighteenth-Century England: A Sourcebook*, 1 December 1999, updated 15 June 2008; www.rictornorton.co.uk/eighteen/dunton.htm; also Norton, *Mother Clap's Molly-House: The Gay Subculture in England, 1700–1830* (London, 1992), p. 19.
7 Anon., *An Account of the Proceedings against Capt. E. Rigby at . . . the Old-Bailey* (London, 1698).
8 Frank McLynn, *Crimes and Punishment in Eighteenth Century England* (Oxford, 1989), p. 283.
9 Huntington Library, no 84175, dated 1712, but actually published in 1723.
10 Trumbach asserts, 'In the first decade of the eighteenth century, England became a society with three genders. This occurred because of a reorganization of the nature of male sexual desire. Before 1700 all western European men had desired women and adolescent males. But after 1700 males were divided into two groups: a majority who desired only women, and a minority who desired only men.' Randolph Trumbach, 'Blackmail for Sodomy in Eighteenth-Century London', *Historical Reflections / Réflexions Historiques*, XXXIII/1, *Eighteenth-Century Homosexuality in Global Perspective* (Spring 2007), pp. 23–39.
11 Lord Wharncliffe, ed., *Letters of Lady Mary Wortley Montagu*, vol. I [1866] (Cambridge, 2011), p. 95.
12 Robert Halsband, *Lord Hervey: Eighteenth-Century Courtier* (Oxford, 1973), pp. 268–9.
13 This quote is from 'An Epistle from Mr Pope to Dr Arbuthnot' (published 1735), lines 331–3 quoted in John Butt, *The Poems of Alexander Pope* (London, 1964), p. 608.
14 In his *Memoirs of the Reign of George II*, Hervey wrote detailed and brutally frank details of the court of George II from 1727 to 1737. He provided a most unflattering account of the king, and of Frederick, Prince of Wales, and their family squabbles although he retained a genuine respect and attachment for the queen and her daughter, Princess Caroline.
15 Hervey's original letters to Fox and the two remaining ones from Fox to Hervey are in the Holland House Papers in the British Library. Hervey saved copies of his letters to Fox at his home in Ickworth, Bury. For ease of use for those with no access to the original papers, I reference the quotes to be found in Lucy Moore, *Amphibious Thing: The Adventures of a Georgian Rake* (London, 2001), pp. 24, 33, 36, 38; see also Norton, *The Trial of Mervyn Touchet,* https://rictornorton.co.uk/touchet.htm, accessed 9 October 2023.
16 Moore, *Amphibious Thing*, p. 40.
17 Ibid.

18 Ibid., p. 73.
19 British Library MS Room, Add MS 51417.
20 Anon. [William Pulteney], *A Proper Reply to a Late Scurrilous Libel; Intitled, Sedition and Defamation Display'd*, by Caleb D'Anvers (London, 1731)
21 Timothy Mowl, *William Beckford: Composing for Mozart* (London, 1998), p. 85.
22 Ibid.
23 Ibid., p. 94.
24 Ibid., p. 98, in MSS Beckford *c.* 31. Letters from Sir William and Lady Hamilton, Beckford Papers, Bodleian Library.
25 Mowl, *William Beckford*, p. 104.
26 *Gazetteer and New Daily Advertiser* (London), 2 October 1781.
27 *London Courant*, 11 December 1781.
28 Joseph Farington, *The Farington Diary*, 4.1175, https://archive.org/details/faringtondiary01fariuoft.
29 Mowl, *William Beckford*, p. 109.
30 *The World* (London), 332, Tuesday, 22 January 1788.
31 *Morning Post*, 25 May 1801.
32 William Beckford, *A Catalogue of the Costly and Interesting Effects of Fonthill Abbey* (London, 1823): accessed online, https://babel.hathitrust.org, Cat ID453377.
33 D. S. Neff, 'Bitches, Mollies, and Tommies: Byron, Masculinity, and the History of Sexualities', *Journal of the History of Sexuality*, 11/3 (July 2002), pp. 395–438.
34 Randolph Trumbach was the first to establish this idea: prior to the eighteenth century, men were allowed to have sexual relations with women and boys without damaging their reputations for manliness but in the eighteenth century 'adult men with homosexual desires' were increasingly presumed to be 'members of an effeminate minority': Randolph Trumbach, *Sex and the Gender Revolution: Heterosexuality and the Third Gender in Enlightenment London* (Chicago, IL, 1998), pp. 6–9. For more debate on what effect the conjoining of sodomy with effeminacy had on Western conceptions of masculinity, see David F. Greenberg, *The Construction of Homosexuality* (Chicago, IL, 1988), pp. 406–10, 416–17.
35 Leslie A. Marchand, ed., *Byron's Letters and Journals* (Cambridge, MA, 1973–82), 10:69.
36 Johann Georg von Hahn, *Albanesische Studien* [1853], quoted in Stephen O. Murray, 'Male Homosexuality in Ottoman Albania', in *Islamic Homosexualities: Culture, History, and Literature*, ed. Stephen O. Murray and Will Roscoe (New York, 1997), p. 188.
37 Marchand, ed., *Byron's Letters and Journals*, 1:231.
38 Ibid., 44.
39 Louise Crompton, *Byron and Greek Love: Homophobia in 19th-Century England* (Swaffham, 1998), p. 131.
40 Marchand, ed., *Byron's Letters and Journals*, pp. 58–62.
41 Fiona MacCarthy, *Byron: Life and Legend* (London, 2002), p. 23.
42 Ibid., p. 36.

43 Marchand, ed., *Byron's Letters and Journals*, 1:210, 67.
44 Anon., *The Phoenix of Sodom; or, The Vere Street Coterie. Being an Exhibition of the Gambols Practised by ancient Lechers of Sodom and Gomorrah embellished and improved with the Modern Refinements in Sodomitical Practices, by the members of the Vere Street Coterie, of detestable memory* (London, 1813), p. 23.
45 Neff, 'Bitches, Mollies, and Tommies', pp. 395–438. Neff suggests he had both containing cases of sodomy and effeminate men.
46 Marchand, ed., *Byron's Letters and Journals*, 5:155.
47 Ibid., 6:40.

9 Quacks, the Pox and the New Sexual Predators

1 Anon., *A Bold Challenge to the Whole College of Physicians; or, A Defence of Those Practitioners in Physick Commonly Call'd Quacks* (London, n.d.), pp. 4, 16.
2 Newspaper clipping pasted in *The Midnight Ramble; or, The Adventures of Two Noble Females; Being a true and impartial Account of their late excursion through the Streets of London and Westminster* (London, 1754), dated 1731.
3 *The Celestial Beds; or, A Review of the Votaries of the Temple of Health, Adelphi and the Temple of Hymen, Pall Mall* (London, 1781), p. 11.
4 The book was in fact entitled *A Narrative of the Extraordinary Delivery of Mary Toft of Godalming, in Surrey* (London, 1726).
5 G. S. Rousseau and David Haycock, 'Voices Calling for Reform: The Royal Society in the Mid-Eighteenth Century — Martin Folkes, John Hill, and William Stukeley', *History of Science*, XXXVII/4 (1999), pp. 377–406.
6 Originally Meibomus, *De flagrorum usu in re veneria & lumborum renumque officio* (1629: reprinted Leiden, 1643).
7 John Henry Meibomius, *A Treatise of the Use of Flogging in Venereal Affairs: Also of the Office of the Loins and Reins* (London, 1718), p. 34.
8 Roy Porter has already thoroughly examined the impact of *Aristotle's Master-Piece* and Venette's *The Mysteries of Conjugal Love Reveal'd* in Roy Porter and Lesley Hall, *Facts of Life: The Creation of Sexual Knowledge in Britain, 1650–1950* (New Haven, CT, 1995), pp. 33–90.
9 Peter Wagner, *Eros Revived: Erotica of the Enlightenment in England and America* (London, 1988).
10 Relating to the works here and the next paragraph, see Julie Peakman, *Mighty Lewd Books: The Development of Eighteenth-Century Pornography* (London, 2003).
11 Ibid., chapter 4.
12 J.T.D. Bienville lived in Holland for most of his life but few other details of his life are known. Various editions came out in French, Italian and German as well as English.
13 Richard Mead, *The life and adventures of Don Bilioso de L'Estomac. Translated from the Original Spanish into French; done from the French into English. With a letter to the College of Physicians* (London, 1719), pp. C2, 16–17.

14 John Douglas, *The Cornutor of Seventy-Five. Being a genuine narrative of the life, adventures, and amours, of Don Ricardo Honeywater, fellow of the Royal College of Physicians at Madrid, Salamanca, and Toledo; and president of the Academy of Sciences in Lapland. Containing (amongst many other diverting particulars) his intrigue with Dona Maria W–s, of Via Vinculosa, in the city of Madrid. [Written] originally in Spanish, by the author of Don . . . , and translated into English, by a graduate [of] the College of Mecca in Arabia* (London, 1748), pp. 50–51.

15 Robert James, Preface, *The Ladies Physical Dictionary; or, A Treatise of All the Weaknesses, Indispositions, and Diseases Peculiar to the Female Sex . . . to Which Is Annex'd, a Practical Discourse on Barrenness in Women, and Impotency . . . in Men . . . Also of Miscarriage . . . Likewise Ample Instructions to Midwives and Nurses . . .* (London, 1729).

16 Robert James quoted in Julie Peakman,'Medicine, the Body and the Botanical Metaphor in Erotica', in Kurt Bayertz and Roy Porter, eds, *From Physico-Theology to Bio-Technology: Essays in the Social and Cultural History of Biosciences* (Amsterdam, 1998), p. 202.

17 Under 'Vagina and Its Disorders' in Robert James, *Medicinal Dictionary, including physic, surgery, anatomy, chymistry, and botany*, vol. III (London, 1745).

18 Robert James, *The Ladies Physical Dictionary; or, A Treatise of All the Weaknesses, Indispositions and Diseases Peculiar to the Female Sex from Eleven Years of Age, to Fifty Upwards*, 3rd edn (London, 1727), p. 57.

19 *Daily Post* (London), Tuesday, 3 January 1727.

20 Anon., *A Practical Scheme of the Secret Disease and Broken Constitution* (London, 1717), p. 3.

21 *Weekly Journal; or, The British Gazetteer*, 7 February 1719.

22 *Pharmacopaeia Venerea; or, A Compleat Venereal Dispensory. By Anodyne Necklace Tanner* (London, 1724), p. 18.

23 Ned Ward, *The London Spy* (London, reprint 1993), p. 99.

24 Philip Thicknesse, *Man-Midwifery Analysed* (London, 1764), p. 10.

25 *London Evening Post*, 26–8 November 1741.

26 Tofts had been taken to London and examined by Sir Richard Manningham and Douglas. Manning published the case but Douglas was concerned that he implied he had been taken in by the deception. He responded in *An Advertisement Occasioned by some Passages in Sir R. Manningham's Diary Lately Published* (1727). A satire came out on Douglas's account of the Tofts affair: *'Flamingo', a Shorter and Truer Advertisement by Way of Supplement, to What Was Published the 7th Instant, Or, Dr D-G-L-S in an Extasy, at Lacy's Bagie, December 4th 1726* (1727).

27 Anon., *The Tryal Between J. G. Biker Plaintiff and M. Morley, Doctor of Physic Defendant for Criminal Conversation with the Plaintiff's Wife. Tuesday the 30th June, at Guildhall London* (London, 1741), p. 3.

28 Ibid.

29 Ibid., p. 6.

30 Ibid., p. 9.

31 Ibid., p 10.

32 Ibid., p. 17.

33 Ibid.

34 Thicknesse, *Man-Midwifery Analysed*, p. 15.
35 *Tryal Between J. G. Biker Plaintiff and M. Morley*, p. 2.
36 *The London-Citizen exceedingly injured; or, A British inquisition display'd, in an account of the unparallel'd case of a citizen of London, bookseller to the late Queen, who was in a most unjust and arbitrary Manner sent on the 23d of March last, 1738, by one Robert Wightman, a mere Stranger, to a private madhouse Containing, I. An Account of the said Citizen's barbarous Treatment in Wright's Private Madhouse on Bethnal-Green for nine Weeks and six Days, and of his rational and patient Behaviour, whilst Chained, Handcuffed, Strait-Wastecoated and Imprisoned in the said Madhouse: Where he probably would have been continued, or died under his Confinement, if he had not most Providentially made his Escape: In which he was taken up by the Constable and Watchmen, being suspected to be a Felon, but was unchain'd and set at liberty by Sir John Barnard the then Lord Mayor. II. As also an Account of the illegal Steps, false Calumnies, wicked Contrivances, bold and desperate Designs of the said Wightman, in order to escape Justice for his Crimes, with some Account of his engaging Dr. Monro and others as his Accomplices. The Whole humbly addressed to the Legislature, as plainly shewing the absolute Necessity of regulating Private Madhouses in a more effectual manner than at present* (London, 1739).
37 *The Trial of a Case between Richard Maddox, gent., plaintiff, and Dr. M----y [Morley] defendant, physician, and man-midwife, before Sir Michael Foster, Knt. . . . at Guildhall, London, 2 March 1754* (London, 1754).
38 Ibid., p. 6.
39 Ibid., p. 10.
40 Ibid., p. 16.
41 Adrian Wilson, *The Varieties of Man-Midwifery* (London, 1995), pp. 343–69.
42 Frank Nicholls, *The Petition of the Unborn Babes to the Censors of the Royal College of Physicians of London* (London, 1751), p. 6, fn. B.

10 Rape on Trial

1 The trial of 30 October 1772 was reported in the *Covent Garden Magazine*, II (1772), p. 27.
2 A fact also noted by Camille Haisell, '"Imprudent Sluts" and "Sober Gentlemen": Testimonial Injustice in Rape Trials at the Old Bailey, 1720–1742', *Ascendant Historian*, VI/1 (2019), pp. 76–89.
3 Anna Clark and Antony E. Simpson's research backs up this assertion. Antony E. Simpson, 'Popular Perceptions of Rape as a Capital Crime in Eighteenth-Century England: The Press and the Trial of Francis Charteris in the Old Bailey, February 1730', *Law and History Review*, XXII/1 (Spring 2004), pp. 27–20.
4 Gregory Durston, 'Rape in the Eighteenth-Century Metropolis: Part 1', *Journal for Eighteenth-Century Studies*, XXVIII/2 (September 2005), pp. 167–79.
5 Sir Matthew Hale, *Historia Placitorum Coronae: The History of the Pleas of the Crown*, 2 vols (London, 1736), vol. I, p. 635; vol. II, pp. 289–90.

6 Jennie Mills, 'Rape in Early Eighteenth-Century London: A Perversion "So very perplex'd', in *Sexual Perversions, 1670–1890*, ed. Julie Peakman (London, 2009), pp. 140–66.
7 These are my calculations from Old Bailey Records Online; see also Anna Clark, *The Struggle for the Breeches: Gender and the Making of the British Working Class* (Berkeley, CA, 1995).
8 Anon., *Select Trials for Murders, Robberies, Rapes, Sodomy, Coining, Frauds and other offences at the Sessions-House in the Old Bailey from 1724–1732* (London, 1735), vol. II, p. 119.
9 Old Bailey Proceedings Online, 28 August 1678 (t16780828–7).
10 See Sylvana Tomaselli and Roy Porter, *Rape* (London, 1986).
11 Durston, 'Rape in the Eighteenth-Century Metropolis: Part I', p. 171.
12 *Rambler's Magazine*, January 1783, p. 33; The case can be found Old Bailey Proceedings Online, December 1782, trial of John Foy (t-17821204–26).
13 *Rambler's Magazine*, January 1783, p. 34.
14 William Hawkins, *A Treatise of the Pleas of the Crown*, ch. 61, at 108 (London, 1716–21), ch. 41, 1 at 108 referenced in Laurie Edelstein, 'An Accusation Easily to Be Made? Rape and Malicious Prosecution in Eighteenth-Century England', *American Journal of Legal History*, XLII/4 (October 1998), pp. 351–90.
15 Durston, 'Rape in the Eighteenth-Century Metropolis: Part I'.
16 Hale, *Historia Placitorum Coronae*, note 13, chapter 58, at 628; but see Hawkins, *A Treatise of the Pleas of the Crown*, ch. 61, at 108.
17 'However, cases of the sort that gained press attention were not those in which women's injuries were consistent with resisting vigorous attempts to have sexual intercourse. They were, rather, gratuitous and sadistic acts of violence deemed disproportionate to the aim of perpetrating rape. These were atypical. Rapes in which these extremes of violence were absent were unlikely to result in prosecution, conviction and punishment'; see Garthine Walker, 'Rape, Acquittal and Culpability in Popular Crime Reports in England, *c.* 1670–*c.* 1750', *Past and Present*, 220 (August 2013), pp. 115–42, 136.
18 Lawson Tait, *Diseases of Women and Abdominal Surgery* (Leicester, 1889), vol. I, pp. 31, 56.
19 Antony Simpson, 'Vulnerability and the Age of Female Consent: Legal Innovation and Its Effect on Prosecutions for Rape in Eighteenth-Century London', in *Sexual Underworlds of the Enlightenment*, ed. G. S. Rousseau and R. Porter (Manchester, 1987), pp. 188–9, 189.
20 Old Bailey Proceedings Online, 25 June 1788, trial of Joseph Fyson (t17880625-93).
21 Simpson, 'Popular Perceptions of Rape', p. 32.
22 Old Bailey Proceedings Online, September 1797, trial of John Briant (t-17970920–12).
23 Ibid.
24 Ibid.
25 Ibid.
26 Ibid.; www.capitalpunishmentuk.org/ng1783.html.
27 Walker, 'Rape, Acquittal and Culpability in Popular Crime Reports in England', pp. 132–4.

28 Julie Peakman, 'Sexual Perversion in History: An Introduction', in *Sexual Perversions, 1670–1890*, ed. Peakman, pp. 1–49, 13.
29 As Sarah Toulalan has found in her study of the cases (see above) in Old Bailey Proceedings Online, January 1675, trial of Edward Coker (t-16750115–3); see also *A Narrative of the Proceedings at the Session for London and Middlesex, Holden at the Old Bailey, on the Third and Fourth Days of July, 1678* (London, 1678), p. 1. Reported only as 'a young fellow', Rowlandson is named in the indictment, LMA CLA-0267; Old Bailey Proceedings Online, December 1678, trial of Stephen Arrowsmith (t-16781211e-2); Old Bailey Proceedings Online, September 1686, trial of John Raven (t-16860901–21).
30 Sarah Toulalan, '"Is He a Licentious Lewd Sort of a Person?": Constructing the Child Rapist in Early Modern England', *Journal of the History of Sexuality*, XXIII/1 (2014), pp. 21–52, 33.
31 *Grub-Street Journal*, 16 April 1730.
32 Trial of Edward Coker (t-16750115–3).
33 Toulalan, '"Is He a Licentious Lewd Sort of a Person?"', pp. 37–8.
34 See Old Bailey Proceedings Online, May 1754, trial of William Kirk (t17540530–3).
35 Old Bailey Proceedings Online, 13 July 1715, trial of Daniel Bonnely (t17150713-35).
36 Walker, 'Rape, Acquittal and Culpability in Popular Crime Reports in England'.
37 Laura Hinton, *The Perverse Gaze of Sympathy: Sadomasochistic Sentiments from 'Clarissa' to Rescue 911* (Albany, NY, 1999), pp. 36, 74.
38 Ann K. Wagner, 'Sexual Assault in the Shadow of the Law: Character and Proof in Samuel Richardson's *Clarissa*', *Law and Literature*, XXV/2 (Summer 2013), pp. 311–26.
39 Anon., *Tryal of Father John-Baptist Girard Cadiere* (London, 1732), p. 8.
40 Peter Mendes, *Clandestine Erotic Fiction in English: A Bibliographical Study* (Aldershot, 1993).
41 See Julie Peakman, *Mighty Lewd Books: The Development of Pornography in Eighteenth-Century England* (London, 2003); see also John Aitkins, *Sex in Literature*, vol. IV: *High Noon: The Seventeenth and Eighteenth Centuries* (London, 1982), p. 91.
42 *The Rambler*, 170, 2 November 1751.
43 *The Rambler*, 171, 5 November 1751.
44 'The case of Colonel Francis Chartres on Ann Bond', in *A Collection of Remarkable Cases for the Instruction of Both Sexes in the Business of Love and Gallantry* (London, 1730).
45 Ibid., p. 25.
46 *Grub-Street Journal*, 5 March 1730.
47 Edelstein, 'An Accusation Easily to Be Made?'
48 Antony E. Simpson, in his article 'The "Blackmail Myth" and the Prosecution of Rape and Its Attempt in 18th Century London: The Creation of a Legal Tradition', *Journal of Criminal Law and Criminology*, LXXVIII/1 (Spring 1986), pp. 101–50, argues that when lower-class women brought rape allegations in the criminal courts, they did so as part of an informal process of negotiation and settlement. Many of these charges were

not malicious in that they were not wholly based on false accusations, but he claims that the goal of these accusations was not to reach a verdict, but to 'make up' – that is, to receive public acknowledgement of injury, and in some cases modest compensation. However, Simpson's thesis does not hold up.

49 Jonathan Swift, *Lines on the Death of Dr. Swift* [1731], at https://jacklynch.net.

11 Seduction, Abduction and Adultery

1 Richard de Courcy, *Seduction; or, The Cause of Injured Innocence Pleaded. A Poem* (London, 1782), p. 9.
2 Susan Staves, 'British Seduced Maidens', *Eighteenth-Century Studies*, XIV/2 (Winter 1980–81), pp. 109–34.
3 Toni Bowers, *Force or Fraud: British Seduction Stories and the Problem of Resistance, 1660–1760* (London, 2011), pp. 11–13.
4 *The English Report*, LXXXII (London, 1908), p. 809.
5 Anon., *The Whole Tryal between Sarah Holt and Know Ward Upon the Promise of Marriage* (London, 1730), p. 3.
6 *London Evening Post*, 21–4 February 1730.
7 *The Whole Tryal between Sarah Holt and Know Ward Upon the Promise of Marriage*, p. 4.
8 Ibid.
9 Ibid., p. 7.
10 Rebecca Probert, 'The Impact of the Marriage Act of 1753: Was It Really "A Most Cruel Law for the Fair Sex"?', *Eighteenth-Century Studies*, XXXVIII/2 (Winter 2005), pp. 247–62.
11 Staves, 'British Seduced Maidens'.
12 Anon., *Trial at Large of the Reverend Mr Scoolt Curate at St Olive's, Southwark, for Seducing Miss Reddie* (London, 1974), p. 56.
13 James Boswell, *Boswell's Column*, introduction and notes by Margery Bailey (London, 1951), pp. 75, 82.
14 *London Chronicle*, 24–7 December 1757.
15 Joseph Farington, ed. James Grieg, *The Farington Diary*, 8 vols (London, 1923), pp. 2, 220.
16 William Black, *A Dissertation on Insanity* (London, 1810), quoted in Richard Hunter and Ida Macalpine, *Three Hundred Years of Psychiatry, 1535–1860* (Oxford, 1963), p. 646.
17 Anon., *A Curious and Interesting Narrative of Poll House and the Marquis of C****** (Late Lord T****)* (London, 1820 [?])
18 Bethlem Hospital Archives ref: Admission papers, 1819 (BAP-006), Medical record, 1819–1820 (CB-006); Incurable admission papers, 1820 (BAP-002); Incurable medical record, 1820–1833 (CBC-01). My thanks to Colin Gale, Bethlem Hospital Archives and Museum Service, for his kind assistance in this case.
19 Howard William Troyer, *Ned Ward of Grubstreet: A Study of Sub-Literary London in the Eighteenth Century* (Cambridge, MA, 1946), p. 36.
20 *Cobbett's Complete Collection of State Trials and Proceedings for High Treason and Other Crimes and Misdemeanors from the Earliest Period to the Present Time* (London, 1811), p. 135.

21 Ibid., p. 137.
22 Ibid., p. 138.
23 Ibid., p. 143.
24 Ibid., p. 140.
25 Ibid., p. 141.
26 Anon., *The Trial of Ford Lord Grey of Werk, Robert Charnock, Anne Charnock, David Jones, Frances Jones, and Rebecca Jones, at the King's Bench, for a Misdemeanour in Debauching the Lady Henrietta Berkeley, Daughter of the Earl of Berkeley, AD 1682*, ibid., p. 129.
27 Ibid., p. 130.
28 Ibid., p. 131.
29 Ibid., p. 145.
30 Ibid., p. 166.
31 Ibid., p. 174.
32 Ibid., p. 176.
33 *Ode Sacred to the Memory of . . . the Countess of Berkely* (London, 1717), p. 9.
34 *London Daily Post and General Advertiser*, 5 November 1734.
35 'The Trials were sold by T Read in Dogwell-Court, White-Fryars, Fleet-Street; ad at the Pamphlet Shops at the Royal Exchange, Temple-Bar, and Charing-Cross'; *London Daily Post and General Advertiser*, 13 February 1735.
36 Hansard, Letter from the Prince of Wales to the Princess of Wales, HC Deb 04 March 1813, vol. XXIV: CC1123–8, at https://api.parliament.uk.
37 John R. Gillis, *For Better, For Worse: English Marriages 1600 to the Present* (Oxford, 1985).
38 Marilyn Morris has highlighted the *Bon Ton* as a precursor to current day 'tabloid journalism'; Marilyn Morris, 'Marital Litigation and English Tabloid Journalism: Crim. Con. in *The Bon Ton* (1791–1796)', *British Journal for Eighteenth-Century Studies*, XXIII/1 (2005), pp. 33–54.
39 *The Bon Ton Magazine; or, Microscope of Fashion and Folly*, 5 vols (London, 1791–5); D. Brewman, 1795–6, v. 479–80.
40 *Town and Country Magazine; or, Universal Repository of Knowledge, Instruction, and Entertainment*, IV (October 1772), p. 513.
41 Ibid., p. 514.
42 Ibid., p. 513.
43 *Trials for Adultery; or, The History of Divorces Being a select trials at doctors commons for adultery, fornication, cruelty impotence etc London from the year 1760 to the present time* (London, 1779), vol. II, p. 5.
44 Ibid., p. 6.
45 Ibid., p. 18.
46 Ibid., p. 40.
47 Ibid., p. 44.
48 Gilbert Burnet, *History of His Own Time* (London, 1823), vol. I, p. 486.

12 Royal Mistresses

1 *Memoirs of Perdita* (London, 1784), p. 99.
2 *The Diary of John Evelyn* (London, 1901), 18 August 1649, vol. I, p. 249, at www.gutenberg.org.

3 Charles Beauclerk, *Nell Gwyn: A Biography* (London, 2005), p. 12.
4 Samuel Pepys, *Diary*, 11 January 1667, at www.pepysdiary.com.
5 Pepys, *Diary*, 28 December 1667.
6 Pepys, *Diary*, 1 May 1667.
7 John Harold Wilson, *Court Satires of the Restoration* (Columbus, OH, 1976), pp. 246–8.
8 Timothy J. Peters, 'The Madness of King George III: A Psychiatric Re-Assessment', *History of Psychiatry*, XXI/1 (2010), pp. 20–37; Timothy Peters, 'Royal Medical Entourages: Analysis of the Roles of Doctors during the Episodes of Madness of King George III', *Court Historian*, XXIV/1 (2019), pp. 48–66.
9 Mary Darby Robinson, ed., *Memoirs of the Late Mary Robinson* (London, 1801: reprinted 1930), p. 21.
10 Ibid., p. 51.
11 Ibid., p. 59.
12 *Morning Post*, 11 December 1776.
13 *ODNB*.
14 Robinson, ed., *Memoirs of the Late Mary Robinson*, p. 119.
15 Ibid., p. 123.
16 Ibid.
17 Ibid., p. 135.
18 Ibid., p. 136.
19 Ibid., p. 139.
20 Mrs. Elizabeth Steele, *Memoirs of Sophia Baddeley* (London, 1796), vol. VI, pp. 177–9.
21 *Gazetteer and New Daily Advertiser*, 21 July 1780.
22 Steele, *Memoirs of Sophia Baddeley*, vol. VI, p. 115.
23 *ODNB*.
24 *Morning Herald*, 5 January 1791, quoted in Byrne, *Perdita*, p. 145.
25 Robinson, ed., *Memoirs of the Late Mary Robinson*, p. 147.
26 *Memoirs of Perdita* (London, 1784), p. 38.
27 Robinson, ed., *Memoirs of the Late Mary Robinson*, p. 154.
28 *Memoirs of Perdita*, p. 27.
29 Ibid., p. 9.
30 Ibid., p. 26.
31 Ibid., p. 29.
32 Robinson, ed., *Memoirs of the Late Mrs Robinson*, p. 171.
33 *Memoirs of Perdita*, p. 152.
34 Robinson, ed., *Memoirs of the Late Mary Robinson*, p. 189.
35 Horace Walpole, *Correspondence*, vol. XXXIII, p. 514, at https://libsvcs-1.its.yale.edu/hwcorrespondence.
36 In fact, three Acts of Parliament stood in his way: the Act of Settlement of 1701, the Act of Union of 1707 (both excluding a prince or princess married to a Catholic from succeeding to the throne), and the Royal Marriages Act of 1772.
37 Arthur Aspinall, ed., *Correspondence of George, Prince of Wales* (Madison, WI, 1965), vol. III, p. 133.
38 At www.turtlebunbury.com/history/history_irish/history_irish_georgeiv.htm, 12 January 2021.

39 Charles Greville's diary quoted in M. J. Levy, *The Mistresses of King George IV* (London, 1996), p. 154.
40 The frontispiece of the drawing of Lady C___ in this work was undertaken by J. L. Marks, a quasi-pornographic caricaturist and publisher who worked for William Benbow for most of 1820. See *The Memoirs of the Celebrated Lady C*****m* (London, n.d [1820]) .
41 The British Library catalogue suggests Mrs Harriet Quentin as the subject of the title. However, she is known to have been called Georgiana. Perhaps Harriet was a middle name.
42 'Edward Eglantine', *Memoirs of Life of the Celebrated Mrs Q* (London, n.d.[1822]), p. 13.
43 *The Times*, 24 January 1811.
44 *Morning Post*, 12 January 1822, quoting from *London Gazette, Brighton Pavilion*, 8 December 1821.
45 'The Kings' Drawing Room' , *Morning Post*, 26 March 1821.
46 *Morning Post*, 10 January 1822.
47 *Morning Post*, 23 February 1822.
48 *Morning Post*, 26 February 1822.
49 *A Peep into Windsor Castle after the Lost Mutton* (London, 1820).
50 See ODNB; and Iain McCalman, *Radical Underworld: Prophets, Revolutionaries and Pornographers in London, 1795–1840* (Oxford, 1988), p. 222.
51 This is pointed out by Lisa O'Connell, 'Authorship and Libertine Celebrity: Harriette Wilson's Regency Memoirs', in Peter Cryle and Lisa O'Connell, *Libertine Enlightenment: Sex, Liberty and Licence in the Eighteenth Century* (Basingstoke, 2004), pp. 161–81, footnote 3.
52 *Confessions of Julia Johnstone* (London, 1825), p. 38.
53 McCalman, *Radical Underworld*, p. 169.
54 BL shelf mark LR. 22c6.

BIBLIOGRAPHY

Primary Sources

'Anodyne Tanner MD', *The Life of the Late Celebrated Mrs Elizabeth Wisebourn, Vulgarly Call'd Mother Wybourn* (London, 1721)

—, *Pharmacopaeia Venerea; or, A Compleat Venereal Dispensory* (London, 1724)

Anon., *An Account of the Institution of the Lock Asylum, for the Reception of Penitent Female Patients, when discharged from the Lock Hospital* (London, 1796)

Anon., *An Account of the Proceedings against Capt. E. Rigby at . . . the Old-Bailey* (London, 1698)

Anon., *An Account of the Tryall of Sally Salisbury* (London, 1722)

Anon., *A Collection of Remarkable Cases for the Instruction of Both Sexes in the Business of Love and Gallantry* (London, 1730)

Anon., *A Conference about Whoring* (London, 1725)

Anon., *A Curious and Interesting Narrative of Poll House and the Marquis of C****** (Late Lord T****)* (London, 1820 [?])

Anon., *An Advertisement Occasioned by some Passages in Sir R. Manningham's Diary Lately Published. 'Flamingo', a shorter and truer advertisement by way of supplement, to what was published the 7th instant, or, Dr D-g-l-s in an extasy, at Lacy's Bagie, December 4th 1726* (London, 1727)

Anon., *Annals of Newgate* (London, 1776)

Anon., *The Celestial Beds; or, A Review of the Votaries of the Temple of Health, Adelphi and the Temple of Hymen, Pall Mall* (London, 1781)

Anon., *The Character of a Coffee-House* (London, 1673)

Anon., *The Character of a Town-Gallant* (London, 1675)

Anon., *The Character of a Town-Miss* (London, 1680)

Anon., *Characters of the Present and Most Celebrated Courtezans* (London, 1780)

Anon., *Cobbett's Complete Collection of State Trials and Proceedings for High Treason and Other Crimes and Misdemeanors from the Earliest Period to the Present Time* (London, 1811)

Anon., *The Constables Hue and Cry after Whores and Bawds* (London, 1701[?])

Anon., *The Countryman's Guide to London; or, Villainy Detected* (London, 1775[?])

Anon., *Drury Lane in Tears; or, The Ladies of Pleasure Mourning* (London, 1740[?])
Anon., *The Effigies, Parentage, Education, Life, Merry Pranks and Conversation of the celebrated Mrs Sally Salisbury* (London, 1723)
Anon., *The Eight and Twentieth Account of the Progress made in the Cities of London and Westminster by the Societies for Promoting a Reformation of Manners* (London, 1722)
Anon., *Farringdon Without. At a Meeting of the Alderman and Common Council of this Ward, At the Inquest Room in Saint Andrew's Church-Yard, on Wednesday, December 11, 1799* (London, [1799])
Anon., *The Genuine History of Mrs. Sarah Prydden, Usually Called Sally Salisbury and Her Gallants* (London, 1723)
Anon., *Genuine Memoirs of the Celebrated Miss Nancy Dawson* (London, 1760)
Anon., *Horse and Away to St. James's Park; or, A Trip for the Noontide Air Who Rides Fastest, Miss Kitty Fisher; or, Her Gay Gallant* (London, 1760)
Anon., *Kitty Attalantis* (London, 1766)
Anon., *Kitty's Stream; or, The Noblemen Turned Fisher-Men: A Comic Satire* (London, 1759)
Anon., 'Jack Lovelass', *The Hoop-Petticoat Vindicated in Answer to the Enormous Abomination of the Hoop-Petticoat* (London, 1745)
Anon., *Life and Character of Moll King* (London, 1747 [?])
Anon., *The Life of Lavinia Berwick, alias Fenton alias Polly Peacham* (London, 1728)
Anon., *The London-Citizen Exceedingly Injured* (London, 1739)
Anon. [Captain Johnson], *The Lives and Adventures of the German Princess (Mary Carleton), Mary Read, Anne Bonny, Joan Philips, Madam Churchill, Betty Ireland, and Ann Hereford* (London, 1755)
Anon., *The Macaroni Jester and Pantheon of Wit* (1730)
Anon., *Memoirs of the Celebrated Miss Fanny M_______* [Murray] (London, 1759)
Anon., *Memoirs of Perdita; interspersed with anecdotes of the Hon. Charles F-x; Lord M-; . . . and many other well known characters* (London, 1784)
Anon., *Mother Needham's Elegy. Who died the 31st of September 1730. Containing, an Account of Mother Needham's Life and Death, Manner of Lying in State, Her Funeral, and Epitaph* (London, 1730)
Anon., *The Midnight Ramble; or, The Adventures of Two Noble Females; Being a true and impartial Account of their late excursion through the Streets of London and Westminster* (London, 1754)
Anon., *A Narrative of the Extraordinary Delivery of Mary Toft of Godalming, in Surrey* (London, 1726)
Anon., *A Narrative of the Proceedings at the Session for London and Middlesex, Holden at the Old Bailey, on the Third and Fourth Days of July* (London, 1678)
Anon., *The Nunnery for Coquettes* (London, 1771)
Anon., *The Oath of a Constable* (London, 1704)
Anon., *Ode Sacred to the Memory of . . . the Countess of Berkely* (London, 1717)
Anon., *The Phoenix of Sodom; or, The Vere Street Coterie* (London, 1813)
Anon., *A Practical Scheme of the Secret Disease and Broken Constitution* (London, 1717)

Anon., [William Pulteney], *A Proper Reply to a Late Scurrilous Libel; Intitled, Sedition and Defamation Display'd*, by Caleb D'Anvers (London, 1731)

Anon., *The Practical Scheme of Secret Injuries. And Broken Constitutions. By Fast Living, Former Ill Cures, Salivations and Mercury. With an Appendix of Gleets, and Other Such Weaknesses in Either Sex* (London, 1719)

Anon., *Reasons Humbly Offer's to the Honourable House of Commons, by the Church Wardens and other Inhabitants of the City and Libertie of Westminster: Against Passing the Bill to Exempt Apothecaries from Serving Parish and Ward-Offices* (London, 1694 or 1702)

Anon., *Report of the Committee of the Society For Carrying Into Effect His Majesty's Proclamation Against Vice and Immorality for the Year 1799* (London, 1800)

Anon., *A Representation of the State of the Societies for Reformation of Manners* (London, 1715)

Anon., *Sally Slisbury's [sic] Garland, Containing Four Excellent New Songs* [n.d.]

Anon., *Satan's Harvest Home; or, The Present State of Whorecraft* (London, 1749)

Anon., *The Secret History of the Green Rooms, Containing Authentic and Entertaining Memoirs of the Actors and Actresses in the Three Royal Theatres* (London, 1790)

Anon., *The Secret Memoirs of Harriott Pumpkin [Mellon], A Celebrated Actress; From Her Infancy to Her Seduction of, and Subsequent Marriage to a Banker* (London, 1825)

Anon., *Select Trials for Murderers, Robberies Rapes, Sodomy, Coining, Frauds and Other Offences at the Sessions-House in the Old Bailey*, vol. I: *1720–24* (London, 1734)

Anon., *Select Trials for Murders, Robberies, Rapes, Sodomy, Coining, Frauds and other offences at the Sessions-House in the Old Bailey from 1724–1732*, vol. II (London, 1735)

Anon., *A Sketch of the Present Times and the Time to Come: In an Address to Kitty Fisher* (London, 1762)

Anon., *Statement and Propositions from the Society for Giving Effect to His Majesty's Proclamation Against Vice and Immorality, Delivered to the Magistrates, At Their Meeting Held at the St. Alban's Tavern, on Wednesday the 5th of May, 1790* (London, 1790)

Anon., *Trials for Adultery; or, The History of Divorces: Being Select Trials at Doctors Commons for Adultery, Fornication, Cruelty Impotence Etc London from the Year 1760 to the Present Time* (London, 1779)

Anon., *The Town Mistress; or The Street-Walker* (London, 1726)

Anon., *The Trial of a Case between Richard Maddox, Gent., Plaintiff, and Dr. M----y [Morley] defendant, physician, and man-midwife, before Sir Michael Foster, Knt. . . . at Guildhall, London, 2 March 1754* (London, 1754)

Anon., *Trial at Large of the Reverend Mr Scoolt Curate at St Olive's, Southwark for Seducing Miss Reddie* (London, 1974)

Anon., *The Tryal between J. G. Biker Plaintiff and M. Morley, Doctor of Physic Defendant for Criminal Conversation with the Plaintiff's Wife. Tuesday the 30th June, at Guildhall London* (London, 1741)

Anon., *Tryal of Father John-Baptist Girard Cadiere* (London, 1732)
Anon., *The Tryals of the Two Causes between Theophilus Cibber Gent and Plaintiff William Sloper* (London, 1710)
Anon., *The Uncommon Adventures of Miss Kitty Fisher* (London, 1759)
Anon., *Whipping-Tom; or, A Rod for a Proud Lady* (London, 1722)
Anon., *The Whole Life of Polly Peachum* (London, 1730[?])
Anon., *Women's Petition Against Coffee* (London, 1674)
Anstey, Christopher, *Liberality; or, The Decayed Macaroni* (London, 1788)
Besant, Walter, *London* (London, reprint 1900)
Black, William, *A Dissertation on Insanity* (London, 1810)
Burgess, C. F., ed., *Letters of John Gay* (Oxford,1966)
Burnet, Gilbert, *History of His Own Time*, vol. I (London, 1823)
Charke, Charlotte, *A Narrative of the Life of Mrs Charlotte Charke* (London, 1755)
Cleland, John, *Memoirs of a Woman of Pleasure*, vol. II (London, 1749)
Colquhoun, Patrick, *Treatise on the Police of the Metropolis* (London, 1796)
Curll, Edmund, 'William Egerton', *Faithful Memoirs of the Life and Performance of that Justly celebrated and most Eminent Actress of Her Time, Mrs Anne Oldfield* (London, 1731)
Defoe, Daniel, *Moll Flanders* (London, 1721)
—, *Some Considerations Upon Street-Walkers* (London, 1726)
Douglas, John, *The Cornutor of Seventy-Five. Being a Genuine Narrative of the Life, Adventures, and Amours, of Don Ricardo Honeywater* (London, 1748)
Dunton, John, *Bumography; or, A Touch at the Lady's Tail. Being a Lampoon (privately) dispers'd at Tunbridge-Wells, in the Year 1707, by a Water-Drinker* (London, 1707)
—, *Life and Errors* (London, 1705)
Eglington, Charles, *The Theatre: A Monthly Review of the Drama, Music and the Fine Arts* (October 1892)
Etherege, George, *The Man of Mode; or, Sir Fopling Flutter* (London, 1676)
Garrick, David, *The Male-Coquette; or, Seventeen Hundred and Fifty-Seven* (Dublin, 1758)
Good, John Mason, *A Dissertation on the Diseases of Prisons and Poor Houses* (London, 1795)
Hale, Sir Matthew, *Historia Placitorum Coronae: The History of the Pleas of the Crown*, 2 vols (London, 1736)
Hawkins, William, *Treatise of the Pleas of the Crown* (London, 1716: reprinted 1973)
Hickelty Pickelty; or, A Medly of Characters Adapted to the Age (London, 1708)
Johnstone, Julia, *Confessions of Julia Johnstone* (London, 1825)
Jones, Charles Inigo, *Memoirs of Miss O'Neill, Containing Her Public Character, Private Life and Dramatic Progress* (London, 1816)
King, Richard, *The New Cheats of London Expos'd* (London, 1780[?])
—, *The New Cheats of London Exposed; or, The Frauds and Tricks of the Town Laid Open to Both Sexes* (London, 1799[?])
Lorrain, Paul, *The Ordinary of Newgate His Account of the Behaviour, Confession, and Last Speech of Deborah Churchill, that Was Executed At Tyburn, on Friday the 17th of December, 1708* (London, 1708)

—, *The Whole Life and Conversation, Birth, Parentage and Education of Deborah Churchill (London, 1708)*
Mandeville, Bernard, *An Enquiry into the Causes of Frequent Execution at Tyburn* (London, 1725)
—, *A Modest Defence of Publick Stews; or, An Essay upon Whoring* (London, 1724)
Mead, Richard, *The Life and Adventures of Don Bilioso de L'Estomac* (London, 1719)
Meibomius, John Henry, *A Treatise of the Use of Flogging in Venereal Affairs: Also of the Office of the Loins and Reins* (London, 1718)
Radcliffe, Mary Anne, *The Female Advocate; or, An Attempt to Recover the Rights of Women from Male Usurpation* (London, 1799)
Salmon, Thomas, *The Chronical Historian* (London, 1723)
Smith, A., *A Complete History of the Lives and Robberies of the Most Notorious Highwaymen*, ed. A. L. Hayward, 5th edn (London, 1719: reprinted 1926)
Spencer, Alfred, ed., *Memoirs of William Hickey* (London, 1913)
Swift, Jonathan, *Lines on the Death of Dr Swift* (London, 1731)
Tait, Lawson, *Diseases of Women and Abdominal Surgery* (Leicester, 1889)
Thicknesse, Philip, *Man-Midwifery Analysed* (London, 1764)
Tickell, R. E., ed., *Thomas Tickell and the Eighteenth-Century Poets* (London, 1931)
Timbury, Jane, *The Male Coquette; or, The History of the Hon. Edward Astell* (London, 1770)
Venette, Nicholas, *The Mysteries of Conjugal Love Reveal'd* (London, 1712)
Walker, Captain Charles, *Authentick Memoirs of the Life, Intrigues and Adventures of the Celebrated Sally Salisbury* (London, 1723)
Ward, Edward, *A Pleasant and Profitable Discourse in Defence of Married Men, Against Peevich, Frerful, Scolding Wives* (London, 1749)
—, *Female Policy Detected; or, The Arts of a Designing Woman Laid Open*, (London, 1695)
Ward, Ned, *The Amorous Bugbears; or, The Humours of a Masquerade* (London, 1725)
—, *Female Policy Detected* (London, 1702)
—, *The London Spy*, ed. Paul Hyland (London, 4th edn of 1709: reprinted 1993)
—, *The London Spy Compleat* (London, 1703)
—, *The London Terraefilius; or, The Satyrical Reformer* (London, 1707)
—, *The Reformer: Exposing the Vices of the Age in Several Characters* (London, 1700)
—, *The Secret History of Clubs Particularly the Kitcat, Beef-Stake, Vertuosos, Quacks, Knights of the Golden Fleece, Florists, Beaus. &c. With Their Original Characters of the Most Noted Members Thereof* (London, 1709)
—, *A Walk to Islington* (London, 1701)
Warton, J., ed., *The Works of Alexander Pope* (London, 1797)
Webb, T., *Epitaphs* (London, 1775)
Wilkes, John, *Wilkes and Granby's Garland* (Darlington, 1774)
Wilson, Harriette, *The Memoirs of Harriette Wilson* (London, 1825)
Woodward, J., *A Rebuke to The Sin of Uncleanliness*. 'By a Minister of the Church of England' (London, 1740)

Secondary Sources

Bartlett, Peter, 'Sodomites in the Pillory in Eighteenth-Century London', *Social and Legal Studies*, VI/4 (1997), pp. 553–72

Beauclerk, Charles, *Nell Gwyn: A Biography* (London, 2005)

Blair, Lowell, ed., *Casanova's Memoirs* (London, 1958)

Bleackley, Horace, 'Ladies Frail and Fair: Sketches of the Demi-Monde during the Eighteenth-Century Metropolis: Part 1', *Journal for Eighteenth-Century Studies*, XXVIII/2 (September 2005), pp. 167–79

Edelstein, Laurie, 'An Accusation Easily to Be Made? Rape and Malicious Prosecution in Eighteenth-Century England', *American Journal of Legal History*, XLII/4 (October 1998), pp. 351–90

Farington, Joseph, ed., *The Farington Diary*, 8 vols (London, 1923)

Gillis, John R,. *For Better, For Worse: English Marriages, 1600 to the Present* (Oxford 1985)

Greenberg, David F., *The Construction of Homosexuality* (Chicago, 1988)

Halsband, Robert, *Lord Hervey: Eighteenth-Century Courtier* (Oxford, 1973)

—, ed., *Mary Wortley Montagu: Complete Letters* (Oxford, 1965–7)

Hatfield, Theodore Merryman, 'The True Secret History of Mr John Dunton', PhD dissertation, Harvard University (1926)

Hawkins, William, *A Treatise of the Pleas of the Crown* (London, 1716–21)

Henderson, Tony, *Disorderly Women in Eighteenth-Century London: Prostitution and Control in the Metropolis, 1730–1830* (London, 1999)

Hill, Peter Murray, *Two Augustan Booksellers: John Dunton and Edmund Curll* (Lawrence, KS, 1958)

Hinton, Laura, *The Perverse Gaze of Sympathy: Sadomasochistic Sentiments from 'Clarissa' to Rescue 911* (Albany, NY, 1999)

Hurl-Eamon, Jennine, 'Policing Male Heterosexuality: The Reformation of Manners Societies' Campaign against the Brothels In Westminster, 1690–1720', *Journal of Social History*, XXXVII/4 (Summer 2004), pp. 1017–35

James, Robert, *The Ladies Physical Dictionary; or, A Treatise Of All the Weaknesses, Indispositions and Diseases Peculiar to the Female Sex from Eleven Years of Age, to Fifty Upwards*, 3rd edn (London, 1727)

MacCarthy, Fiona, *Byron: Life and Legend* (London, 2002)

McLynn, Frank, *Crimes and Punishment in Eighteenth-Century England* (Oxford, 1989)

Marchand, Leslie A., ed., *Byron's Letters and Journals* (Cambridge, 1973-82)

Mendes, Peter, *Clandestine Erotic Fiction in English: A Bibliographical Study* (Aldershot, 1993)

Merians, Linda E., ed., *The Secret Malady: Venereal Disease in Eighteenth-Century Britain and France* (Lexington, 1991)

Moore, John Robert, *Defoe in the Pillory* (Bloomington, IN, 1939)

Moore, Lucy, *Amphibious Thing: The Life of a Georgian Rake* (London, 2001)

Morris, Marilyn, 'Marital Litigation and English Tabloid Journalism: Crim. Con. in *The Bon Ton* (1791–1796)', *British Journal for Eighteenth-Century Studies*, XXIII/1 (March 2005), pp. 33–54

Mowry, Melissa, *The Bawdy Politic in Stuart England, 1660–1714* (London, 2004)

Murray, Stephen O. and Will Roscoe, eds, *Islamic Homosexualities: Culture, History, and Literature* (New York, 1997)

Neff, D. S., 'Bitches, Mollies, and Tommies: Byron, Masculinity, and the History of Sexualities', *Journal of the History of Sexuality*, xi/3 (July 2002), pp. 395–438

Nicholls, Frank, *The Petition of the Unborn Babes to the Censors of the Royal College of Physicians of London* (London, 1751)

Norton, Rictor, *Mother Clap's Molly-House: The Gay Subculture in England, 1700–1830* (London, 1992)

Novak, Maximillian E., *Daniel Defoe. Master of Fictions: His Life and Ideas* (Oxford, 2001)

Parks, Stephen, *John Dunton and the English Book Trade* (London, 1976)

Peakman, Julie, *Amatory Pleasures: Exploration in Eighteeenth-Century Sexual Culture* (London, 2016)

—, *Lascivious Bodies: A Sexual History of the Eighteenth Century* (London, 2004)

—, *Mighty Lewd Books. The Development of Pornography in Eighteenth-Century England* (London, 2002)

—, *Whore Biographies, 1700–1825* (London, 2006–7)

—, ed., *Sexual Perversions, 1670–1890* (London, 2009)

Peters, Timothy J., 'The Madness of King George iii: A Psychiatric Re-Assessment', *History of Psychiatry*, xxi/1 (2010), pp. 20–37

Picard, Liza, *Dr Johnson's London* (London, 2002)

Postlewait, Thomas, 'Autobiography and Theatre History', in *Interpreting the Theatrical Past: Essays in the Historiography of Performance*, ed. T. Postelwait and Bruce A. McConachie (Iowa City, ia, 1989), pp. 248–72

Probert, Rebecca, 'The Impact of the Marriage Act of 1753: Was It Really "A Most Cruel Law for the Fair Sex"?' *Eighteenth-Century Studies*, xxxviii/2 (Winter 2005), pp. 247–62

Rauser, Amelia, 'Hair, Authenticity, and the Self-Made Macaroni', *Eighteenth-Century Studies*, xxxviii/1, 'Hair' (Fall 2004), pp. 101–17

Rayner, J. L., and G. T. Crook, eds, *The Complete Newgate Calendar*, vol. ii (London, 1926)

Reynolds, Elaine A., *Before the Bobbies: The Night Watch and Police Reform in Metropolitan London, 1720–1830* (London, 1998)

Rousseau, G. S. and David Haycock, 'Voices Calling for Reform: The Royal Society in the Mid-Eighteenth Century. Martin Folkes, John Hill, and William Stukeley', *History of Science*, xxxvii/4 (1999), pp. 377–406

—, and R. Porter, eds, *Sexual Underworlds of the Enlightenment* (Manchester, 1987)

Shesgreen, Sean, ed., *Engraving by Hogarth* (New York, 1973)

Simpson, Antony E., 'Popular Perceptions of Rape as a Capital Crime in Eighteenth-Century England: The Press and the Trial of Francis Charteris in the Old Bailey, February 1730', *Law and History Review*, xxii/1 (Spring 2004), pp. 27-70

Speck, W. A., 'The Harlot's Progress in Eighteenth-Century England', *British Journal of Eighteenth-Century Studies*, iii/2 (1980), pp. 127–39

Staves, Susan, 'British Seduced Maidens', *American Society for Eighteenth-Century Studies*, xiv/2 (Winter 1980–81), pp. 109–34

Straub, K., *Sexual Suspects: Eighteenth-Century Players and Sexual Ideology* (Princeton, NJ, 2006)
Tomaselli, Sylvania, and Roy Porter, *Rape* (London, 1986)
Thompson, Grace E., *The Cyprian: The Life of a Covent Garden Lady* (London, 1932)
Toulalan, Sarah, '"Is He a Licentious Lewd Sort of a Person?": Constructing the Child Rapist in Early Modern England', *Journal of the History of Sexuality*, XXIII/1 (2014), pp. 21–52
Troyer, Howard William, *Ned Ward of Grubstreet: A Study of Sub-Literary London in the Eighteenth Century* (Cambridge, MA, 1946)
Trumbach, Randolph, 'Blackmail for Sodomy in Eighteenth-Century London', *Historical Reflections/Réflexions Historiques*, XXXIII/1, *Eighteenth-Century Homosexuality in Global Perspective* (Spring 2007), pp. 23–39
—, *Sex and the Gender Revolution, Heterosexuality and the Third Gender in Enlightenment London* (Chicago, IL, 1998)
—, 'Sodomy Transformed: Aristocratic Libertinage, Public Reputation and the Gender Revolution of the Eighteenth Century', *Journal of Homosexuality*, XIX/3 (1990), pp. 105–24
Wagner, Ann K., 'Sexual Assault in the Shadow of the Law: Character and Proof in Samuel Richardson's *Clarissa*', *Law and Literature*, XXV/2 (Summer 2013), pp. 311–26
Walker, Garthine, 'Rape, Acquittal and Culpability in Popular Crime Reports in England, c. 1670–c. 1750', *Past and Present*, 220 (August 2013), pp. 115–42
Waller, Maureen, *1700: Scenes from London Life* (London, 2001)
Wharncliffe, Lord, ed., *Letters of Lady Mary Wortley Montagu*, vol. I [1866] (Cambridge, 2011)
Wild, Anthony, *Coffee: A Dark History* (New York, 2005)
Williams, Tassie, 'Female Fraud: Counterfeit Maidenheads in the Eighteenth Century', *Journal of the History of Sexuality*, VI/4 (1996), pp. 518–48
Wilson, Adrian, *The Making of Man-Midwifery: Childbirth in England, 1660–1770* (London, 1995)
Wilson, John Harold, *Court Satires of the Restoration* (Columbus, OH, 1976)
Woods, Gregory, *A History of Gay Literature: The Male Tradition* (New Haven, CT, 1998)

ACKNOWLEDGEMENTS

I want to thank my publisher, Michael Leaman, for seeing what I might do with the subject of *Libertine London* (as well as all the other books of mine he has published) and his patience in troubled times; I am indebted to Martha Jay for correcting my errors. When I was researching and sourcing the images in the book, Reaktion's Alex Ciobanu helped find alternatives or replacements and I am grateful for all his input. It has been a difficult couple of years for many people and I am indebted to the Wellcome online library, which was invaluable to me for allowing me to access eighteenth-century books and providing free images for this book. I am especially thankful to the Society of Authors, who were kind enough to give me a grant to enable me to take extra time to write this book; they have been such a wonderful support for members, keeping the writing community together and offering us all training, conversation and support through COVID-19. I am ever grateful for the support of my family and friends, who make life more joyous, stimulate discussion and creativity, and generally make the world a better place. You know who you are. I particularly want to thank my brother, Paul Peakman, for lunches out as a break from working, and to reset my mind to good food, wine and non-eighteenth-century conversation.

The stalwart by my side is always Jad Adams, who keeps me going through difficult writing times, helps me with edits and suggestions, and more importantly feeds me dinners and opens the wine. We have run through many libertine times together in London, and hopefully we will run through many more.

PHOTO ACKNOWLEDGEMENTS

The author and publishers wish to express their thanks to the sources listed below for illustrative material and/or permission to reproduce it. Some locations of artworks are also given below, in the interest of brevity:

Beinecke Rare Book and Manuscript Library, Yale University, New Haven, CT: pp. 66, 123, 302; Boston Public Library: pp. 14, 167, 170, 240; The British Museum, London: pp. 97, 106, 113, 124, 164, 209, 256, 281, 299, 305, 307, 311; David Rumsey Map Collection, David Rumsey Map Center, Stanford Libraries, CA: pp. 8–9; from Daniel Defoe, *The Fortunate Mistress; or, A History of the Life of Mademoiselle de Beleau* (New York, 1904), photo Joseph F. Smith Library, BYU–Hawaii, Laie: p. 122; from William Egerton, *Faithful Memoirs of the Life, Amours and Performances, of that Justly Celebrated, and Most Eminent Actress of Her Time, Mrs Anne Oldfield* (London, 1731), photo Getty Research Institute, Los Angeles: p. 137; Ickworth Estate, Horringer: p. 196; from Captain Jesse, *The Life of George Brummell* (London, 1886), vol. I, photo University of California Libraries: p. 162; Lady Lever Art Gallery, Wirral: p. 200; Lewis Walpole Library, Yale University, Farmington, CT: pp. 17, 31, 36, 40, 44, 68, 75, 84, 148, 174, 176, 177, 228, 266, 272, 274, 286; Library of Congress, Prints and Photographs Division, Washington, DC: p. 95; Medical Historical Library, Harvey Cushing/John Hay Whitney Medical Library, Yale University, New Haven, CT: p. 239; The Metropolitan Museum of Art, New York: pp. 48, 52, 92, 151, 184, 222; National Galleries of Scotland, Edinburgh: pp. 258, 273; National Gallery of Art, Washington, DC: pp. 112, 132; National Gallery of Ireland, Dublin: p. 264; National Maritime Museum, Greenwich, London: pp. 116, 217; National Portrait Gallery, London: pp. 77, 153, 165, 192; The New York Public Library: pp. 53, 74, 81, 93, 126, 219; private collection: pp. 109, 150, 168, 188, 199, 287; Rijksmuseum, Amsterdam: pp. 24, 144, 253, 254; Royal Collection Trust/© His Majesty King Charles III 2024: pp. 189, 205; Science Museum, London: p. 87; Temple Newsam, Leeds: p. 309; University of Illinois Library, Urbana: p. 145; Upton House, Warwickshire: p. 198; Victoria and Albert Museum, London: p. 135; The Wallace Collection, London: p. 291; Wellcome Collection, London: pp. 20, 23, 32, 35, 49, 54, 79, 101, 117, 128, 129,

152, 181, 183, 214, 216, 218, 220, 225; William Andrews Clark Memorial Library, University of California, Los Angeles: p. 160; Yale Center for British Art, New Haven, CT: pp. 18, 57, 108, 141, 194, 236, 265, 282, 283.

INDEX

Page numbers in *italics* indicate illustrations